To Ginnie,
A fellow member of the Booth
Chapter of Collectors' Anonymous
Best wishes,
Johnny

Close Encounters with ANTIQUE FURNITURE

A Restorer's Story

Close Encounters with ANTIQUE FURNITURE

A Restorer's Story

DAVID HAWKINS

Sage Creek Press

Traverse City, Michigan

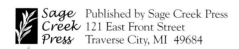 Published by Sage Creek Press
121 East Front Street
Traverse City, MI 49684

Publisher's Cataloging-in-Publication Data
Hawkins, David, 1922-
    Close encounters with antique furniture ; a restorer's guide
    / David Hawkins. – Traverse City, Mich. :
Sage Creek Press, 1999.

            p.   ill.   cm.

    Includes bibliographical references and index.
    ISBN: 1-890394-13-0
    1. Furniture – Collectors and collecting.
    2. Antiques. 3. Furniture – Styles. 4. Antiques business.
    I. Title.
NK2240 .H39 1998   97-62534
749'.2 – dc21   CIP

PROJECT COORDINATION BY JENKINS GROUP, INC.

03 02 01 00 * 5 4 3 2 1

Printed in China

To Jimmy Little, 1872-1961,
and all my other old boys,
one or two still present.
I doubt we shall ever see their like again.

CONTENTS

Foreword   *ix*

Acknowledgements   *xi*

1
THOUGHTS   1

2
THE WOODS   11

3
QUALITY   25

4
THE TRADE
AND MACHINES   39

5
THE WORKSHOP   55

6
VENEER   73

7
VENEER AND
THE PITFALLS   85

8
THE DECORATED SURFACE   91

9
BOULLEWORK, OR BOULLE MARQUETRY   99

10
METALWORK   117

11
FAKES (MOST ARE WISHFUL THINKING)   131

12
THE CARE AND ATTENTION OF FURNITURE   145

Epilogue   160

Glossary   162

Appendix I   164

Appendix II   165

Bibliography   166

Index   167

Order Information 169

FOREWORD

$\mathcal{M}$UCH HAS BEEN WRITTEN on antique furniture by academics trained in historical research, by museum curators, by dealers, and by other "experts." However, what books exist written by a fully trained cabinetmaker who began as an apprentice starting at age fourteen, was taught by and knew the "old boys", many of who had themselves received their training in the late nineteenth century? World War II interrupted those early days. Unlike many, this cabinetmaker returned to the bench after those years and continued to follow his trade until his recent retirement. It is no exaggeration to say that David Hawkins' training, observations and teaching are only two generations of mentors removed from the early nineteenth century when "hand" craftsmanship was at its zenith.

It is incredible that so few who write about antique furniture have consulted with the men who restore furniture or were trained by men who made furniture in the same way that the "antiques" were constructed. The reason is the traditional reliance placed by research on published or written material.

Never forget primary sources. That is what David Hawkins is, and he is one of the best.

The skill and experience of David Hawkins and the other "old boy" restorers like him are what make the high end market in antique furniture possible. After all, most antique furniture that museums and collectors purchase re-appear, prior to sale, in a shocking state. This is natural, as the best will always carry their history of use, wear and repair. It takes years of experience, skill and training to know how to restore old furniture without destroying either the old color or the integrity of the construction. All this work to revive these items occurs BEFORE they are returned to the art market. For this reason the collecting public, curators, and academics who understand how to "see" the physical history of these items are way ahead of the game.

Let this book be your peek behind the antique market's curtain into the work of the back rooms.

John Booth
Grosse Pointe, Michigan

ACKNOWLEDGEMENTS

*T*HIS MUST BEGIN with John and Becky Booth. They made all this possible, their faith in what I could do has never ceased to amaze me.

Second, must be all my customers over the years who trusted me with such a diversity of things. Even now, I find it hard to believe just how fine some of those things were.

The late Lady Elsie Stoddart-Scott, President of the Chippendale Society who was directly responsible for giving me the opportunity of talking to so many thousands of people about the trade and workshop side of it all. This was in village halls, social centers large and small, conference centers, lecture theatres at universities, museums, etc. A distinction given to few.

My wife Sheila, her support through thick and thin has been total. The finest thing I ever did was to stop and offer her a lift at a bus stop early one rainy morning in October 1959. We have been together ever since! She is also just about the best wax polisher I know.

Our family who still seem to think that we are about 50 years old.

Richard D. Barnsdale, mate of 47 years. Farmer, ex POW, Slade scholar, artist as was his late wife Angela. Simply one of nature's gentlemen. He has been telling me for years that I should try and put something like this together. Well Dick, my son, I have.

David Hawkins
September, 1998

Chapter 1

THOUGHTS

*T*HAVE ALWAYS SAID THAT I WOULD NEVER WRITE A BOOK LIKE THIS. The reasons are many. One of them was not knowing how to put onto paper something that became almost second nature to me. Another was the trouble of opening doors to my sort of workshop and of showing what we got up to! Honour? Something like that. Probably the biggest reason of all was not knowing how to do it without pointing a finger at so many things that should have had a finger pointed at them! However, I will try to tell it how it is, from the bench, from the people who made it, kept it in good condition, saved it from disasters and created a lot more of it along the way. This is from someone who has followed the long traditions of the Cabinet trade, if you like. It is simply a tradesman's story and how he thinks.

History I shall leave to you and will assume that you know the dates and periods as used by the writers of furniture history, the writers of catalogues, and the purveyors of the goods themselves. I will also assume that you know of the Jensens, Channons, Vile and Cobbs, Ince and Mayhews, Chippendales (18th century variety), Seddons, Moores, Bullocks, Gillow, Edwards and Roberts and that you know a Queen Anne batchelor chest, a Georgian bureau or a Regency library table when you see one.

So if you know all this, what is the point in me putting more down on paper?

The answer to that is simple. Do you know if these things are what they are supposed to be? Does your nose tell you, "Yes!" or does it twitch a little and say to you, "If this is what I hope it is, why is it like that?" If it does, read on.

I retired from the workshop for the third time at the beginning of 1994. All my working life apart from flying aeroplanes during World War II had been a practical one. In my case it revolved around furniture, antique, or old furniture as I prefer to call it. I have repaired it, restored it, fiddled it, carved it, cut marquetry and Boullework for it. You name it and I could have done it. On occasions I bought and sold it. This was usually when the workshop's eye spotted something that other eyes had missed. (An example of this and the most memorable was an overmantle in a beaten up house in Fulham. When that was finished, I sold a very good serpentine commode in Satinwood that had started its life in the 1780's, apart from the stiles or frames of the back. It was all there, built in, almost from floor to ceiling, covered in dark reddish brown varnish around the fireplace. That was do-it-yourself from the late 19th century, with a vengeance.) I have designed and made furniture, chairs from short sets to long in all shapes and styles, and I must confess that I have on occasions made it up to deceive. And since I have heard nothing more about those it can only be assumed that I got away with it!

The name for people like me in the antique game is "restorer," a posh name for someone who can repair something in such a way that it can be difficult and sometimes impossible to see what has happened unless you are told. Having said that and believing in putting your money where your mouth is, or in this case your pen,...

The front cover of this book shows a typical and simple example. The top picture is a sewing box brass inlaid into rosewood, typical quadrant nulling from the time, it comes from the early days of the 19th century, from about 1815. It is in nice condition and also, suprisingly, contains all the necessary bits and pieces, scissors, silk and cotton reels, etc. for sewing.

The lower picture is that box as it was given to me, brass inlay panels have to be cut and laid for the top and one end of the sarcophacus shaped top, quadrant nulling, (nulling is the name given to these small decorative mouldings, they can be quadrant or half round) had to be made up as we had quite a lot of loss. This is made by glueing four squares of rosewood together and turning them to shape in the lathe, to get them apart without breaking them after the turning you put a piece of paper in the join and glue that. The paper is much weaker than the glue so it fails and the join is easily and safely broken. How it has always been done. I will say it for the first time now: If it is not simple it cannot be successfully and more importantly, quickly done.

This little box took about eight hours to repair and about an hour to clean and polish.

An obvious question is how does something get into that state in the first place? The answer is the same for most things old, it is, I am afraid, value. The owner of this box bought it over twenty years ago and paid twelve pounds or about eighteen dollars for it. She tried to find someone who was prepared to take it on. When she did the cost of doing it far exceeded its market value. She had kept it, wrapped up, for the best part of sixteen years when I met her and was asked to look at it. I asked her, did she want it repaired and was astounded when she said that it was not worth it. She did change her mind when I asked if I could buy it. The job was done as you can see. The extraordinary thing was that my price was not very much more than that quoted all those years before. I was around seventy years old at the time!

That little box today in the condition it now is, has got to be worth seven to eight hundred pounds or one to one and a quarter thousand dollars. My end of it was a days work, about two hundred and twenty pounds. My customers original investment of twelve pounds has turned out to be a very good investment indeed.

The ability to do things like that comes after more years than you care to remember of having your head stuck inside old furniture. That furniture had been good, bad, some of it just plain awful, and my conclusion is that they made just as much rubbish in the 17th, 18th, and 19th centuries as we have in the 20th! However, on many occasions I have been entrusted with the finest that the world of the decorative arts has had to offer. Because of this and my intimate association with it I am today called an expert. If that is so, then I am possibly a rarity, a white-haired one who is 74 years old!

When I seriously began trying to earn my living at the bench, seven or eight pounds or twelve to fifteen dollars per week at our present rate of exchange was good money. This does sound ludicrous I know, but when I first began before World War II, a top man on the bench was on about £2-75, or £2-15-00 in old money. Me, the boy, was on 38p or 7/9 and this was for a five-and-a-half day week of 52 hours. Yet no matter what is said today, in my opinion they were good days. We were in work and in my case I was learning a trade. I do not believe that we had the stress imposed on the youth of today, either. And as I remember it, a clip round the ear worked wonders!

This story, if that is what it is, begins around 1950. Then an antique had to be before 1830. Goods were plentiful that is to a degree not understood today. There were many. And they were so varied and cheap it is hard to imagine, unless you were actually involved. People are always asking me, "Why on earth did you not salt some of it away?" The answer to that is simple: "Where on earth would the money have come from? And anyway, who could possibly have forseen the world of art as it is today?" Today, anything, no matter how tatty, if it has some age about it, seems to make money. A couple of years ago a Dinky toy which had cost a tanner, two-and-a-half pence 60 years ago sold for £12,500-. The reason: it was the only one left. Now, I ask you, how can anyone possibly know that? I know one thing: when the next one turns up, and it more than likely will, I would not touch it with a bargepole!

A very important point must be raised here. In those days of plenty, none of it was regarded as something special. There was a vast quantity of large, often ugly, and mostly unwanted goods about. Where has all of that gone? One answer is that we made a lot of it into smaller, more attractive and saleable goods that more often than not carried more than their fair share of age. A lot of that is today sailing under false colours. Some of it is under very false colours indeed. Also apart from an awful lot of furniture there were an awful lot of people like me. And you will be surprised when I tell you that forty-odd years ago every Saturday of my life was spent touting for work among the antique shops and business houses of London.

The media alone is a phenomenon that would have been incomprehensible to anybody then. Who would have believed that twenty percent of our population (1950) would be watching a television programme called the ANTIQUES ROADSHOW. If you had gone around proclaiming like that I think the men in white coats would have been knocking on your door. It is even more amazing that goods from my childhood that were bought trashed and thrown away would now be sought after, bought, collected and analysed in the new offering from the media, "THE GREAT ANTIQUES HUNT". It was this offering and the obvious lack of understanding by most of the participants when it came to furniture that did concern me, so when it was suggested that I should put my way of looking at it on paper, it was this sort of thing that stirred me from building my steam engines and made me fire up the word processor and to try once again to see if I could describe my way of looking at furniture. I say once again because I had been asked to try a few years ago. It came to naught because I tried too hard to be an author (which I am not). However, I can talk and in my own way pass what I know across to an audience. What has been put together this time are the talks, lectures if you like, that I have been privileged to give to so many people.

One point about the media coverage: when it all began thirty or more years ago the name of the offering was "GOING FOR A SONG", and I can remember the guest on one of the programmes was the late Ted Ray, a much loved comedian from the time. He was given an object to look at and just said, "I don't like that."

He was immediately told off by the guy in charge, "What do you mean you don't like it, it's old!"

I could not believe it, and for me the attitude that something old must always be better than something new was born as, frankly, that was never the case before. The huge interest in antiques began to escalate. My workshops were in Farnham, Surrey, at the time, that rather nice little town had one old and well established

Antique shop, a couple of lesser ones and the usual junk emporium. In 18 months, within a couple of miles around us we sported 13! Shops sprang up everywhere. Where the keepers suddenly got their know how from was always a mystery to me. Oddly enough it did me a huge favour because it very rapidly made me change course. The reason was that they were buying up the cheap and cheerful – our livelyhood if you like – the breakers. Also at this time, right out of the blue, I was asked to take on a very complicated restoration job. A superb piece of 17th century French marquetry from the Gobelin had been found. In fact, I was asked to authenticate the age of this rather sad and neglected thing that had once been so magnificent. Happily the job was successful. That sort of thing, working with the top echelon of furniture, became the pattern for the rest of my working life.

From that time I have been a fortunate man. My trade has been kind to me and my family. It has taken me overseas, all over the Continent and America. I have met people who are international names in the world of fine furniture. I have been entrusted with fine pieces from this country, the Continent and America. But possibly the most unusual thing about it all is that for the past 30 years I, an Englishman, specialised and worked on some of the finest French and German furniture that the world of the decorative arts has had to offer.

Although I have retired, I have discovered that you can never really do that. I am still asked to lecture and talk about it all. I talk about veneer (the workshop has some very different views about this often decried material), the extraordinary technique of Boullework (this has all the mysteries and old wives tales taken out of it), fakes and fakery (I fought shy of this one but eventually I was persuaded and was astounded not only at people's interest but also their naivity) and quality (this is a rare thing because it needs so many things to all come together on one article). Yet out of it all the surprising one was peoples wish to know how to look after their furniture. They all seemed to think that there

was some sort of workshop secret about it all. It was a huge surprise to discover that it was still shrouded in the "mystery of the trade and its secrets". Because of this, what I really do is to simply talk about my trade.

The questions I get from an audience have prompted me to try again and put it down as the workshop sees it. After all, workshops like mine did make it all in the first place, a point easily forgotten when you see the colour pictures in the books and catalogues. Those pictures from the salerooms often make my hair stand on end. And the estimates, dear Lord above! I also find it difficult to listen to the hype and almost reverential way that a lot of people talk about old furniture. I have often been tempted to say that a couple of days in a workshop would soon change that.

The questions are so often about the simplest of things. Wood, the basis of it all does, sometimes seem to be a complete mystery. Many times I have had a piece of furniture brought in for me to look at, and it is the sheer interest and pleasure that the people seem to get when it is dissected by (surprise surprise) someone who can actually make it. That has made it all very worthwhile.

People do forget that people like me made it all in the first place. A few years ago, I had a group of students with me in the workshop for two-and-a-half to three hours a day for four days. They were nearly ready to be released into the academic and commercial world. They could lose me with the history of it. Yet when it came to my side of it – how a piece of furniture was made, the when and why of it – their understanding was very limited and in one or two cases almost nil. It was the same with veneers. They knew the woods came from trees and that some of them were ecologically threatened, but their knowledge of the why and when of wood in furniture was almost nothing. It was a huge surprise to me and I am afraid that the rose-tinted spectacles of the classroom were severely fogged after a visit with me to the local auction room. However, it has now fallen to my lot to be involved with students and I have discovered just how difficult it can be to try and pass the workshops know-how across when you are not actually in one.

Because of my work in the trade, many buyers do use me to have a look before they commit themselves. How this happened is in its own way extraordinary. It began when I went to see what the cost of repair work could be. On many occasions I would point out that this was wrong or that was wrong, this had been altered, or a fiddle had happened. People were often genuinely surprised that someone from a workshop would have this sort of know-how. Some of them I have now worked with for years in an advisory capacity and it is nice to call them friends.

It has always surprised me how the average furniture buff is for some reason very unwilling to accept that furniture is a utilitarian thing, and, as with anything in almost constant use, is going to suffer to a greater or lesser degree. They find it difficult to believe that a piece of furniture, if it carries any sort of age, will usually need some work on it or will have had it already happen.

Having seen thousands of pieces in the rooms, private sales, collections large and small, museums as well as my workshop, I will agree with Herbert Cescinsky, who wrote in 1926, four years after I was born, "There is more 18th Century mahogany furniture shipped to America in one year than could possibly have been produced in the whole of that century". Now 70 years later I think that he would say that we seem to have more 17th and 18th century furniture than could possibly have been produced during those centuries!

The pitfalls of old furniture are varied and many. Most are caused by the lack of one vital ingredient: experience, from the buyer and very often the seller. Experience can only come by handling thousands of things, understanding the cabinet trade and completely understanding age and what it does to things.

My own understanding comes from this and also something else. Few people will know what a restorer can do. You would be astounded at the mess things can be in. Most times the thoughts about us in the workshop is that we put bits back, wash its neck and clean its teeth and make it all nice and shiny. Sure, this is our function. But more often than you would imagine the work is radical. This is where the other part of my understanding comes from. Some pieces have to be totally taken apart and stripped down. In my case this has applied to many, many things from the 17th, 18th, and 19th centuries and on two occasions the early 20th century. Because of this you get an understanding of the smell of it, a complete insight into the cabinet trade and how it developed. You learn to know that how they did something in 1750 was done in a quite different way 50 years later. You learn to read the trade. This is of vital importance to any serious restoration job. It is a bit daft to repair something from 1700 using techniques from fifty or one hundred years later. So the man from the workshop will develop an understanding that is unique. This is why I have had a very close encounter with antique furniture. This and Steven Spielberg's movie gave me the title for this book!

When people hear that I have retired the inevitable point that is brought up is, "How many people have I taught or am now teaching?" The answer is "none" and I am continuously taken to task about it. My reply to this is twofold: (1) even if I did teach someone, they could not be me. Some of the things I can do now I could not possibly have done 30 years ago. (2) I could not have put trainees on some of the work undertaken during the past 25 years. I think that I would have been irresponsible if I had. I do not like to think of your reaction had you been the owner! The way to learn is to work alongside the experienced man. My friend Doug in Michigan is an example of that. He has a good pair of hands which are coupled with a wish to learn. I can remember once doing some work with him when he showed me his "notes". Dear God, he had almost written a book about the work we had done together. It was brought home to me then just how important my beginnings and experience are to someone like Doug.

I hope this story will show you what I mean. I first retired in 1986 and we went to teach a short course in America. More than anything this course was to show ways of surface conservation other than stripping and refinishing. People ask, "Why not in England?" The answer to that is very easy: "Nobody asked me". I think it was a success, hard work and a lot of fun. But we decided that enough was enough, and again retirement beckoned.

We had not been home in the West Sussex countryside for more than two weeks when I was asked to do just one more restoration. I had no workshop. Everything from my closing down was in store. This, and the fact that I was retiring was explained and the solution was as usual when something is urgently needed, in this case it was me. Money was thrown at it, and another small workshop was opened near my home. The piece arrived in early 1987. I had heard about it. It was a double-sided Bureau Plat from about 1685. It carried six drawers on one side and seven on the other. It was veneered with classical marquetry into an ebony ground, the eight legs veneered on all sides with pewter and Celadon grey cowhorn. These had been mounted with a combination of Gilt bronze and pewter. When the pewter was cleaned, it looked uncommonly like silver! It carried all the hallmarks of the Gobelin workshops of Paris. It was very large and the reason for me being chased up was obvious – it was in one hell of a mess!

There was just me in the workshop with my ever patient wife, Sheila. She was the holder-upper and provider of the extra pair of hands that are so often vital. She was also the receiver of the invectives when patience wore a bit thin. The job was completed. It took us just under twelve months to complete and was sold for over seven figures of money. When finished, it was magnificent.

It has always amazed me how things happen in your life. This piece was the last really serious and complicated job I undertook. The first, all those years ago, was from the same era and workshop. Some of the birds in the marquetry were identical in each piece and I am convinced that they were cut by the same hand. I would have loved to have had the opportunity to really see if I was right.

My own view is that if the need is there to develop your skills you will develop them. This is very much how it was with me and is exactly how it has been with Doug.

There is another side that does cause me sadness and is something that most trainees will not benefit from. It is much to do with how I began. I am now I suppose an old buffer who is supposed to know it all. Fat chance. But who taught me? Who did I work with when I began? Now I was in a workshop with a lot of skilled men. These men were people like me, people with a lifetime of experience. Some of them had begun as long ago as the 1870's, two of them had been in workshops that made the Edwardian satinwood furniture that is now making serious money. They were paid 2p per hour. By just being with them, seeing them work and observing the discipline of how they worked was something that I have always been grateful for. It is something that will probably be missing from any training scheme today. An apprenticeship was then five years. (The war put paid to mine. I did not help, I suppose; I volunteered.)

Many people take me to task for saying that I would not have been very responsible to put trainees on some of the pieces that we handled and many have said to me, "But surely you worked on other peoples furniture when you were a boy". My answer was, "Of course I did, but none of it was worth over a million quid!"

It was one of these men from my past that I shall always remember. He knocked on my workshop door in 1952 and asked if there was any part time work. He being a mere youngster of 82 I took him on and we worked together for 4 years. What I learned from him was extraordinary, yet oddly enough he learned from me because I taught him all the tricks and dodges of brass inlay and the use of the piercing saw. The sadness has to be that the experience of these men was never written down. People ask me why. The answer is as usual a simple one: there were thousands upon thousands of them and as usual, sadly, it was always left just a little too late.

This lovely old man, James Little, apart from being highly skilled had a profound understanding of furniture old and new. He understood age and how to preserve it. This was, as with me now, almost inbuilt. The question I have always asked myself is, "Who had taught him?"

Before anything more is written two things about old furniture must be put down and fully understood. As a tradesman, craftsman, restorer – call me what you will – I will say that anything created by my trade during the 17th, 18th, 19th, and early 20th century can be created today and in some aspects will be better. You can imagine how a statement like that has, more than once, got me into trouble. However, there are two things that cannot, or at least I cannot successfully do.

1. Recreate old colour if it is destroyed

2. Recreate old polish and patina that may have been on that old surface.

Old colour and its patina and polish are rare. Patina is especially so. Good, old-fashioned, spring cleaning with vinegar and water would have made sure of that. People do not usually think about that when they hold forth about old surfaces! Old colour is something else. It is not commonly understood that the difference between old and new is tiny. The lovely mellowness of true and genuine age is about EIGHT THOUSANDS OF AN INCH in thickness, or the thickness of a piece of scribbling paper. Below this thickness the wood will be very much the colour it was when new. Woods in furniture can begin their lives in colours from black to white. If the pieces are left alone and just live with us they will all take up this rich mellow golden tone. The darker ones will fade down. The paler ones will warm up until they will all carry this mellowness. The one possible exception is ebony, yet I have seen it in some of that, especially when it has not been ebonised. (Yes, they did black polish ebony.)

Old polish is much rarer. You have your

home redecorated, and furniture, a utilitarian thing, it will get tatty and used, just as your home. This will show and it will be put right usually by repolishing. It has always been so and for some reason when old furniture is talked about this fact is never mentioned.

There used to be itinerant French Polishers who would call at your home and go over the pieces as necessary. A team of them would be sent to the very large houses. This was commonplace. Whether it still goes on I do not know – it more than probably does. When I was young they were called fad floppers. (A fad is the name given to the polishing pad a polisher uses.) Time and again we have found evidence of this polishing when under a skin of dark brown shellac, which is their polishing, has been a lovely old surface waiting to be revived.

The finishing of furniture is the maker or breaker of it. It is absolutely vital to the restorers art. If I could be in charge of the training of restorers, I would not be seriously concerned about how good they were on the bench – they would have to have some skill to get onto the bench in the first place. The first thing I would make really sure of would be that they understood finish and how to polish and conserve surfaces. Something, I am afraid to say, is very often lacking in the work I see today.

The usual and often quoted way of the 18th century was to oil it, then polish it with beeswax. In the Cabinet Makers Book of Prices from 1793 to wax polish with hard wax, (a lump of solid beeswax) was 3d per foot. To wax polish with soft (wax softened with turpentine) was 1d per foot. You try the former and you will see why they wanted three times the money to do it. Spirit varnish was about in the 18th century although this applied more to the Continent than England. We began using this when Marquetry and decorated surfaces began in earnest around the 1770's with the Neo-Classical revival. (Dear me, I am getting all historical.) Spirit varnish gradually became more and more refined, and it became French polish. I am sure that you do not need me to tell you how vulnerable that can be. Because of these points, I have said on many occasions that the use of the word "original", especially when applied to the finish, should be seriously thought about when used in the context of antique furniture.

Out of the thousands of things that have come through my hands during my working life, I have only seen 48 pieces of furniture that were truly original. Possibly I am a hard task master, but my 48 had never been repaired or repolished. The miracle of them was that they did not need any repair or repolish. They were perfect and ready to go. All that was needed was a gentle clean and wax polish. They were then ready for another 150-200 years. Everything else needed repair to a greater or lesser and sometimes a radical degree and always a repolish, or, there was evidence that this had already happened. Some were fakes. Of these, some were silly, some were very good indeed, many, many pieces were the ones I have already mentioned, things made up to live with our society today. Many of these things that carried signs of age would never have been made in the time they were supposed to come from. They just did not make pieces like that! It all needed our know how to a greater or lesser degree.

Because of this it is no surprise to me that when you view the things that have survived and are now in houses, museums, gallerys and dealers' showrooms, the one name you will rarely, if ever, see is that of the restorer or his workshop!

Once in America I was introduced to an audience as the antique dealers secret weapon – a touch off-putting to say the least.

One of my 48 pieces of original furniture was a truly superb Louis XV Commode by the Ebeniste Joseph. The Ebeniste Joseph was a German working in Paris, named Baumhauer. The commode was veneered in bois de bout marquetry of kingwood into a satinee ground. The carcass was entirely of oak. The drawers were lined with fine walnut and the carcass was fully mounted with the finest gilt bronze which was mounted into veneered reserves of purpleheart. It was stunning. It also carried its original varnish. I found it hard to believe what I was looking at, if anything carried its history on its face this did.

From a commercial sense it was not much use to me. The bronzes were removed and washed with mild soap and water. The carcass surface was also washed and wax polished. The inside was left exactly as it had come to me. The bronzes were put back. (Even these still had their original fixings.) It probably cost more to move it from London to me and back than my bill for washing its neck.

Two years later I saw it again. I just could not believe it. So harsh and gaudy, it looked brand new. I had bent over backwards to preserve the old colour and original varnish. Now, somebody had stripped off that varnish and cleaned the gilt bronze to a degree that made it look like brass. Worst of all was that the old colour had been scraped back to new wood. That precious 8,000 parts of an inch, the authenticity of age if you like, was gone. Here was something that had been made about 1750, survived the turmoils of that century, sold in the revolutionary sales during the early 19th century and eventually been purchased by, I believe, the Rothschild family. They had looked after it through war and peace until it was bought and came to me. After all that history, it ends up having some idiot doing that to it.

Had I done that I doubt if I would have been allowed to touch anything again.

This sort of thing does, I am afraid, happen far more often than it should, usually because of a lack of understanding. And it has fallen to my lot to try and get rid of the harshness and put this problem right on far too many occasions.

Woods can obviously be bleached and treated chemically to recreate an old colour. This is being done all the time and a fair fist[1] can be made of it. But it will never be as lasting or look as good as an authentic and natural old colour. Give the artificial one the test of time and in a year or two it will start to show. When I began, repair was done whenever possible with materials that carried old colour. Goods were so plentiful and cheap it was common practise to buy something not wanted that matched and use that. These are the BREAKERS

[1]Fist. Slang for job, result or just trying to do something and not quite succeeding.

from the days of "Going for a song". My own stock of old materials was huge, and I had a goodly collection of odds and ends when I finally shut up shop. However, in retrospect, I cannot help but feel ashamed at how short-sighted we were.

ILLUSTRATION 1: *Rosewood drawer 1720. Authentic old colour.*

This can only be a problem for the person who is for whatever reason trying to create age. For those of you who are not and are looking for the authentic, if the colour is right then you have made

ILLUSTRATION 2: *Another drawer from same piece. Old colour scraped off.*

a good step in the right direction.

I have found it impossible to explain old colour. Happily we in this country still have a few houses stately and otherwise where the goods have been left alone. Many of the smaller museums are true eye openers. This mellowness will be obvious when you see it.

ILL 1 shows a drawer front from about 1720, it is French and comes from a commode or chest of drawers, it was bought years ago as a BREAKER. The parquetry surface is veneered and has had its polish removed and the colour is right. It is the colour that results from 280 years of being left alone. ILL 2 shows another drawer front from the same piece of furniture, all I have done is to scrape the old colour off in the top right quadrant. The

authenticity of age, that vital 8,000 parts of an inch has gone and that quadrant is how it would have looked when it was new in 1720.

I can imagine your reaction if you owned the piece!

Having two drawer fronts illustrated like this is good for another reason, no two pieces of wood are the same even if they come from the same tree. At first glance these two drawer fronts look alike, just look at the surfaces and you can see the small and often subtle difference there is in the appearance between each piece that makes up the surface. I call it reading the wood. It would have been impossible for these two surfaces not to have been veneered at the same date. Learn to look at and think about wood like this. The veneer is East Indian Rosewood. All woods will behave like this to a greater or lesser degree. The fading will begin from the day a piece of furniture is made. It will eventually take up its colour as in our picture and will stay like that. How long will this be? I honestly do not know other than it will be much more than my lifetime. One certainty is this: ILL 2 will not look remotely like ILL 1 in three score years and ten, and I have a sneaking feeling that it will take a lot longer than that.

Obviously this is completely a matter of choice, but why bother to buy something 150, 200, 300 years old if it looks brand new? For what it is worth, keep old colour and you will keep value.

My advice can only be to do as little as possible and remember that a piece of old furniture will carry its history on its face.

This is much my own view and very much the view of my customers. In fact one of my major customers was converted to this view. Oddly enough it was with a late 17th Century Bureau Plat in untouched ebony. I refused to do the usual thing in those days of taking the surface back and then polishing it like a mirror. To this day I am not sure why he agreed to my way of thinking. Happily he did, and the piece went to London. It sold immediately, much to my delight and the amazement of my client. Enough to say that old colour was always maintained from then on. I worked for him for the rest of my time on the bench and handled all the things for them that were in my field. My life blossomed and that company became a byeword for the finest. However, there always has been a trend for articles to be re-finished to a greater or lesser degree and today being brought to something being called "mint condition". This can cover a multitude of sins and can often be taken to a degree where much of the mellowness has gone. It is not my intention to show how this is done. If some of the advice being given, for example, the use of abrasives, various concoctions for stripping and some of the new ways of refinishing, the use of caustics etc, it will take you a very short time indeed to destroy any semblance of age that you

may have, and having had to try to rectify some of these efforts, my advice to do as little as possible is very sound advice indeed.

More and more it seems that these views of mine about old colour and finish are being noticed. Time and again these days people are coming up to me and voicing their concern. Surprisingly the concern and sometimes complaints are about the furniture and articles in our national collections. The most common criticism is that the goods are over-cleaned, and this has run from looking tarted up to looking downright gaudy. Recently, after a lecture a lady came up to me, she had been in America, and she referred to the furniture in a museum collection over there as looking brand new!

However, no matter what is done cosmetically, whether you agree with it or not, it does not affect the piece. If it has been fiddled with, no matter how much repair is there, it will not affect the signs that the makers have left behind. What now follows are things to look for. They are I suppose the rules of a trade and how it developed. It is the discipline of that trade, but as in any trade there will always be good and bad – the cowboy of today. (No, not really that.) There is good and bad and just because it is old does not matter. They did create the shoddy. And just as today, everything had a price.

Anything that has been around and used for a hundred years and often much, much more than that has to be a survivor. Much of that survival has in part been due to workshops like mine over the years, and because of that I shall include some of the simple and basic rules for the care and attention of these survivors.

They are rules that have served me well and I am sure that they will also serve you. I will do my best to explain the Trade, the discipline and often rigidity of it, if you can understand that and how it was done and developed and when that development happened and why, then you will look at furniture, hopefully, through my eyes, and be able as I do when someone tells me that something comes from 1780 I just simply ask him, or her, to tell me WHY!

Chapter 2

THE WOODS

HEN I FIRST TRIED TO RETIRE IN 1986 and closed our workshop down I can remember, almost with sadness the remnants of nearly 40 years stacked around me. Sheila and I were waiting for the removal men to collect and put into store what, at first glance were crates and tea chests full of rubbish, old iron and firewood, the latter being the last knockings of the old furniture bought and broken up – the Breakers that had been such an essential part of the job.

My tool chest was there, clamps of all shapes and sizes, jigs and gadgets made up for specific jobs and never thrown away because as soon as you do they will be needed again, (the origin of sod's law I suppose) a small anvil and forge, a wood lathe that had many a dodgy leg and fruit-shaped tea caddy that it could talk about. (Why I had kept it I do not know, as all my other wood working machinery had been sold) My small engineering machines I was keeping. My sideline and hobby of model steam engines I reckoned would keep my hands and mind busy in the time to come. One thing was missing: my two rolls of carving chisels, about 80 in all, mostly 19th-century, many of them still had their original sharpening slip and scraper. They had been given to me and collected over the years. They were much prized and had been stolen twenty years before and I do not doubt that they now grace some collectors cabinet. To collect the tools of a trade is understandable, but to steal them from someone who uses them, for my money, is just not on. I have never carved anything of significance since then. That was sad. Whoever has got them now would never have thought about it. Some of the tools were replaced, some were not replaceable. The thing was that not one of them ever felt right when they came to your hand.

Apart from the breaker wood there were bundles of 19th-century sawn veneer. Kingwood, Tulip, Ebony and Purpleheart had been sorted and parcelled. Some of this was so rare to see it should possibly have been in a museum. The modern knifecut variety lay with it. Inlays and strings were neatly tied up for the first time in years and laid by the wood. A box of pearl veneers, some flattened cowhorn plates, a few scutes of turtle shell, bits and pieces of Ivory left

11

over from the days when you could go up to the Minories[2] in London and come home with half a tusk. (Happily those days are long ago as are the days of turtle shell.) A box full of old locks, hinges, bolts, castors of all shapes and sizes but not a full set amongst them, old screws and nails, another box full of furniture mounts. Gilt bronze lay alongside the lacquered variety. Brass, copper, pewter and black iron sheet packed and braced to keep it flat. It was quite a collection going into store. Why store? As events have turned out it seems that people like me do not retire. More likely we join the old soldier and just fade away.

This lot of dusty rubbish was the result of almost a lifetime's work on all kinds of furniture from all sorts of countries, and yet I doubt if there were more than thirty different woods and materials lying about me. Now I have seen it written that about four hundred different woods can be listed in furniture, and long lists are presented by veneer merchants today. Why, I had to ask myself, had I seen and handled so few.

Because of this and the near mystique that tends to surround things old, I suppose it is inevitable that I am expected to know and recognise every wood there is. What a hope. If I do not know I call it "treewood" and if the matter is that important, I will find out. A tiny sample sent to Kew Gardens will usually do the trick.

Chapters such as this can be a bore. Persevere. Since wood is after all the basis of furniture, an understanding of it, no matter how basic, will be useful. After all, I doubt if any of us could bake a cake without some knowledge of the ingredients, this is probably the wrong way of looking at it today with our instant this and that, but then I still find food superstores mind-boggleing Understandable I suppose; my father was a small grocer in the 1920's. My list is not long. It is simply the woods and materials that I have come across on a regular basis over the years. There will be confusion; there has to be. And I have been surprised on many occasions at the almost non-

chalant attitude toward this basis of it all – wood.

I have worked on famous things, things recorded in history, written about, photographed etc, yet sometimes I have found that they are not of the wood that they are said to be. On one or two occasions the pedigree had a few hiccups in it as well! This does not really matter or surprise me, but it does matter when money could change hands, and matters hugely when you have to repair them.

This nonchalant attitude was brought home to me with a pair of bookcases on chests. They were in the rooms. Enough to say that we were in Londons West End, and that they were catalogued as English, veneered in rosewood, dated 1770 with an estimate of 25,000 to 30,000 pounds. The problem was that the bottom or chest parts were in solid East Indian rosewood, the top or bookcase parts were veneered in the Brazilian or West Indian variety. I queried it with the guy in charge only to be asked what was my problem with that. As far as I was concerned, this was, in furniture, akin to asking the difference between black and white. I was so astounded that all I could think of in reply was that the difference was about 11,000 miles! To this day I do not think he understood why I was bothered. The reason was simple. These bookcases were said to be English and I have never seen a piece of English furniture made out of solid Rosewood, not large things like this. A Canterbury maybe. Here you see the chest parts were solid everywhere —carcass, drawer linings, feet, dustboards, backboards, everything. The only time I have ever seen this was with furniture that came from the East Indian part of this world. The tops or bookcase parts were made of pine and veneered with the Brazilian variety of Rosewood, and I cannot remember seeing any English furniture veneered with that before around 1790. If someone bought these as English 1770 I would love to be a fly on the wall when they tried to sell them. I do not know the outcome of this story. I suppose I should have found out. But my thoughts now are as then. If they got away with that one, then this chapter is of vital importance. Persevere.

[2]Minories. A street of warehouses in the East end of London, they sold Ivory, tortoiseshell, pearl and exotics in general, from the days of the Far Eastern trade.

Wood, being so common, is forgotten as the incredible material it is. A tree is alive until felling kills it. But we do not know how long it will last when stabilised by seasoning or kiln drying. It is difficult to think of any other growing thing that has been put to so many uses. Sadly, as with so many living things, it is temperamental. One of its major failings is that it takes too long to grow! At this time we are at last trying to come to terms with the ecological problems that constant felling are causing. This, to most people's minds, is something new. Far from it. For my money this began with the felling of Ebony 400 odd years ago, and that has not recovered to this day. Wood in its utilitarian life is temperamental and, rather like us, does not take kindly to rapid changes in temperature and humidity. In our modern living conditions it can and will soon show you that it is unhappy. However, this is not the place to go into these sorts of problems. They will not be forgotten and will be talked about later.

One thing I am not going to do is put in the Latin names, which does seem to be the case, for some reason, with so many books about furniture. I can imagine the reception I would have got at the timber yard if I had asked for five cube of Dalbergia, the Latin name for Rosewood. Obviously I have looked them up, but not only could I not pronounce them, not once in my life have I ever needed them.

After all these years woods are such familiar things to me, or they were until I began trying to teach people how to recognise them. Sitting here trying to put it down on paper, I am realising why you cannot learn very much about them from books! I am afraid that at the end of the day it will all boil down to the old, old chestnut, experience. That experience will give you the feel and weight of them, if you can get into workshops you will get the smell of them. There is just so much that cannot be put into words.

However, all is not lost and we all have to start somewhere. I have decided to explain the woods that will turn up nine times out of ten in the world of furniture in the years that we are talking about. The reason for doing it this way is the reaction of students when I get onto the subject. They always seem to imagine that we are going into some new and mysterious world, which, as you can imagine does make it rather difficult. For the last few years I have given them a list of the woods that will turn up on our nine out of ten occasions. Then I tell them to go out and become as familiar with them as they possibly can. They do have a big advantage over us, because of the samples that they can see and handle. Their list is simply this:

1. Pines
2. Oaks
3. Walnuts
4. Mahoganies
5. Rosewoods
6. Satinwoods
7. Acers (sycamore, maple)
8. Beech
9. Birch
10. Yew
11. Kingwood (bois de violette)
12. Tulipwood (bois de rose)
13. Purpleheart (amaranth)
14. Satinee (faux acajou, or fake mahogany)

This short list is enough and you will see these used somewhere on practically all furniture. The last four will appear mainly on Continental furniture and of that France must be the leader. The other ten will appear on our nine out of ten pieces somewhere in furniture from Europe and America. I shall be accused of simplifying it all, but just go and look; you will soon see what I mean.

1. PINE

With the abundance of pine furniture shops, the now-popular, flat pack and put-it-together-yourself vogue, it should need no explanation. There are many varieties. The ones that had long clear growth on the trunk were the ones sought after, this meaning that there will be a lack of knots and other imperfections. The size of the pine used in the world of old furniture, American especially, has to be seen to be believed. It is not like that today. Modern machines and the quick harvesting of the timber industry make a large and clear board a rarity. Boards made up of small strips glued together are very much the norm.

Uses

Pine furniture as just pine furniture is comparatively rare. It was used mainly as the carcass work for painted furniture until the practice of stripping pine, made painted furniture virtually disappear. However, it is now starting to reappear, some in the traditional styles. Some nice modern approaches to it are also appearing which are good to see.

Used as a secondary wood from the beginning of cabinet making, secondary wood means the wood that is not seen, or the wood used for the backs, bottom boards, dustboards, drawer lining. The latter is usually found in lesser quality furniture, frames for drop in chair seats, glue blocks etc, The best cheap and easily worked utilitarian wood.

Pine was used as the ground wood for veneering from the earliest of times. In the 17th century a red pine, very similar to the Douglas fir, was used with great success on the early Flemish and French furniture which was veneered with ebony and the other early exotics. However, as is usual, lesser quality and cheaper pines were used more and more for this. The results usually showed, which had much to do with veneer getting a bad name.

When new, pine is almost white to a very pale yellow. Left alone it will darken down to a rich golden colour. Old pine will very often have a pale almost greyish colour, caused by the common practise of washing this almost utility furniture down with water and soda! The same effect will also be seen on pieces that could have gone through the stripping tank.

Pine is susceptable to woodworm. I recently had a nice bracket clock brought to me made of solid Mahogany except for the bottom board which the movement stood on. This board collapsed because of worm, the movement dropped, the clock fell over and the damage was serious. The clock was from 1810 and valuable. Someone had filled the worm and covered it over in an attempt to hide it. This had been done about 40 years ago.

This stupid practice is commonplace. Old things must always be original to the collectors of them. Be careful.

2. OAK

Oak should need no introduction and from the beginning has been used for everything from buildings to ships and back. Furniture is really a minor part of its use!

Possibly with pine, oak was the first wood used for furniture. This I am sure can be said for this country. However, in my opinion our indigenous oak does not lend itself well to cabinet work. As the trade developed the use of imported oak became the English preference. It would seem that the Continental makers had the same ideas as Baltic, French, Austrian, Hungarian, Persian and in the late 19th century, American oak is common. Do not let this confuse you. Oak is Oak and they are all very similar in appearance.

Uses

All forms of furniture, chairs and stools, used as drawer linings for better quality furniture through the years. However the early makers forgot how hard Oak is and often allowed the much harder Oak drawer to run on the stiles and runners of the carcass that were made of pine. Watch for this. The wear can often be huge and repair is more often than not unsightly.

Oak was used as a ground for better quality furniture that was to be veneered. This has applied especially to French furniture, and because of this the weight of some of it is unbelievable.

Oak will not be thought of as a decorative wood. Yet it was used in inlay work from the earliest of times. One of these was Bog Oak, the other Green Oak. In this case the tree was infected by a fungus that turned the wood to a pale green. As veneer developed the decorative side of Oak began to be exploited and in the early stages of the 19th century Burr Oak makes its appearance along with the Pollarded and Root Oaks.

When new, its colour can range from almost white to fawnish brown. With age they will all become a darker brown. Oak furniture that has been left alone and just matures will take up a beautiful rich golden almost chestnut brown that is impossible to create artificially. Man-made "old" oak always seems to appear to be black, something that I call the "olde world pub look". One tip here: when looking at old Oak if there is any wear, for example where a door rubs or the colour is worn away, if the Oak looks white then it is not going to be very old.

A good powerful and stable wood that has allowed man to create amazing things. Oak well deserves its title: the KING of trees

3. WALNUT

Not really a native English wood, the finest walnut comes from the warmer climates of Europe. This, too, should need no description. I will not try to describe the quality and beauty of some of it. Just look at the stock of a top quality, sporting gun.

Walnut is a dense and easily worked wood. If a wood had to be designed when furniture began, it would have been something very much like Walnut. If it has a failing, it would be the fact that the furniture beetle likes it.

Where English furniture began with Oak, furniture on the Continent, especially in the Southern areas, was made with Walnut extensively. This was in the solid form. English furniture in solid Walnut will be rare.

Uses

On the Continent Walnut was used to make all kinds of furniture and chairs. Its ability to be carved made sure that the finest would be created in it. It carried paint well and this means that it also lends itself to being gilded. When veneer came into common use during the late 17th and early 18th centuries, the English and German makers began to seriously use it. In English goods it was chairs that showed us its ability to be carved. The wood for this was not over-exciting in its appearance. The practice of veneering the face work began and on the finest parcel gilding was sometimes used. This is the use of gold leaf to enhance or emphasis an area, for example, the knee of a chair leg between the carving. With American furniture the use of it follows very closely the pattern of European usage.

I have never seen it used for a veneer ground. The French used it extensively for drawer linings, and never, like England, seriously exploited it as a veneer.

With English furniture it was the introduction of veneering from the Continent that determined our way ahead. Our high style furniture began with chests, escritoires, tallboys etc, veneered with oyster pieces. Walnut was often used for this. It was the first few years of the 18th century however that determined the style of English furniture. Our use of veneer was not as it had usually been. Now, almost for the first time, the English began to use wood for its beauty alone. The use of curl and crotch veneers began to be seen. Burrs and other highly decorative parts of the Walnut began. It is this side of the English cabinet trade that I consider highly important. It was something that they were not given the credit for.

The English use of Walnut died out around 1720-30's to reappear in the middle of the 19th century when the furniture industry began to become really industrialised and veneer became very cheap to produce. Shipping and trade grew. American walnut became prevalent. Significantly, 150 years would have been long enough for the regrowth after the great frost of 1709. (Just a thought.)

The colour of old walnut should be a superb honey golden colour that has a lot of depth. The reason for this is the thickness of the early veneers. If the colour has an orangey tinge without much depth. Be careful. Faked up walnut is produced with concoctions of Nitric acid to take out the natural tones as when it is new the colour of it can range from a rather weak fawn colour to a dark brown almost purple tone. American black Walnut carries this purple tone.

We cannot leave Walnut without mention of Red Walnut, or Virginian Red Walnut, very often mistaken for mahogany. It was quite commonplace in English furniture during the 1720's. Whether it was used as a substitute for mahogany, I do not know. I think it was taken up by our trade because it carved well. It also was very good for the chair maker. And I will probably be howled down for saying this, but it could well be the poor man's mahogany!

Walnut, probably the most important wood in the early history of furniture, was certainly the first wood used for its decorative quality alone.

4. MAHOGANIES
If Oak is the king of trees then Mahogany is the king of woods, not only in furniture but in any other trade that it was used.

The source of the first Mahogany was the West Indies and because of our interests there the English and probably the Spanish were the first to use it. It begins to seriously appear about 1730 and coincides almost exactly with the end of the Walnut era. It is said that the great frost of 1709 killed our Walnut trees and caused the end of Walnut furniture. This I find hard to believe. It probably helped, but, if the frost killed the trees it would not of killed the wood! However, having worked with wood most of my life I would say that the moment West Indian Mahogany was available and the trade discovered what it was like and what could be done with it the days of Walnut were numbered.

Many varieties are named for furniture. We really only need two. The Cuban or San Dominican variety is the best, being heavy and hard. The lighter and softer varieties can be called Honduras. These two are always mentioned when 18th and early 19th Century things are talked about. Brazilian varieties began in the late 19th century and are prevalent today. Many species from Africa are also in common use.

The first of the wood to come in was often quite plain and uninteresting. It was called Bay Wood. It is said that it came in as ballast for our shipping. It's hard to believe that a ship would come back from the West Indies in ballast! The arrival of the other varieties and, as usual, veneer allowed it to blossom and to show us the beautiful wood that it is.

It really came into its own with chairmaking, its stability, strength and adaptability to carving made it the most important wood for English furniture and I do not believe that the English trade could have developed as it did without it. Without a wood such as this I doubt if Thomas Chippendale would have designed the chairs he did. Just look at a mid 18th Century ribboned back chair and you will see what I mean. I doubt if such a thing would have been created in any other wood.

Uses
Early 18th century work used the hard and heavy varieties for the show work, ie, tops and drawer fronts of case furniture. The sides were often in Pine and painted to look like Mahogany. It was expensive and veneering began early on as with Walnut, not because of the expense but because of the highly decorative wood that the tree contains. It was about 1760 that the very stable and straight grain of the Honduras wood began to be used for carcass wood and the grounds for veneer, especially when marquetry began. It began to be used for drawer linings, a practice that has continued to the present day. The use of the Honduras moved into chair making toward the end of the 18th Century and lent itself well to the smaller chairs of the early 19th century and Victorian era. It was a wonderful wood when the 18th century reproduction chair trade really got going.

A workshop thought: without mahogany with its size and stability I do not think that dining tables would have developed as they did, and I personally do not think English furniture would have developed along the path it did without it. I think that this also applies to American furniture.

Their work and use of it in the 18th century was superb, and the skill of their carvers allowed a distinct style to develop, this leading to a style in the early 19th century of combining their carving skills with veneer to a very high degree of style and quality.

It is strange that it took almost fifty years for it to be seriously used on the Continent. When it did begin the results were stupendous as the work of Jacob, Weissweiller, Roentgen and company can show us today. No matter what your taste or preference in furniture is, it is their usage of this king of woods that will never be surpassed.

One important point in comparing Mahogany with Walnut is that it is not attacked by the furniture beetle when in its solid form.

Colour when new is a pale brown to pinkish colour that rapidly darkens to a mid brown tone. When left alone it produces again this marvelous rich deep golden colour. This is the rarity rather than the norm and most Mahogany will be a rather drab brown colour. This is from the habit of repolishing everything when antiques became popular at the beginning of this century. Brown Mahogany was the norm and pieces were stripped and stained with Van Dyke or Walnut crystals, a colour that does not fade. Years ago, a certain road in West London was known as the Brown Mahogany Mile!

The felling of the wood during the 18th century was such that by the 1850's the fine Cuban woods were to all intent and purpose extinct. Its common use was not possible anymore. In my working life I have never been able to buy Mahogany of a quality that the 18th century makers must have taken for granted and many other varieties have been introduced. It is not generally known that a plantation of the Cuban wood was set up in India in the early 1820's. It is being marketed today in small quantities. I have used some of it. Sadly, 180 years is not remotely enough to produce a tree that can be ten feet in girth that the 18th century makers were fortunate enough to use. Unhappily that is something that will not be seen today or more than likely ever again.

5. ROSEWOOD

We have the age of Oak, the age of Walnut, the age of Mahogany, and the age of Satinwood; we should also have the age of Rosewood.

There are several varieties, but the two that concern us are the East Indian and the Brazilian. My first sight of its use was in German, French and Flemish work dating from the 1600's onward. It is probably the latter along with Portugal who first imported the East Indian variety. It was used extensively throughout the 18th century with Continental work, usually in a decorative veneered form. This is the Pallisander wood of France. The natural darkness of the wood made it a wonderful foil for the Continental habit of mounting with gilt and lacquered bronze.

The first serious use of it in England began in the latter stages of the 18th century. Again the purple darkness of it made it a foil for inlay when our marquetry revivals began. It is strange that at this time we were beginning to move away from Mahogany while the French and German shops were beginning to exploit it.

The Brazilian wood started to make an appearance around 1790 and into the Regency when it really came into its own. The Brazilian wood carried startling grain patterns and colour changes, and the emergence of brass inlay work was a natural progression for a wood such as this. The hardness of it made it a firm favorite for the mechanical inlaying techniques that began in the early days of the 19th century.

I personally have never seen it used on American work of the 18th century, but have seen it used in a veneer form on work from around the 1820's onward. However, I am sure that it or some of its varieties would have been used in the southern part of that huge nation.

Uses
All kinds of furniture and chairs were made of Rosewood since its introduction. It lent itself superbly to the small and often very delicate chairs of the Regency era and when the couch or day bed made a serious appearance. In furniture,

solid wood will sometimes be found in the legs of tables – sofa, card, work, breakfast etc. You can, however, expect to find its use to be predominantly in a veneer form.

The 19th century used it extensively and it became a popular favorite for the spoon-back dining chair, sofa and easy chair. During this century it has been a favorite with some of the more expensive makes of furniture.

Colour

The Brazil wood when new is a rich dark purple colour with areas of much lighter hues, these areas are often outlined with striking and random black lines. The East Indian is usually darker than the Brazil and does not carry such striking colour changes and the black grain lines are not so predominant. They both have one thing in common: a sweet cloying smell that gave it its name – Rosewood.

Workshop tip

This is the wood illustrated in Chapter 1. So if you have a piece in Rosewood that has taken up its pale golden colour, or even if it is comparatively new and it should need work carried out, make sure that you or the workshop you go to fully understands the difference between old and new colour.

6. SATINWOOD

Again like Rosewood there are two varieties of Satinwood: the East Indian and the West. Serious appearances of it was much the same as Rosewood in England. The West Indian was used first, when old looks remarkably like Mahogany. (I have seen it mistaken for it on occasions) The East Indian was used later in the 18th century and has a more quilty or satin look. Use was sporadic during the 19th century with reproductions that were often painted. This fashion in the second half of the century meant that many fine 18th century pieces were also painted.

Edwardian Satinwood became very popular. This used the East Indian variety of the wood. Remember that Edwardian furniture is 20th century and is made with that technology and machinery!

Uses

As for Mahogany and Rosewood, Satinwood was also a very popular wood for the ground veneer in Marquetry work. It was much favoured in the Neo-Classical revival of the late 18th century in England. Use in American work was sporadic, and mainly as a decorative veneer.

Colour

When new it is a pale butter colour. The East Indian tends to carry a very faint greyish hue. Years ago I was asked if I wanted to buy a couple of railway sleepers. Curiosity made me go and look. I had not a clue what they were except that they were not railway sleepers. So they were bought. If I remember right they were £4·00 and heavy. It took three of us to move them. The moment they were cut the smell of Satinwood was all over the workshop – a sweet almost butter-like smell. I could not believe it, but I had bought two huge baulks of the West Indian variety. They had to have been at least 150 years old and where they came from I never found out. They were sawn to veneers and what happened to it is another story. Enough to say that this was the one and only time that I had bought let alone seen the West Indian variety in a new condition. The colour was a pale buttery colour with the satin effect showing up as pale honey. It was quite beautiful and far better than the colour that it takes up when old. The East Indian on the other hand improves with age and warms up to a rich golden tone with all the greyish hues not showing anymore.

Workshop tip

If you find an 18th century piece that has been painted later, do not try to have the paint removed. The area where the paint was will always show. This is the reason why an 18th century piece unpainted will be worth an awful lot more than the one that has been painted. It has all to do with the medium used in the paint in the first place. I have on occasions been taken to task by customers when I have refused to strip this 19th century painting off.

7. ACERS

The name given to the sycamores and maples. Maple was used in America to a far greater degree than Europe. Understandable. I had never heard of maple syrup until my first visit to America fifty-five years ago. It is a tough wood ideal for chair making, is very stable and decorative. Tiger maple can be quite startling, and I am sure birds eye maple needs no introduction.

Sycamore is an unobtrusive wood, the mainstay in the world of stringed musical instruments. Fiddle back needs no explanation. It is used as a decorative wood, almost a poor man's satinwood. It is a startling white when new, is dense and takes a polish well. In England it came into its own with the Neo-Classical revival and the world of marquetry. It takes stains and chemical reactions well. Harewood is sycamore treated with ferrous oxide which produced a startling pale silver colour in the wood.

It became very popular in early 19th century France with the era of Charles X furniture.

The colour of Acers, as with all pale woods, warms up with age to this pale golden tone. Because of its denseness it is often mistaken for Satinwood.

8. BEECH

Often called a soft wood, Beech is nothing of the sort. It is a tough close grained wood that is superb for the chairmaker and the mechanical work of the cabinet trade. It was used for knuckles to support the flaps of sofa and Pembroke tables, screw threads for small table tops etc. It was also used extensively by the woodturner for all kinds of work.

Beech was used continuously since furniture began and right across the chairmakers trade, yet rarely will you see a Beech chair as just Beech. Usually they will be painted, gilded or grained to look like Rosewood or Kingwood. Graining came into its own in the Regency era for the small dining chairs so popular in that era. It was also used on legs, feet and often the columns for table stands. You can usually see when this has happened, Rosewood fades, the graining does not.

Used for the frames in upholstered chairs, it is the obvious wood for this, dense enough to take nailing easily and well. Unhappily it does carry one serious flaw. It is probably the furniture beetles favourite wood. Probably the only time that you will see wormholes in Mahogany is through the veneered Beech rails of chairs. Always check for worm with anything that has Beech in it.

Colour

It is a very pale yellowish pink when new and goes a drab pale brown when old. I cannot remember ever seeing a piece of Beech furniture just polished. It has always had some surface colour added.

Workshop

The fact that something old is worth more than something new can really be shown here. The lengths that people go to to try and save worm eaten chair rails is laughable. (Excellent for me!) We have tried to saturate them with glue, pump them full of modern styrenes, wrap them in canvas, all sorts of things to try and do the one thing you cannot do – salvage a wormy and rotten chair rail. The men in white coats from the laboratories will say that is rubbish. Okay. They can almost fossilise something that is falling apart, it is being done with the Mary Rose.[3] (But who is ever going to use her?) A chair is only as good as the tenons in the joints and how you are supposed to get them out in one piece to treat them has never been explained to me. My advice if you get the problem: re-rail and be damned! I know one thing, I would not have a seriously worm eaten chair in my house, and if I saw one for sale, I would not buy it at any price.

When I was working with Jimmy Little and we were confronted with a very wormy chair rail or infested piece of wood, he would say, "That is just drix, useless". I never had the cheek to ask

[3]Mary Rose. Flagship of the navy in the reign of Henry VIII. It capsized and sank in front of him at the entrance to Portsmouth harbour. She was located and raised in 1982. Her remains are being preserved. Some wonderful artifacts have been found. One, the surgeon's box, had a pot of ointment in it with a finger mark left when a smear of the ointment had been applied!

19

what in the hell was "drix". It took me a lot of asking and visits to libraries to discover that drix is an old-fashioned word (early English, I imagine) for rotten wood. I have never heard it used since those days.

"That is a really drixy chair". Now that could catch on!

9. BIRCH
Birch is a very close cousin to Beech and used much for the same purpose. It looks much like beech and became very popular in the late 19th century when the furniture industry really began. The times I mean are when department stores sold bedroom suites made of something called "Satin Birch". They looked all the world like satinwood until you scraped the surface back. The wood then polished to a beautiful pale peach colour.

Used successfully as a veneer, Birch is very difficult to tell from Satinwood when it is old. I have a Scottish longcase clock from about 1800 with two small panels of a curl birch veneer set above and below the door of the case. When students came to my workshop and then my home these birch panels were always called satinwood if I asked them what they were.

10. YEW
I suppose the archers or bowmen of England have made Yew a wood known to everyone.[4] It has been used from the beginning of furniture. It is usually associated with country goods and certainly folk art, love spoons and treen.

It is a lovely wood to use when new. When old it is as hard as old Oak if not harder. I have seen almost everything you can think of made of Yewtree. This is from a joint stool from about 1650 to a five pillar dining table from the late 18th century. This table was in a lovely house in Hampshire, the owners telling me that the wood had come from the Estate. This I can well believe. The size of the wood was massive.

Yewtree has a very long life indeed. Used as

[4]Dozens of yew bows were found and salvaged when the Mary Rose was raised.

a decorative veneer for crossbandings, the Burrs were much favoured by makers both English and Continental where it is sometimes mistaken for Thuya that was very popular during the latter stages of the 18th century.

Uses
Very popular in the chair trade for bentwork in Windsor chairs, Yew is a very heavy and dense wood that will polish to a rich sheen with little effort. Finest examples for me are the Gothic Windsor chairs made from the mid-18th century onward.

Prominent in the world of treen, the density of it makes it a good material for very small pieces, snuff and patch boxes etc. These are not over-difficult to fake. Be careful. Over the past twenty to twenty-five years it has been a favorite in the reproduction world. Almost everything that was made in the realms of everyday furniture has been produced and veneered in Yewtree. The denseness of it makes it a natural for modern veneer technology. Because of this the veneer on some reproduction work can be very thin indeed.

Colour
The colour of Yew will be from a pale yellow to pink and sometimes almost purple with large areas of an almost white sapwood. When old, it will come down to a dark chestnut brown. This can sometimes be nearly black, and I believe is caused by the wood being dyed or stained when the piece was first made. The surface will often be so dense and smooth it can sometimes, except for its colour, look and feel like ivory.

If Yew is of a fairly pale colour it will not be very old!

11. KINGWOOD
Kingwood is in the Rosewood family and carries all the problems that are in that wood. It is called Princes wood, Royal wood, Purple and is the Bois de Violette of France.

Kingwood never gets to a large size and because of that has been used almost always as a veneer. I have only seen it used in the solid once, and this was a set of Dutch chairs from the early 18th century. They were not really satisfactory. Kingwood has a tendency to crack and split like Ebony, and this showed here. By their appearance they had been continuously repaired and were a bit of a problem for the workshop.

Kingwood is a small tree and you will never get a large piece of it. It will be rare to find a piece of English furniture veneered with it. It made its first appearance with the practise of oyster and butterfly veneering a few years before and after 1700. Used spasmodically for crossband decoration work, it then began to appear in the last stages of the 18th century and appears along with rosewood during the first 30 years of the 19th. Out of a couple of hundred pieces from that time one might be Kingwood. It is rare.

This is not the case in France and it will be quite common to find their high style furniture veneered with it or in combination with other wood. It was used for end grain wood in marquetry. The straightness and accuracy of the grain lent itself to parquetry.

The colour of Kingwood is startling when new: a rich mauve to purple with very definite grain lines. Kingwood is also just about one of the hardest woods to work that you will come across. I made up a parquetry table for a client with a bundle of late, 19th-century sawn veneer. The veneering was the most difficult job I have ever undertaken. It was like trying to lay sheet steel. How the 18th-century men veneered their serpentine and bombe shaped pieces I have no idea. It is said that they used heated sand bags made of leather. I have also used them but they would not work with this one. I have had to put kingwood over complicated shapes like they did on three occasions. Thank goodness for the late twentieth century. I made up fibre glass moulds.

Old colour is much as rosewood. Disturb that colour, and you will not have any luck at all in trying to recreate it.

12. TULIPWOOD
Not the tulip tree, Tulipwood is a very hard wood remarkably like Kingwood except in colour. The early uses of it were the same as with Kingwood. However, I have never seen a piece of English furniture veneered with it as I have Kingwood. The use was mainly for decorative work, crossbands etc.

The continent is a different story, and it followed their usage of Kingwood. It has that wood's properties, even down to old colour. However, new colour is a different story. It is garish, a yellowish white with rich reddish stripes running through it. I have often shown people the difference between old and new with this one and on many occasions I am not believed, something that I have never understood. I have never had any luck whatsoever in trying to recreate age with tulip and have had to revert to the age old way of painting out repairs with coloured polish. This, as anyone in my game will know, is a complete waste of time with furniture veneered with these woods. If you see a repair that sticks out like a sore thumb you can bet your bottom dollar that you will be looking at a paint out.

13. PURPLEHEART
Purpleheart is very rarely seen on English work. In fact, I have only seen it on half a dozen occasions and this was crossband work and stringing on a couple of Pembrokes and as long grain decoration on satinwood.

It is not the same story on the continent. The French used it regularly. The rich purple colour made it a natural foil for gilt bronze. Again, it takes up a colour much the same as King and Tulip when left alone. My advice here is to leave it alone!

Purpleheart comes from South America and when felled is a rather bright orange brown colour. When sawn and exposed to the air it rapidly takes up this rich Royal purple tone. I used to hate working on pieces veneered with it.

14. SATINEE
Again predominantly Continental in its use, when new it can carry all sorts of colours, from bright red to a sandy colour. I have only ever seen it in a veneer form. It was used frequently as the

ground for marquetry work and also lent itself superbly to parquetry. I have always called it Causarina. This is a tree indigenous to South Europe and North Africa. It is said to be fast growing. You will only see it in its antique clothing. It is not very exciting. Because of repair work I have been fortunate to have seen it as the day it was made. A piece of 18th century furniture made of this would take your breath away if you could have seen it then. I have said that old colour should be preserved: but if it had arisen and I had been asked to bring a Satinee piece back to a new condition, I would have done it without question. If there was ever a wood that would have shown you the wealth and grandeur of the 18th century, satinee would have done that.

These fourteen woods are the ones that my workshop handled continuously during my working life. Obviously there are others. This list has to be put in; if they are of interest you can look them up, or do what I did, find out when I saw them:

1. Elm is similar to oak and follows much in its footsteps for its use. It produces some highly decorative wood which was used for veneer, some of this was dyed and became Mulberry. I have worked on four Mulberry pieces, one of them famous. Three turned out to be dyed Elm. I believe that this was done deliberately. To reproduce the effect, I soaked my Burr Elm veneer in a concentrated solution of tobacco juice. It was perfect!

2. Ebony will need no explanation.

3. Chestnut: I have only seen one piece of furniture made of this. It was an Edwardian wardrobe. It looks very much like Oak but is lighter in weight. Its usual and popular use is for drawer linings, etc.

4. Poplar: The tree itself will need no explanation. It is used much as pine, but does not carry knots as does the pine. It is a good utilitarian secondary wood.

5. Box should need no explanation. It is often used for string lines. Box is a very hard and dense wood which makes it a natural for turn-

ing. It never grows to a large size. The best is Russian. An essential part of marquetry was that the hardness of it accepted sand burning or scorching like no other wood.

6. Fruitwoods: The most prevalent in use was the Cherry. Very good furniture has been made out of it, and I have seen some good examples in America. I have never seen a large cherry tree in England. Yet some of the wood used in making this American furniture must have been huge. Apple, pear and plum have all been seen but mainly in turned work. Our frequently-seen and often dodgy, apple- and pear-shaped, tea caddies will be made of them.

7. Cedars must be put in. They are very distinctive in smell and usually found where clothing will be kept. They are much favoured for drawer work when the smell of the pencil sharpener will be very noticeable. Western red cedar should need no explanation.

8. The rare ones, often called exotic, which I think is a silly name for them, will be rarely seen. It is often just used as a decoration or in the box and caddy trade.

According to my records and old invoices, these are the ones that I have seen and handled and the number of times that I have seen them (remember that I was involved with old furniture all the time): Laburnum once, Fustic three, Partridge six, Amboyna five, Thuya seven, Camphor once, Sandal twice, Mulberry once, Olive four, Coramandel six, Silkwood once, Palm once, Maccassar ebony three, Green oak twice, Bog oak twice, Snake once, Alligator once, Greenheart once, Padauk three, Abura three. In the sale of the pair of cabinets in rosewood at the beginning of this chapter there was a colour picture of a fine pair of small and very rare corner tables, said to be veneered in mahogany, estimate 5,000 pounds. They went for 18,000 pounds. They were veneered in Abura: at least a couple of people must have known!

I cannot think of any more. I shall be surprised if there are many more that really matter.

Also, I will bet my bottom dollar that one or two have slipped my memory. I reckon I am entitled to have that happen at my age!

The problem is that most of them that you see will be old and carry that age, so you will have to give them more than a cursory glance. This is quite simply because all woods will start to change colour from the day that they are made into something. The change will be imperceptable to you and there will be a time, if left alone, when they are all very much the same. A friend of mine put it rather well: "Dave, when motor cars began you would know instantly what make it was. That industry is quite old now, and they all look much the same. You have to give them a closer look to be sure what make they are".

Old wood is very much like that if it has been left alone. As has been said you cannot put into print the smell of it, the weight of it or the feel of it. This can obviously only come with your familiarity with it. It is a fascinating material that will pay handsomely those of you who do delve into it a little more deeply.

One did slip my mind: Lignum Vitae. I have only seen one piece of furniture made from it. I found it in London and John now owns this rather nice, tiny, three-drawer kneehole, which I suppose should be called a Lowboy. It is said to have been made in Jamaica, and I would not argue with that mainly because the making is very English. I suppose that I should illustrate at least one very rare one. But no. Photographs do not follow any of the rules of wood.

Chapter 3

QUALITY

---

*I*T SEEMS TO ME THESE DAYS that almost any piece of tat furniture will make money. Tat is a polite word for junk. Our word in the workshop was a much cruder one than that.

A few months ago I accepted the invitation to visit an auction saleroom and join a group of people who were currently attending an arts course. Arrangements had been made for the visit to be a private one during the evening. The reason for going was to listen to the students' assessments of the furniture. I still find it difficult to put into words the things about old furniture that I take for granted and have found that listening to their remarks has been a great help. It was a very good visit, and I learned one thing: not one of them had the bottle to say what a lot of rubbish most of the furniture was. I also realised that they did not know what a good piece of furniture should be – understandable; no one seems to have told them.

Rarely do I go to the rooms to buy for myself. It usually begins with a telephone call from a client. We have a discussion and I am given the lot numbers involved. So I am mostly in the position of not having a catalogue, which is good because I have a rule not to look at one until I have looked at the piece. This is ridiculous I know and hardly practical for anyone unless they are in my situation. But in my situation I learned years ago that I do not want the catalogue telling me what it is supposed to be!

I did not have a catalogue during this visit and I was appalled at the things on offer. These rooms have a sale every couple of weeks, so I am sure that I had not been unlucky and copped a bad one. There were a couple of things that I could not understand. First, thirty-odd years ago, 85% of this stuff was in the province of the junk shop and the lower end of the secondhand furniture shop. Nothing as far as I was concerned had changed that for me. The only thing that could have changed was the lack of junk and secondhand shops or the attitude of the buyers. This I found sad. After all, a piece of junk will always be a piece of junk. No amount of hype, fashion or advertising can change that – except possibly understanding what makes a good piece of furniture and applying it. The second thing I did not understand was the estimate of price. That was something else.

If you do not know about or have not experienced the attitude that something old must be better than something new and therefore more valuable, I would suggest that you view a sale like this. And do it my way, without a catalogue. Put your own price on things. Then have a look at the catalogue.

The catalogue with the estimates of price is something that we did not have thirty-odd years ago. If you wanted to know the price, you had to go and ask. I am amazed that the public today let the auctioneers prime them up with a price. But then it is 1997. I suppose the be-all and end-all of something old today is always "How much?" On this particular visit, there was a small, rectangular, centre table. It had been made up from the end of a Dutch armoire, veneered in typically rough, cube parquetry, cross-banded with the cheapest, peeled Walnut. This made a top mounted onto a turned American whitewood stand from the early part of this century. It was also falling apart. Estimate: £400-600. Dear God. And the description? Grimms Fairy tales had nothing on it. It should not have been given house room.

The dismay of some of the students was sad to see and it really did shake some of them. One was the son of a dealer and even he found it difficult to understand. There is a huge difference between a saleroom and an organised visit to a stately home or museum! This was reality. When I used to have groups visit my workshop they were often surprised how rough things were when you really looked at them and very surprised when we had something that was of the best quality.

Today it seems that the auction room rules. And if something good had been in those rooms that evening it would have stuck out like a sore thumb. Now, I have to contradict myself because good does not mean quality and getting the two together is rare indeed.

I live near Chichester. It is a lovely city, and now that it has been pedestrianized, (if there is such a word), it is even nicer. To get from our usual car park to the shops is a short walk that goes past the entrance doors of an auction room. It is a branch office of one of the big four. During a visit about four years ago, Sheila and I passed the doors of this place and something pale caught my eye. We got about three or four paces before I stopped and went back. This sounds like some old codswallop I know, but then stories like

this often do. Instinct. Sticking out like a sore thumb, it was superb. We found ourselves looking at a cylinder bureau veneered in Satinwood.

Obviously I had no catalogue and went to the office to enquire. It was said to be English and had an estimate of £1000-1200. It probably will sound strange but we have never bought a piece just for ourselves in the rooms. It has always been either for clients or bought, worked over and sold on. We took a deep breath and reckoned that we had to try for this one. It called for a visit to the pub and we decided that we would go to £5000 for it. It was an awful lot of money for us, but also a lot of money for an English cylinder bureau.

People often assume that we have a home furnished like a museum. I always say that I could never afford my prices! The truth is that we are like the cobbler who wears shoes that need repair. When we had something good, it was sold on. However, we do have one or two nice things. This was something else. Not only was it good it was also very rare because it had quality. It looked like being an expensive walk from the car park!

The sale was two days later. Lot 301 began at £1500. Just one other was bidding and it took just about a minute to go for £5500. The last three bids were in £500. Someone wanted it as much as I did. My second rule of thumb is to never go beyond your price. We were sad. But if it is good it will shine; if it also carried the subtle touch of quality, it will glitter. Who bought it I do not know. Whoever it was knew about quality, and I reckon it would have run. I would have loved to have had the money to take it on. However, that's life.

Now, why was this something special?

Cylinder bureaus are usually rather large and lumpy things. Just the action of the cylinder rolling back can cause that. Also they are usually large. They have the image of the managing director sitting at his desk controlling it all. They are also very English.

This one was German.

It was veneered with superb West Indian Satinwood, the colour pale golden tan. It looked so much like fine Mahogany I could understand it being mistaken for it. The cylinder and the four drawers were cross-banded with Tulipwood into Boxwood and Ebony lines. It stood on a hollow moulding with four splayed feet that had Hepplewhite written all over them. So why German?

These pieces have a writing slide. Usually there are two handles that you pull and as this is done the slide comes out and the cylinder rolls back. Usually they are and feel heavy. Because of this the handles will show signs of being repaired, replaced, sometimes removed and cup handles screwed onto the cylinder itself. Handles like this became common practice on the later 19th-century versions. This one had two oval knobs about one and one-quarter inches across. They were cast and chased in a floral pattern and were fire-gilded. No damage could be seen and when I pulled them the cylinder rolled back as if it was silk. This could only mean one thing: it was balanced – and superbly balanced, which meant that some good mechanical work was hidden behind the Harlequin of drawers that came forward with the slide. After the slide pulls, it was the mechanics that made me think German. They were the masters when it came to the mechanical side of things.

The inside was a shock. You do not expect in this day and age to see something that has been little used and also lovingly cared for. I first thought that maybe it was one of those things that had not seen the light of day for generations, but the outside colour discounted that. The inside was a bank of six small drawers, veneered as the front, but as fresh as the day they were made. They were identical in size and of a proportion that made them appear smaller than they were. Small pigeon holes were set above the drawers. These were faced with Satinwood as was the carcass of the Harlequin. Each drawer had a smaller version of the gilt bronze knob on the writing slide. The drawers were lined with Walnut as was the carcass of the Harlequin,

another pointer to Germany. This piece was good and of quality, because you do not put fire gilt hardware on anything but the best, and the best can only mean superb cabinet making. You could take any one of these six drawers and interchange it with any other. Also, you could turn any of them upside down and they would still interchange with any other. That takes some doing. It is engineering in wood and is always a sign of quality and workmanship of the finest.

Before we leave the inside, the back of the Harlequin had been made curved so that the cylinder fall could fit snugly behind it as it was pulled forward. Nothing had ever touched anything which means that the timbers used were the best and had been selected so that the chances of any movement in them was minimal.

This bureau was by cylinder bureaus standards small. It was two feet, nine inches wide but was so beautifully proportioned it looked perfect. Usually with small things the wood is not correspondingly thinner. For example, a three-foot bureau will have wood the same thickness as a four-foot one and it does not matter very much. But make one at two feet with the same thickness, and it will really show. It is probably why I have never been over fond of miniature furniture. It is very clever, but you cannot use miniature wood and that is where it fails. Working as I do with models, this sort of thing is always a problem.

The four drawers in the carcass were lined in Walnut which had been prepared down to about 5/16 inch. That is thin for drawers of this size. And they were proportioned in their depth with the bottom one about seven inches deep. The dovetailing was not the very fine almost pinched style of the English at the end of the 18th and early 19th centuries; it was a little bolder, very tight and accurate with a touch of quality as the back dovetails were mitred on the top or show joint. Also, because of the thin walnut the bottom boards were in two pieces with a nicely-made, small muntin. These usually have a rounded edge moulded on. This one carried a hollow moulding, which dated the whole thing, or dated it for me, to have come from the first twenty years of the 19th century. Also, the tops of the drawer linings had been slightly rounded, another pointer to German origins.

The only thing you can really examine in a situation like this are the drawers. These were quality. You could not interchange them obviously, but you could turn them upside down. They were not stopped in the English way of two small blocks on the drawer stile; instead, they had a small block fixed at the back on either side behind the drawer. These did their duty and each drawer duly ran upside down. (People must have thought we were mad.) The final accolade to the makers of this piece of furniture was the fact that these carcass drawers could be pushed in from one bottom corner either left or right. That is the ultimate sign of the best. Try it next time you are faced with an empty drawer from a three foot bureau.

The handles were as the two knobs on the writing slide.

The carcass was heavy in its weight. It is surprising sometimes just how heavy some pieces are. In this case oak had been used for its veneering ground. A surprise to me were the dustboards between the drawers; they were Walnut. The final surprise was the back; it was panelled. When you see this it is usually two panels, sometimes four; this piece had six! This I have only seen on massive pieces of furniture. This little desk had it all. And yes, the back was made of Walnut!

The last consideration must of course be the condition. I have seen a lot of fine furniture in my time. It has always been in a condition that needed my services, very often to a serious degree. Yet whenever it has carried this other side of quality, very little is ever needed and there is rarely any evidence that anything has ever been done. This was no exception. There were about four or five lifts on the crossbands. All the veneer was sound – no hollow taps anywhere. Had we been lucky enough to have bought it I would have used a mild reviver on it. That would have been enough.

It had lost its keys. I would have made up a slender kidney bow for it. Nothing looks nicer that a delicate key with its colored tassle hanging down. But the key would have all the wards cut in it and look the part – except it would not work!

A serious tip for you here: NEVER LOCK A PIECE OF FURNITURE. And if you do, leave the key in. No cabinet lock ever made will withstand a burglar's jemmy and I can assure you that the damage can be tragic.

The veneers and woods used here were of the finest. And reading this through the things that I use when trying to explain quality are all here. I call them the Four W's: wood, weight, workmanship and wallet. The latter is the least important. I have worked on things worth thousands upon thousands yet they were a long way down the ladder. Money will not give quality to you. I have been amazed at the number of people who think it will. It is the first three things that work together.

When you see top quality wood that is highly decorative, it will almost always be in a veneer form. And time and again it will carry evidence of damage. This can often be severe: shrinkage, warping, faults in the ground showing through. This often applies to the best and is a problem to the workshop. In fact, I have advised people not to buy when there is this problem unless they are prepared to accept and live with it. These pieces will rarely carry our second "W", weight. When you do find a good veneered piece that is heavy, the heaviness caused by the quality of the ground wood, you will be surprised how much better its general condition will be.

When a piece is of solid wood and small, it will really show.

A few years ago, during my first visit to America when I had not gone to repair something, I had been invited to undertake a short lecture tour. I began at the Detroit Institute of Arts where I met a young couple who invited me to their home for dinner. This was a gorgeous house on the shore of Lake St. Clair. Over a large scotch I was looking around with my host and he put a small carved tripod table in my hand. I nearly choked, (or spilt some of my scotch which would have been worse) because I was told that it had been purchased at some vetted antiques fair, was fully authenticated from around 1760 and a lot of dollars had been paid for it. I can remember that I did not even have to look at it. It weighed nothing – and I mean nothing. I was as usual asked for my opinion, and since we had not eaten, it obviously had to be a nice one! I learned years ago to keep shtumm when this sort of thing happens.

The couple are of course John & Becky Booth and are now friends. I have bought for them, restored for them, made an elaborate piece of furniture for them, driven them around some of our stately homes and met up with them when they visit this country. Over the years I have advised them, resulting in a fine collection of furniture that continues to grow.

Illness kept me away from America for almost three years. Luck or fate decreed that I had to go to the Detroit Institute of Arts. The movement of a very fine clock whose case I restored had gone wrong. I was with Jean, a horologist from Paris helping him take this movement out and came down my set of steps (the clock is French and about nine feet tall!) to be confronted by John, who is one of the museum's trustees. It was dinner again at that lovely house on the lake, and, the first question was, "You did not reckon my tripod did you?" I did not even have my scotch this time. Anyway, he said that some English dealer had recently told him it was a wrong one.

John is a lawyer. He recalled that my face had given it all away when he gave me his tripod and I hefted it in my hand. He wanted to know why. I told him about the four W's. The first one is that quality of wood means weight and if a carved one from 1760 is not heavy it will usually mean that it is not from 1760. It is as simple as that. I think it was at this point I discovered that John has an amazing memory!

I have always admired this young man because he has kept his strop. Me, in that position, would have been rather annoyed to say the least. However, this was all a few years ago now, and the person who carved up this not very good copy (it was not good enough to be called a fake) had copied one illustrated in a book of English Furniture. This one has got a broken fret on the top edge. The copier did not know this and copied the broken bits as well! If John ever did sell his tripod, what a good selling point that would be. But I would not be in the least surprised if he had not thought about that already.

They tell me that people collect fakes. I suppose eventually they will start faking the fakes. Dear me.

Because the wood was so light in weight, it means that it will be soft. This table was carved. Soft wood will never carve well and that was immediately obvious in this case. The work was poor. Always with these little tables, if they are right, the carving will be superb and because of that the wood will be dense and very heavy indeed. On the best of these, and there are very few, the carving looks to all the world as if it is carved from stone. The wood is that dense and hard.

Carving should look as if an edge of it could cut you!

I have seen a lot of these tripods in my time and of the 18th-century ones a few have been excellent. There are 19th century copies and many of these have been the base of a pole screen with a later top. I have to confess that a few of these were put together in my working life. Yet out of the ones that I have seen and handled only one was really of quality.

A tripod will be a good one by the proportions. Most of them, the modern ones especially, are unstable. Usually this is caused by the diameter of the feet. You will be surprised just how stable one from the 18th century is. The diameter around the feet is surprisingly large when compared to the top, and yet it does not look out of place at all. My tripod of quality made me look at it the moment I saw it because it had an oval top. It stood by an armchair with an upholstered back and was on suite with the others in the room. They came from the 1750's, were in Red Walnut and had all been carved by the same hand.

I can remember sitting down and picking up this table. The carving felt like cut glass. Today I would need two hands to lift it; it was that heavy. It had never been touched and was an object lesson in the best. The oval top would have worried a few people, for sure. After all, that does not fit well with three legs. But if you get it right and make the size of the tripod bold enough, it is superb. This table was so proportioned that I doubt if it could have been knocked over. I tried. Most of us will know how easy it is to topple these little tripod tables. This one was so beautifully proportioned it had to be deliberately pushed over.

ILLUSTRATION 3: *Boulle table and shavings. None of it was any big deal.*

Having got into this chapter, it is gradually dawning on me that I have not seen very much furniture that I can put in this category – understandably, I am going to be criticized for expecting far too much. But you must remember that I have had a vantage point given to few people.

Quite recently a lady who is a docent with the National Trust came up to me and was rather worried that a lot of the furniture did not really stand up to close inspection. She knew my history and I asked what she meant. She could not understand why so much of it was really very rough and of poor quality on the inside, and where it could not be seen. She asked if I had found this sort of thing. My answer had to be yes. I could not bring myself to tell her what I really thought and that if I made her a piece of furniture in the image of the things she was worried about I doubt if she would have accepted it!

Few people can accept the fact that very few pieces of furniture from the days we are talking about could command the money needed to produce the finest. Today the huge money paid for things is Rarity and History. If quality played a part in it, the story would be a very different one.

What the eye does not see, forget it. You will have to accept this rough and often crude appearance. It is part and parcel of old furniture.

A few years ago a boullework console table came through my hands. The top had to be taken off to be repaired. The inside was the biggest mess you can imagine. We were the first people to take the top off since it had been made in about 1725. You do get used to seeing the almost rubbishy interiors of fine French furniture but this one was the worst, so bad that I photographed it. It was also of interest because they had left some walnut shavings in one end. There were huge glue runs everywhere and in one corner they had spilt the glue pot and not wiped much of that up, ILL 3 I would love to have shown the owners what they had got for about a quarter of a million dollars.

Our last "W" is the workmanship. When it is of the finest, wherever you look it will be hard to find fault. Attention to detail is the secret. I have seen few things that come up to the very exacting standards that I have tried to explain here. When I have seen them, I have nothing but admiration for the people who created them. I suppose it is like saying there have been thousands of artists but very few Rembrandts.

ILLUSTRATION 4: *Fustic Pembroke. C1780.*

It sounds strange but there are no more than five pieces of furniture that I shall never forget. Maybe I am a hard task master. Or possibly I have seen an awful lot of stuff that did not stand looking at it too closely! These five pieces all stood out as they all contain the Four W's, one of them cost over a million pounds. Out of the other four Sheila and I could have afforded a couple!

The first is a Pembroke table from 1780 veneered in Fustic. It was quadruple-banded in Tulip, Sycamore and Purpleheart. The veneering and banding I have never seen bettered. It had been heavily French polished. When this was removed, the end result was exquisite. Age had done its part and for me it is the finest quality Pembroke that I have ever seen. ILL 4 Apart from this side of it, it was the shape of the top – neither oval nor round, just a continuous curve. It is difficult to explain, almost a rectangle with gently curved sides. I expect the shape has a name, but I doubt it because I have never seen another. Similar yes, but never one that looked so right. The top was as flat as the day it was made. Yet the veneer was at least 1/8 inch thick. ILL 5 The ground wood was Mahogany and only 1/2 inch thick. It had been clamped as

you would expect and the edges crossbanded with Tulip. All that was missing were two small pieces at the end of the rule joint. The quality and stability of this ground must have been something else. It is the only table that I have ever seen with such a heavy veneer on such a thin top that was still perfect. It was the shape that was so unusual because it was a shape for a dining table I made up for Sheila some years before. It was nice to see that I got the top of our table nearly right.

Another, or number two I suppose, was a large double-sided writing table, also English, or said to be, and from a similar sort of date. This was in a superb, very tight, Mahogany curl veneer. It carried six drawers, three on each side and two dummy's at each end. Each drawer surface was butt-veneered down the centre with tight curls of Mahogany. It stood on four tapered legs that looked so thin I wondered how they

ILLUSTRATION 5: *Veneer and 20p piece. The coin is 75% actual size in this photograph.*

could support anything. These were finished in castors that looked to all the world like delicate tulips. The carcass was made of Oak and faced around the drawer stiles and the dummy's with really dense Mahogany that also made the legs. The tops of these had been carved with the most delicate oval fans, the edges of which stood proud by no more than about 1/32 of an inch. There were eight of them, perfect and carved on the legs, not planted. This piece was so good that the drawers were all made of superb, dense, Mahogany. The moulding of the top was a hollow into a half round which was so proportioned that the top looked really thin. The weight of it was huge and it took two men who knew what they were doing to move it. The handles were the simplest of swan-neck pulls. The top carried its original leather. This top was made of Oak and made flush panelled with about eighteen squares of wood all opposed in their grain direction. Because of this nothing had moved.

Over the years I have often wondered about this one and if indeed it was English. In the workshop we had a lot of superb late 18th century furniture in Mahogany from France and Germany and having worked on it, it would never surprise me if this one had those origins. The top, the Mahogany drawers, the castors and the workmanship were all clues. It has been valued, assessed, insured and all the other things that a fine piece of furniture warrants today. And so it is "English". It does not matter, it is just one of the finest things that I have ever seen. It is also one of my 48 pieces of original furniture.

It is strange that the next two are both roll tops, both in mahogany. One is German, the other English.

I must confess that I do like a good cylinder and tambour-topped desk. Because of that it is about time that I confessed to something. Out of the two baulks of West Indian Satinwood all those years ago three small desks were among the things produced. One was a cylinder, two feet, three inches wide on four tapered legs. Another was the same size but with a tambour about six inches high. They were nice and were sold to pri-

vate customers. The third one was a little naughty. It was prompted by my third piece of furniture that I had seen a few months before. It was thirty-six inches wide, made as a centre piece and had a low tambour that rolled back and down behind three drawers set up as a kneehole. It also was on legs and castors. This one was different because the castors were old, as were the drawer linings. It was set up to deceive. The age old treatment to warm up Satinwood, bichromate of potash, was used and the polishing was spread out over about eighteen months. A surprise, maybe, but you would be astounded at the results when a piece is stripped and repolished a few times and a little bit of fakery is included each time. It was sold – how does not matter except that it was under the hammer. I did not see it again until years later. One day there it was in the window of a shop in Mount Street.[5] I went in and must confess it had worn well. The price was very healthy as well. It was about eight years ago when I saw it again in a rather posher shop in Madison Avenue.[6] This time I did not go in. Frankly, I wish that I had kept it as there was no way I could have afforded to buy it.

It is the English, tambour, writing table that I used for this Satinwood one that is number three. It was three feet, nine inches wide, which is very wide for a desk like this. A tambour is, after all, strips of wood glued onto canvas that roll in grooves on either side of it. They are not very condusive to constant use and to find one that has not been repaired and rolled so freely it had to be restrained is something else. This little table (no it was not little it just looked that way) was perfect in its construction. It followed all the rules. However, it was the tambour that I found so surprising. The desk was deep, very deep indeed because it did not have a writing slide. It was again a centre piece and was two feet, nine inches from front to back. The tambour stopped

[5]Mount Street is an exclusive street in London's Mayfair. It has the Connaught Hotel, Purdeys the gun makers, and Scotts restaurant. (It also had one of the finest butchers you are ever likely to see.)

[6]Madison Avenue, another exclusive street, this time in the upper East side of New York City.

at the front of the nest of drawers inside and was only eight inches high. To do that it had to roll down the back and under the drawers in the frieze. That was rare to see and would have caused a few problems without engineering in wood. She was a large piece of furniture but looked small. Again the proportions were exactly right. The legs were again tapered onto castors, all the metal was gilded. The final touch were the rather Chinese-looking brackets, eight of them, set in the angles where the legs joined the frames. I was in the house doing some work and some people – I have no idea who they were – stopped by my desk. My desk? Well, why not? I heard it referred to as "Dutch", "Far too heavy for English", and "I would get rid of those brackets if it was mine." I hope they were not in the trade!

Again the piece was really heavy and the timber was that dense San Dominican Mahogany that after two hundred odd years of being left alone carried a depth of colour and polish that can only be achieved by being left alone. This piece is also in my list of forty-eight.

Number four is a cylinder desk in plum pudding Mahogany. Plum pudding – only the English would think of that; the French call it Acajou Mouchette, so much nicer. This piece was hugely expensive, or hugely so for me. I had the misfortune to work on the first piece of furniture that had topped a million pounds. I will let you guess why I have said that! (History again and do not point fingers.) This one was another, priced at one and a quarter million, and worth every penny. Stupendous. I suppose it is only money, and if we returned to the 1780's when it was made, it would have been hugely expensive then and comparatively could well have been more than one and a quarter million!

This piece was huge – well over five feet wide – and stood on twelve legs! Fully mounted with the finest gilt bronze with the added touch of two colour gilding. Two handles were pulled and this huge cylinder rolled back to reveal an interior that can only be described as the steps leading up to a Greek temple. It had just arrived from New York when I was introduced to it. And I will be rude enough to criticise such a magnificent thing because someone had repolished it. New French Polish can look very harsh. But then you cannot expect it all.

This desk is one, I believe, of five that came from the workshops of David Roentgen, for my money a genius. He invented a method of marquetry that did not depend on artificial ways of animation. He let the wood do the talking and, for the first time, the human form could be successfully created. The success of this work was such that it can look for all the world like a painting. It is brilliant. However there is another side of it that puts this piece among the finest for me. Herr Roentgen was also a mechanical genius.

You would be surprised at the number of times I have been asked what we do when something like a lock, fitting or handle is missing. The usual assumption is that we have an endless supply of old bits and pieces. The people who ask are genuinely surprised when the answer is that we just make up what is needed. After all, if you have a Louis XVth commode that has lost a complicated lock that has been designed to lock both drawers, you cannot just go to an ironmongers and buy one. So you turn the clock back, get your bits and pieces of black iron, a small anvil, some heat, hammer, files, go to work and make one just as they did. Because of this they look remarkably like the ones from the period – just new metal. However, with the use of acids, a bit of gentle rusting and pitting of the surface (not moving away from how they made them) the results can be surprising. Frankly, unless you have been told you will often not know that it is a modern copy.

Recently a piece of furniture sold for over half a million pounds. It carried five locks of a complicated nature. No one would have believed me if I had queried a couple of them, and believed me less if I had said that I had made them about ten years ago!

Apart from the usual side of my trade a mechanical and metal side developed to a degree that virtually anything could be made. It was because of this that I came face to face with number four, this huge desk.

It began as usual with a phone call, "Maestro, the desk has arrived, and we cannot open the drawer; come up and have a look". I was faced with this stupendous thing. I had seen another one but not so magnificent. The drawer in trouble was about two feet wide, seven inches in height and set as a raised piece in the centre above the cylinder. The key was on the side. It was explained to me that it was a mechanical drawer. I asked what that meant. The explanation was so garbled that I did not believe it! The desk was a centre piece which means a back finished much as the front. The back of the drawer had another keyhole. This I unlocked, took the panel out and was confronted with what can only be described as some of the finest late 18th century mechanical work that I had ever seen or am ever likely to see. I cannot describe it; the illustration will say it all. ILL 6

It was driven by weight and it took me a couple of hours to follow what would happen when the weight was triggered. The problem was the usual one: being moved. One spring near the key had been nudged fractionally out of line. I nearly gave myself a heart attack because I moved the spring, turned the key and all the mechanism in front of me shot forward and the drawer front had turned into a reading and writing slide. Two other drawers had appeared with inkwells, sanders and quill trays. As they moved left and right through 180 degrees their lids opened and a reading slide slowly slid into position. ILL 7 You pushed the slide gently back, closed the lids and everything slid back into place with that satisfying click that a good mechanism makes.

I will say it again; Herr Roentgen was a genius.

There are many tales about the tribulations of these pieces of furniture and the journeys and travels they make about the world. Two hundred years ago a piece was made, delivered and probably stayed where it remained for generations. It is not like that now and many niggling problems

ILLUSTRATION 6: *Roentgen lock.*

ILLUSTRATION 7: *Roentgen drawer open.*

can happen because of it. Some are tragic, some funny. One of the latter happened to this desk.

It was sold and was to be shipped to the Continent. You would be surprised at the casual way this can be carried out. Again it was a phone call – would I go to so and so as there is a small problem with the desk! I arrived. The shippers who I knew had their offices alongside a railway. The warehouses, packing works and stores were in the railway arches opposite. The desk which had been flown from New York was now waiting for its next journey when a brick from the top of the arch was dislodged by the 4:30 train from Victoria Station. It fell and naturally the corner caught the cylinder a nasty thump. It was so bizarre I could only laugh. That went down like a lead balloon, I

ILLUSTRATION 8: *Saunier secretaire after restoration.*

it was veneered in some of the finest mahogany I had ever seen. It was about three feet, six inches wide and panelled on the sides to match the fall that had two doors below it. The corners were inlaid with three brass flutes and veneered over. This had made sure that the eighteen inlays had never moved and were as good as the day they had been put in. The fall, doors and side panels were all framed in the finest, matt, gilt bronze. The top was a piece of pale, grey-white marble, framed in gilt bronze. The marble was over an inch thick and, thank God, it was removable. The whole thing stood on four bronze lions feet. ILL 8

The fall was of such quality that it has always reminded me of a really wild sea breaking on the shore. When it was safely upstairs and it could be really looked at, the surprises began. The fall had a key which was original. When this was turned the fall was so balanced that it slowly came down to the writing position. You were then confronted with eighteen drawers surrounding a central box to keep files in. A surprise here was that some of the horizontal partitions were still in place. I had never seen that before. The eighteen drawers were veneered from one huge piece of Mahogany, just as the fall. These were made from Mahogany throughout and just as I suspected each and every one was interchangeable rightside up and upside down. ILL 9 You took the

can tell you. How the problem was got over does not matter. Enough to say that the cylinder has now got two more plum pudding spots in the veneer than it had when Herr Roentgen's workshop veneered it in the 1780's!

Money has very little to do with quality. Number five, my last piece, came through my hands about 22 years ago. It was bought for 1,100 pounds in the days before it all went mad.

I shall never forget this one. It was a secretaire à abattant (I think that is how you spell it!) It is a low piece of furniture, low enough for you to comfortably rest an elbow on the top while you have a chat – the French really did think of it all. It is imprinted on my memory just from the weight of it. Three of us struggled, and I mean struggled, to get it upstairs to the workshop.

The date of it would be about 1780 and

ILLUSTRATION 9: *Saunier open. Top left, bottom right interchanged and upside down.*

ILLUSTRATION 10: *Center box turned over, refer to Ill. 9.*

ILLUSTRATION 11: *Saunier drawer bottom.*

second drawers left and right out and on the side by the central box were buttons. A push on both and the box slid gently out. When removed, there was a well with four secret drawers hidden in it. And of course you could take the box and put that back upside down. ILL 10

ILL 11 shows the bottom of one of the drawers. See the face mark and the mechanical sawing. (Ready for the next chapter!)

Below in the bottom cupboard was a shelf and below that two drawers with locks that would have made them almost safes. The whole piece had been made out of Oak and the veneer that had never been touched was at least 1/8 inch thick. The back, also of Oak, was four-panelled. Even the champhering of this was hollow-moulded. It was the finest thing I had ever seen and to this day I have not seen anything better.

I have said that I will be criticised for wanting too much and even this piece had a flaw. The reason it came to me was because it had a split across that superb wild sea of the fall. Nothing else on the piece had moved.

When the leather on the fall was removed, the reason for the crack became clear. They had made the fall of Red Pine. The reason I reckon was simply that had they made it in Oak, the weight would probably have been too much for a balanced fall. When they made this in 1780, they knew nothing about steam heating, or even imagined that it could be around nearly 200 years later! Think about that; few people do. Pine is more susceptible to movement than Oak. A joint in the Pine had failed giving us this very nasty, ragged crack through the veneer.

I do not doubt that we have all seen the attempts to repair cracks like this. They are rarely a success. I decided to try something that I had wanted to try for a long time. The reason for the crack was the Pine just got too dry. So did the Oak but it would not shrink as much. I had always wanted to see if you could reverse the process. If it did not work, it would not matter. I could go back to the usual ways. If it did, I could really earn money! I just wanted to see if I could reverse the shrinking habits of the wood.

A polythene tent was built. The fall was put on trestles. Three bowls of water were put under them and electric black heaters raised the temperature to around 75 degrees. The humidity after a couple of days had reached nearly 70%. I put a couple of loose wedges in the crack and after three days they were still loose. I began to think that I was wasting my time. It was after a week and frankly I had forgotten about it. But when I tried them again on the Monday they were tight! The ground was moving. The crack running through had been about a full eighth of an inch. In six and a half weeks it had closed up so that it could be cleaned on the edges and glued. This was done using synthetic glues and pressure. Six dovetail keys were put over the join on the back. The problem now was what will happen when it is gradually brought back to normal temperature and humidity. The answer was what I hoped. The crack was a join from 1780, this could not move anymore and about six fine cracks developed in the wood itself. These were very fine and with this very heavy veneer none ever showed on the surface. The doing of this was spread over about twelve weeks.

I have seen this piece on occasions over the years. It still carries the hairline mark through the fall where the ragged crack had been. The method works and I have used it successfully on many other pieces since. This sort of thing is just a part of your experience. And that experience will tell you when it has a good chance of working or not. It is a method that I can recommend trying before the more drastic and often cosmetically bad repair work is carried out.

On another occasion, I was asked to look at a piece of furniture that had a similar problem. I reckoned that there was a 60-40 chance of success. It was worth a try since it was a world famous thing in a well known museum and it would look the same if it was not a success. It was a shock to be told by a young lady about 25 years old from the conservation department that I was talking rubbish, and she had never heard of such a thing. But then, neither had I when I was 25.

Crack through the fall or not, this little secretaire had it all. When it was cleaned and polished it was stunning. She came from that era of French cabinet making in mahogany that has, for my money, never been surpassed. She has been attributed to Adam Weisswieller. Fine. But under one of the brackets that supported the fall

I found part of an invoice and plain to see in the rusty ink of the time was the name SAUNIER. Who knows?

You may well ask what was some paper doing packing up a bracket hinge? This guy must have made a cock up to have to do that. I would agree until I measured the brackets. The blacksmith had made one a little thinner than the other. I know that when I am given a pair of hinges I doubt if I measure them both before I mark out and cut them in. Anyway, that is my way of covering for these men, whoever they were. This was the best.

It was the 4th of October, 1995, when John came over. A sale in London had tickled his fancy. A well-known collection was being sold. I met him virtually from the airport. He had been up all night and was as fresh as a daisy. Me, I would have been dead. It makes you spit.

It has got to be sod's law, luck, fate or whatever, but the first thing I found myself looking at was a double-sided, low-topped, tambour desk in Mahogany. It sits on eight legs fitted with brass castors and leather wheels. The tambour works. This is a bit of a miracle because it is forty-eight inches wide. However the thing for me was that it was double-sided, a centre piece which is always a little special. I gave it a very quick look as did John. It had to have begun its life in the late 18th or early 19th century. Everything about that time was there.

As said, I do not look at catalogues before the event and was more than surprised to see it written up as Late Victorian! Had it been, it would not have been that colour or that genus of Mahogany. And another thing for sure, the cabinet makers from that era, the likes of old Jimmy, would not have made it that way. An example of not understanding the trade, one classic pointer are the mouldings that make up the tambour. There are seventy of them. Two hundred-eighty feet of moulding had to be made. It is all hand-worked with a scratch stock, something that would not have happened in the latter stages of the 19th century.

The catalogue also said, "the later locks are stamped R. Barron Patent". For the life of me I still do not understand this one. Locks can and often do get replaced, something that does not worry me. However if whoever it was had looked a little closer he would have seen on the lock for the tambour a faint, hand-engraved triangle around the initial B, a classic example of a locksmiths mark from the early days, or at least a long, long time before the times of the late Victorians.

John came down to dinner that evening and at the station waiting for his train back to London he said, "How much for the desk Dave?" I must say that we were tempted, but I could not see it going for a price in our bracket. John can be a little persuasive when he wants, and we gave him a price that I did not for one minute imag-ine would come off. He called the following evening. He had not gone mad, as has been known, and the desk was ours. It was delivered four weeks later. It got into our home with a fraction of an inch to spare and proudly sits in our living room. There is some justice in this world, because it was a lot cheaper than the one we were outbid for in Chichester. There is a lot to be said for not believing a catalogue!

We are not about to move, but I cannot help but wish that we had a larger house. I would love to give this piece the status it deserves and use it as the centre piece it was designed to be. But you cannot have it all. And anyway, if anyone had told me thirty-seven years ago when Sheila and I got married that we would one day own something like that, I would have said that they were well and truly off their trolley.

Chapter 4

THE TRADE AND MACHINES

*T*MUST CONFESS that I have been fighting shy of this chapter. The reason is that I have got to break some of the rules, tradition and almost folklore that seems to surround our subject and the production of it. My problem is that I have nothing to refer you to. That is understandable as again I have not really looked! I prefer, arrogantly maybe, to just put it down as I have seen it, and how I think it must have been. Then you may be the judge.

Why we have so little put down about a successful trade and how it worked is to me a bit of a mystery. After all, the cabinet trade and those associated with it did create most of the decorative arts that are so revered today. Probably it was such a common thing that it just did not warrant any putting down. I suppose people will not get very excited about a lorry and its driver, but put a coach and four on the road and all will stop and stare. Recently there was a hold up on the Chichester by-pass. What was it? A beautifully restored steam lorry from the 1920's.

This idea was brought home to me in a most unusual way. On my last trip to America I successfully did what will probably be my last restoration. I do not like flying over much these

days and find sleep impossible. It was about 4 AM and I was using the stewards seat on the port side right at the back of a 747 Jumbo 400 series Boeing. At least there you get some leg room. The captain came down to stretch his legs. We got talking and he invited me up to the flight deck. I stayed there until we docked at our gate at Heathrow five hours later. How many rules that broke I have no idea!

To me it was a revelation. This complete, state-of-the-art aeroplane was an Alice in Wonderland experience that will stay with me forever since it culminated in a completely automatic approach and landing! Now the reason for a diversion such as this is that the Captain, when he heard that I had been a pilot and had flown

Mosquito fighter bombers, treated me to a barrage of questions that made me dig very deep into what memories I have left from those days. Here was someone with just a co-pilot, controlling a mind boggling piece of technology, asking a 71 year old bloke questions. Questions such as "What was the engine torque like on take off and how did you control it?", "What was your single engined capability like?", "Were they aerobatic?", "How did you fly so low at night and also cope with a total blackout?", "What navigation aids did you carry?", "What sort of range did you have?", "How good or bad was the forecasting of weather?", "What were your servicing intervals?", "How good was your reliability?", "What happened when you fired four 20 millimetre cannons?", "How did you cope with icing?" or "When you dropped 2000 pounds of bombs from low level and what was low level?" (I think he was a little sceptical when I said that it was often below the height of this cockpit when landed!) He seemed amazed when I said that all we could do was use our experience and try to get out of the icing conditions as soon as possible. There had certainly been many casualties because of it. It was an extraordinary experience for me. Flying, the war and my part in it was a long time ago and has become an almost taboo subject. I do not need to tell you why.

Before I thanked him and said goodbye I asked him why he was so interested in my era of aeroplanes. There have been so many books, films, documentaries and people agonising about the rights and wrongs of it. I found it strange that a man of his experience should be interested in the near archaic flying of my youth. His reply was something that I shall never forget: "David you were there and know how it was. I shall never fly a Mosquito and you are the first pilot I have met who flew the early ones as you did. You must remember that your aeroplane fifty years ago was as advanced then as this 747 is today. What we have been talking about has not been written down as you have told it to me today and that is understandable because there were an awful lot of you then just as there are an awful lot of us today".

I could see what he meant. The extraordinary thing was that I had probably started flying before he was born. And yet we seemed to understand each other. We spoke almost the same language. No matter what your views, I had nothing but admiration for these two young men who sat and controlled such an incredible piece of machinery. They were two highly skilled men following their trade.

I think that this says it all. After all, there have been an awful lot of cabinet makers in the trade over the last 300 years!

Right. We will see what can be done. We have our materials. These then go to merchants and from there to workshops large and small, good and bad, where they are prepared and put together to create our furniture. The purpose of that is to hopefully make money, pay wages, pay for the materials and at the end of the day make a profit or enough money to start all over again! You are entitled to think, "Dear God, has he taken leave of his senses. We all know that". And you would be right, except that you would be astounded at the number of times people say to me, "But Mr. Hawkins, you are a craftsman and must really love your work". And many times I have got a very frosty reception when my reply has been that the nicest part of it has been paying the cheque into the bank! The thing about loving your work is understandable. The end result is usually such that the piece does look as if it has been lovingly cared for over the years. You do not see the worries and problems it caused along the way; they are not there to be seen. If they are you have failed. Also, you do not have an open cheque. Frankly the problems of running a small business in this field are so varied that now, with it all behind me, I know that it was a success only because it was always regarded as a job, not something special. It was done as fast and as efficiently as possible, and the work was totally in keeping with the piece being restored. We just followed our trade, while following the trade as it was at the time.

The open cheque did happen on a couple of occasions. The condition and rareity of the pieces made it the only way to work. But no advantage was taken of the situation. There is just no point in that. It gave us something far more important: time to get it right! The problem of getting the price for the job was always with us. This did not apply overmuch to me but it has been a common complaint heard from other people in the field. One classic complaint was, £250 to service my car, yet I could not get fifty quid for repairing a chair worth a couple of grand. Then I suppose a car is more important than a chair like that in this day and age.

You will be surprised how often pieces of furniture are bought without any thought of the condition. For me, one of the biggest aggravations was to be presented with a job which had cost the owner well into six figures of money, often in a horrible condition and being asked for an estimate to put it all in order. Love? It does not come into it.

Rightly or wrongly, I always call myself a tradesman and am taken to task for it. I do not understand why. After all, I and my father signed papers for me to be taught a trade. It has a lot to do with the days before the last world war. If you had a trade you could, with luck, go virtually anywhere in the world and find work. You were a tradesman. It is not like that today. In sixty years it seems to have turned full circle. Most of my era did not have a very long schooling. Jimmy Little had left at the age of twelve and one of the most skilled men I ever knew could hardly read or write. Few, if any, had money behind them.

One of my reasons for being stubborn about trade and craft was brought home to me recently. I have been putting together a chapter about Boullework. In there is a description of two-part sawing and how I think it has been made from the beginning. The presenter of a television programme was on a walkabout in Wiltshire and fetched up in a small town near the Savernake forest. We were taken into the workshop of a local craftsman, furniture maker and designer. He put forward the argument that it was difficult to compete with the 18th century designers and

also the makers of modern reproductions of those designs. Here I will agree with him totally. He, as seems usual today, was a very well educated young man. He told the presenter that he had had some success with cutting boards, bread and serving boards. These were made out of two woods. I could not believe the next part of this when he very seriously explained how he put two boards together – just as the marquetry and Boulle cutters of 300 and more years ago would put their two materials and veneers together and saw out their pattern. He sawed his shape with a bandsaw, very carefully mind you, then interchanged one with the other and glued it all together and got two for the price of one. Good luck to the young man. I wish him well, since he did admit that he found it hard going to run a small workshop and get his ideas across.

I do wish that he had said that he had taken his ideas from the trade of all those years ago and used it, along with a fairly modern machine, a powered bandsaw plus the advantage of modern waterproof glues to make something that was of use to us today.

Cynical, maybe, but I cannot really remember how many times I have been asked about the difference between craft and trade. I think the best way to describe it would be like this. A workshop in the late 17th century employs thirty Boulle cutters. I am one of them. We are all working away piercing our particular task and the man working alongside me has a heart attack. The boss asks me to finish the work he was doing. I do. We were both trained in the trade of Boullework. It will be very doubtful indeed if you could ever tell the difference between his work and mine. That is a tradesman.

I have been told that these views have a sour flavour. But think about them before I defend them. My first point in that defence is that I come from a workshop and I have employed cabinet makers. Now put yourself in my position. You employed people who, when they got down to work, did it in a completely different way one to the other. For example, you made chests of drawers and you had one man making the drawers one way and another made them in a different way. That, I am sure you will agree, would cause all sorts of aggro and problems to you and your business. Now, having employed people from the trade who had served their time, you would know that how they worked would be the same as you, or so close it would not matter. But more important even than that is that you talk a common language. You do not have to continuously explain. It is the discipline of the trade. So, as this is a book to help you know if the article does come from the time it is said to come from, it is going to be important that you have a rough idea about how they would have made the thing in the 17th century as opposed to the second half of the 18th century and then the difference in the 19th century. This then is the importance of understanding a trade and its tradesman.

We will start at the beginning with something that all woodworkers will understand. It is called a facemark, sometimes a benchmark (ILL 11 previous Chapter).

Once in America I bought a book about New England furniture. I have a fondness for American furniture because you can see in it a freedom from the hidebound traditions of Europe. On the other hand, corners have often been cut to hurry up the process! Money again rears its ugly head you see. Not much love is there. And I will let you imagine how that goes down with the furniture buffs! However, in this book is a photograph that shows the bottom of a serpentine chest of drawers and on it is a chalked "vee" with the top of the "vee" pointing to the front, chalk has been used from the earliest of times and seems to last forever. ILL 14A and B It was for me a facemark, a mark put on the wood that points to the place or edge that everything is marked out, measured and squared from. This means that every other person involved in the making will also know where to measure from.

ILLUSTRATION 14A: *Facemark, American C1760*

ILLUSTRATION 14B: *Facemark, English C1760. Top left corner, a rat has gnawed it. Charming.*

Cock ups will be eliminated as long as everyone knows and follows the rule.

I found it difficult to understand the point of such a picture and, as usual, when all else fails you read the instructions. In this case the text said, "It remains a mystery to this day why the craftsman who made this piece chalked these vee letters on his wood". I suppose the authors of the book could have asked a cabinet maker or carpenter. For my money they had not, so I wrote and told them what the mystery was. I did not get a reply. Not much point after publication, I suppose. Besides, I cannot possibly have been the only person who had picked them up on one of the first things that you are taught when you begin. At least I sincerely hope that this was not the case. However, some books about furniture do seem to have been put together by people who, I am afraid, have little idea about the trade that produced their subject.

This was brought home to me recently. This point had been brought up during a lecture. Afterwards I was talking to a young lady who had been researching Bostonian furniture. The researchers had constantly seen these marks and nobody knew what they were. She herself had done a short course in cabinet making and had not been told this. The gist was, "How can you be so sure? Can you prove it?" It was very difficult to be civil. Anyway, I told her to go and talk to someone else in the Trade if she could not bring herself to believe me!

Many people today talk about the hand workshop of the old days. It is surrounded with mystery and old wives tales. Once I was at a function, the dinner before a television recording the next day, when one of the people taking part was very seriously telling someone, "In Florence, you know, there are workshops making up antiques almost while you wait, mostly in walnut. They use 18th century wood (walnut) and 18th century tools. It's almost impossible to tell the difference". Lord have mercy. Thank the Lord that he was an expert in porcelain! How this idea originated I have no idea. I will say however that it would only have come from someone who has not worked with their hands. If they had they would have known that the hand tools of the 18th century are identical to mine in their function. No new ones have been invented to my knowledge. Just the technology of making them has improved. In fact, the way I have carried out my job in my working life is to all intent and purpose the same as a cabinet maker from the 18th century.

I was recently given a couple of books about tools of the 18th century. In it were illustrated planes, routers and chisels. The authors would have been surprised to see the array of identical tools that I have on show and would be more than surprised to hear that they were mine and had been in use throughout my working life. The fact that tools need to be constantly sharpened and therefore get worn out, broken and replaced would have never occured to them.

Let me show you what I mean. Suppose that by some miracle a man working in a workshop in 1820 could suddenly be transported to mine. He would feel at home, that is assuming that he survived the shock of our modern society. Obviously a circular saw that did not have to be treadled would surprise him. But he would have soon got used to electricity. My mortice bumper would more than likely have been similar to something in his shop. The drill press would not be a surprise, nor the lathe. The bandsaw would have been a surprise, yet had the miracle happened in about 1860 even that would be very similar. The difference is that his would have been powered by hand. All my other tools would have been similar and some identical to the ones he had left behind, or better still.

Suppose he could have transported his tools with him. They would have made him a small fortune if he put them into the rooms! (That makes me wonder what mine could be worth.) A thought to this fantasy. If he did put his tools into the rooms and took the money back with him, what a wealthy man he would have been!

A final thought for you is this: suppose he also brought with him a pair of sofa tables veneered in Rosewood, tastefully inlaid with brass. Now, having sold his tools so well he could be well tempted to sell his tables and I think he would have got the shock of his life at the problems he would come up against. They would be new. And to sell them well he would have to somehow put a fair dollop of age into them! That, I do not think he would understand. I certainly did not when it happened to me over 40 odd years ago.

This little fact about handwork is important since the evidence of handwork, and its tools will be very much the same no matter what century it comes from. It is the way they did the work that is important. So my emphasis on understanding age, its colour and feel becomes very important indeed.

It is also a surprise to people when I say that our visitor from nearly 200 hundred years ago, would not, in my opinion, be very surprised by my machines. The reason is that all woodworking machines as I understand them had been invented and patented by 1790. And since I have been skirting around them, my own views and the part they have played must be put down.

Lathes are accepted without question. These were more often than not human powered, very often by a treadle. I am sure that you have heard about the pole lathe that only cut on the downward stroke of the treadle. That must have been a pig to get used to. Because of this action it never turned anything very round. Remember this when someone tells you that the little turned leg stool or stick back chair that has caught your eye had been turned on a pole lathe by a bodger. Just run your hand around the turning. You will be surprised how unround (yes, unround) that a pole lathe one will feel.

What is a bodger? He was the turner who worked in the woods, felled his timber and turned the legs and bits and pieces on site as it were. He took his lathe with him and sprang a sapling over the lathe with a rope. The rope was wound around the workpiece that was set up between the centers. The other end of the rope was attached to the treadle of the lathe. When he pressed the treadle down the rope would turn the work and pull the sapling down. When he released the treadle, the sapling sprang back and pulled the treadle up for the next downward stroke to be made. An ingenious machine, it has been around since history has been recorded.

Apart from this sort of power they were also driven by a wheel and belt, the wheel is usually presumed to have been turned by a lad. My own opinion is that they must have had some very strong lads. The work would more than likely have fallen to the man you never hear about, the workshop labourer.

While on the subject of lathes, I quite recently heard someone holding forth about the spiral twist legs on a late 17th century chair. The point being made was about the huge amount of work needed to make them and how accurate they were one to the other. I wish I had been in the position to tell him that a copying lathe had been invented in the time of Elizabeth I. This had been designed to make barley sugar twists. And I have a few quid to say that even though this is common knowledge in the trade I would not have been believed. Power, apart from manual labor, was supplied by wind, water, tide, animals and weight or gravity. The thought, where old furniture is concerned, often seems to be that there was not any power until steam became a practical proposition.

Before we leave a barley sugar twist, I recently saw on television an open one, one with two twists, being described as being turned on a pole lathe! Dear me. The turner of that would have needed at least four legs!

Before we move on, why "bodger?" I must confess that I did not know for sure. My own idea has always been that the life of these men and women have been one of continuous make and mend. That I have always called bodging. You bodge (or botch) something up, I suppose. That is a pretty accurate explanation. As with antique furniture where you do not hear about the restorer, in publishing you do not hear of those who make your scribbles all nice and shiny! The one who sorted out my awful grammar and punctuation bothered to look up "bodger" for me. He tells me that the word "botch" comes from the term "bodger". This came from the Middle English "bocchen", which meant "to patch". Bocchen, in turn, came from Old English, Old French and Old Dutch that basically meant "a swelling" or "a boil!" The English, French, Dutch and German all used pole lathes.

My thanks to Mike Henry for his time and trouble.

The drill press would also be common. The

power for it was as for the lathe, the mechanics of a wine press utilised to produce the downward pressure vital for its success. Drills have been mechanised from the earliest times. The bow drill is still in common use today. You can buy a drill today that uses an Archimedes screw for its motive power, and a drill driven by a bow is still common all over the world, the function just the same as the sapling on the pole lathe.

The mortice machine, or bumper, was nothing more than a hand mortice chisel set up in a wooden frame and weighted over the chisel. It had a foot-operated lever that lifted it up on a cam, just like the Chinese water hammer of a thousand years ago. The cam let it down with a thump onto the mortice being chopped out. It was tricky to get the hang of it. But once you did it was very much quicker than by hand. Again you see it is time – and time is money. Because of this and since it was simply a machine made up to copy the function of a man, the end result at the bottom of the mortice is to all intent and purpose identical to the one chopped out by hand.

The next stage in these machines was the hollow chisel, a device that will drill a square hole! A simple idea (most good ideas are). You take a square of steel, drill a hole through the middle of it leaving as thin a wall on the four sides of the square as possible, make a drill to go through the hole, sharpen the bottom of the square of steel on the inside, mount it in the drilling machine, or drill press as it is better known, and feed it down onto the work. The drill makes a hole and the chisel around cuts the hole square as it goes down. So should you see the bottom of a mortice that has drill marks instead of chisel marks on it and you are told that it is before about 1860-70, it is not.

The obvious remark is, "How in Hell am I going to see the bottom of a mortice?" The answer: you are not unless the workshop opens one up for you. However we do live at the end of the 20th century, and if the matter is of importance try x-raying it! I have.

Planing machines were invented by 1790

and were in their own way a tremendous advance because they did not try to make a machine that would copy the function of a man planing wood. They made a flat disc about eighteen inches in diameter and a couple inches thick, mounted two cutting edges on the perimeter opposite each other, put a shaft through the middle of it, mounted it vertically in a wooden frame and drove it with wind, water or animal power. When it was spinning fast enough, the wood was laid on a table and fed under these two spinning, cutting edges. It must have been horrendously dangerous and would obviously have left marks of its use behind. This machine was developed in the 19th century and became known as a spindle, which for my money is one of the most dangerous machines ever. I would never have one in my workshop. In fact, if you saw a woodworker with a couple of fingers missing and you asked how it had happened the answer was very often, "I was a spindle hand".

There is one of these planing machines from the early 19th century in the Henry Ford Museum at Dearborn, Michigan. You would not have gotten me to operate it for a fortune!

The next stage with a planer was to put the cutters, usually two, into a horizontal roller, put guards over the top and pass the wood over or under the cutters. These leave very fine ripple marks on the surface and these bruise the surface. Often, even after the machine-planed surface has been planed up by hand, cleaned up and polished, these bruises can show. They show as very faint ripples under the polish. Years ago I got a customer their money back on a piece of furniture which was supposed to have come from the Regency simply because of that.

Probably one of the naughtiest tales from the workshop was about a dealer customer of mine. He arrived and we unloaded a very nice, small, Italian chest on stand, veneered in walnut, ebony and purpleheart. The drawers were lined with walnut and had their faces veneered with red shell banded in ebony. It came from about the 1830-40's and was choice. It was also in lovely condition and I obviously asked what was the problem. He gave me a drawer and said, "Look at that". I did and could not for the life of me see anything wrong. He was not well pleased and in no uncertain terms said that surely I knew a circular saw mark when I saw one! It was on the drawer bottoms. And there for all to see were the marks of a circular planer head, or a Ruffler as I think they were called. Anyway, he wanted them taken away. I protested. I do not know why I bothered. I was well used to the near paranoia of machinery by this time and told him what they were. The usual thing happened: I was talking rubbish; he had never heard of such a thing. I am afraid that money is money and we did his bidding. It is amazing when you think about this. We had to take the drawers apart before we could plane the marks out, then faked the bottoms back as best we could. Just the planing said bye bye to any age that had been there. We delivered it, got paid, and forgot about it.

The following June, Sheila and I were given tickets for the Antique Dealers' Fair in London's Park Lane; there was our pretty, little, Italian job in all its glory. The problem was it was now dated 1720! How this could be got away with baffled me. The drawers were classics from the 1830's. They simply did not make drawers like that one hundred years before. This was several years ago, before I realised that things like this were not considered important and in some places not understood. It is a funny and sometimes a rather bent world.

There is another machine that was invented which also did not try to copy the functions of hands. This one is early and comes from the beginning of the 17th Century and made its appearance on Flemish furniture, or rather I first saw it on furniture from that part of the world. These pieces of furniture carried mouldings that rippled, or waved as they are also called. The accuracy of them is such that they could not possibly have been created by hand.

A machine said to have been designed to make them is illustrated in the 18th century treatise by Roubo (or Diderot, I do not remember which; I suppose I should). This shows a scraper set up with the necessary shape formed on it. The piece of wood to be moulded was fixed on a bed below the scraper. The bed could be wound under the scraper by a handle and a cam under the bed made the piece of wood being moulded rise and fall as it moved along to create the rippled effect.

A superb piece of furniture from 1650 came through my hands and as usual it was in a bit of a state. It was in Ebony veneer laid onto Red Pine. It had Beech columns veneered with Ebony and its drawers lined with Fruitwood. Worm had done its thing, which was bad enough. Naturally, about forty-odd feet of the ripple moulding in Ebony was missing. A machine similar to the engraving I had seen was fabricated, the necessary Ebony prepared, and it did not work. We tried everything we could think of but just could not get over the simple problem that a scraper will not cut against the grain of wood. Rightly or wrongly, for my money, someone somewhere had got it wrong – probably me.

Looking at the old mouldings we were trying to copy under magnification, it was obvious that they must have been cut with a revolving cutter.

ILLUSTRATION 15: *Ripple mouldings, modern. Top two are from 1650*

I made up a cutter to match the moulding, put it into a router, set it up over my lathe and fixed the Ebony on a board that was moved past the cutter. This board was made to move in and out to follow the same ripple as the ones from 1650. It worked and under my glass it was impossible to tell the difference. ILL 15 It worked because we had speed of the cutter. When you see the vast quantities of this moulding that was produced in the 17th century and beyond, I have a funny feeling that a system very much like mine had been devised by the early Flemish makers.

Who knows? But then history does have a funny habit of repeating itself on occasions doesn't it?

The commonest tool of them all, whether it is hand or machine, has got to be the saw.

Almost the first thing that I was shown was how to sharpen and set a saw. My first lesson was with a tenon saw that was an early member of my tool kit, and I was justly proud of it. You can imagine my shock when I was told not to use it until it had been sharpened and set. I argued the toss. After all, at the age I was, you do know it all. So I did use it. To me, it seemed fine. But I found it a bit tricky to start on a cut. I asked Bill Bunce, my charge hand, why. He took it away, and I watched him set it up in a sharpening horse. To my horror, he filed the teeth almost flat. He then nonchalantly reshaped them, every other tooth down one side, turned it around and did the same to the ones in between. This took about ten to fifteen minutes. He then sat down and set the teeth. Giving it back to me, he just said "Try it now". Even for a youngster like me, it was an experience. No effort at all was needed. The problem of starting the cut had gone and it cut so accurately it cannot really be described. It took me a long time to be able to sharpen and set a saw like that. Today not many people have or need that sort of skill. The days of the throw-away-and-start-again saw are with us. But for anyone who is interested in wood and works with it and does not have the know how to be a saw doctor, acquire it. You will be amazed.

I used up three tenon saws like this one. They were just sharpened away. See what I mean about old tools?

The variety of saws is almost absurd, but they do all have a specific job. We have rip saws, panel saws, pit saws, tenon, dovetail, pad, keyhole, hack, bow, betty, coping, fret, piercing, gents, warding, flooring, band, horizontal, circular, skil, pruning and flexible. That is more than enough to be getting on with.

Time without number it has been said to me that a saw is difficult to use. "It is hard work, will not cut straight, seems to get stuck in the wood!" This is understandable because comparatively few people will have had the pleasure of using a saw that has been correctly sharpened and set. We will all know what sharp is and my American friend, Doug, found out when he first used a small dovetail tenon of mine. He cut a finger and I never did find out how he managed it. Doug is left handed and I can remember calling him a cack-handed so and so. I am probably fortunate because I am ambidextrous, in the nicest possible way! However, it is possible that setting will not be so familiar. To describe it will not be the easiest of things, since you often use different sets for different saws and the work they are to do. Also, it can be dependant on the number of teeth per inch that the saw has. Setting is the slight bending of alternate teeth to one side of the saw, and the ones in between bent to exactly the same amount to the other side so that when you look down this cutting edge you can see a "vee" running down the length of it. The teeth are now wider than the blade of the saw. This allows it a clear passage as it cuts through the wood. So, if it seems to get stuck, set it correctly and the problem will go away.

It is the set of the saw that leaves saw marks or kerfs on a surface. Learn to recognise what saw leaves what. Then know roughly the dates when that sort of saw was in common use and you have another little string to your bow.

In my list of saws before I got carried away with sharpening I left out the most important

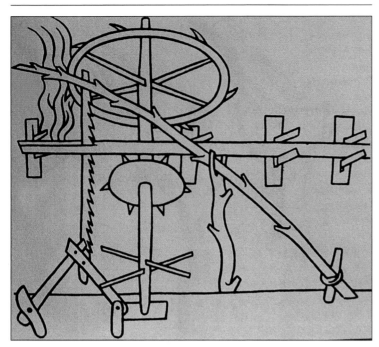

ILLUSTRATION 16: *D'Honnecourt saw. C1150 AD!*

saw, as it had been set in the frame, was replaced with wood. A saw blade was fixed to replace a side of the frame and the other side was set up to be tensioned, usually with a cord tourniquet. These you will see time without number in the depictions of medieval life. Yet you can go to a tool shop today and buy a saw that is identical. Its function has never been bettered. That function? To be able to cut around shapes.

Strangely enough, the saw we will all know today is the one with its nice, shiny, hand-grip handle. This one was not in at the beginning. I think the reason was that the technology of metal and its working had to catch up with the idea!

When very large timber was sawn, obviously a large frame saw was needed and the method was to have two men doing the actual pushing and pulling movement of the frame on one side and one man on the

one. It is the earliest of them all. You will have seen them on paintings from medieval times and in illustrations from the ancient Egyptians. A tube station in London, Charing Cross I think, has its walls decorated with murals depicting the 15th or 16th century. Building is going on and you can see the carpenters using these saws.

What are they? They are frame saws and have been in use before the two handed pit saw was thought of. They are exactly what the name implies, a wooden frame with the saw blade down the centre of the frame set up so that it can be tensioned. They can be of all sorts of sizes, large enough to need two men on each side of the frame or small enough for one man to comfortably handle without getting tired. Getting tired is something not often thought about (unless you are the one getting tired).

The bow saw is a derivation of the frame, and is as early. All these saws needed to be tensioned. This one was different since the cutting part became one side of the frame. The

ILLUSTRATION 17: *D'Vinci saw.*

other who actually guided the saw. It was the problem of moving massive trees about and getting them into a position to be sawn that brought about the pit saw. It was easier to manhandle the tree over the pit, which in the beginning was probably nothing more than a trench in the ground for the engine to be put in. The engine was actually the one or two men doing the work for the sawyer on top who was guiding the saw.

You do not need me to tell you what a long-winded and costly business this must have been. The sheer quantity of timber that has been used just over the last 400 years must mean that machines were common. Early machines were usually attempts to copy the actions of man. The frame saw was an absolute natural for this. They simply took the frame saw and put it into another frame so that it would slide up and down. A bench was put on either side of the frame. Power from an axle and crank below the frames drove the saw frame up and down in the outer frame that guided it. Timber was laid on the bed and fed into the saw. The mechanical pit saw was born. Power could have been water, wind, tide, animal, gravity, even human (when you have seen a treadmill in operation). There is one in Beaumaris Castle, Wales, that still works.

One of the earliest prints that I have ever seen was dated 1151. It was French and by a monk by the name of D'Honnecourt. It so impressed me that I turned it into a slide transparency. ILL 16 One of its most important features was the fact that it used the age-old principal of the springy pole of the pole lathe to return the saw after a cut. 1151 is a long time before Leonardo Da Vinci.

He, Da Vinci seems to have invented most things and among his drawings is a framed saw that is to be driven by water. In Italy, there is a model made up from his drawing. ILL 17 You need to keep saws sharp. This is done with a file, so he left a drawing of a file striking machine for good measure.

In the time of Elizabeth the First, a mechan-

ILLUSTRATION 18: *Print of saw from the time of Elizabeth I.*

ical saw like this was a fact. And there is a print to prove it. And surely if they could invent a copying lathe, a mechanical saw would be no problem. In 1621 they could have gone over to Holland and copied the one that they had working. Happily for our story they still have one that works for the tourists today. And yes, the date on it is 1621, and original. ILL 18 is my drawing of that print.

The thing about these early machines is that they began to exploit their potential from the beginning. The saw in Holland has got three saw blades in its frame so you can put an eight inch plank through it and have four pieces come out the other side. I never had a saw in my shop that could do that. And I have seen a print of a machine that was in use at the end of the 18th and early 19th century that carried ten saws in its frame. Now that really was something (The

ILLUSTRATION 19: *Bradley saw.*

History of Machine Tools, Ian Bradley). ILL 19

My own evidence of early sawing machines is wide. The folk museums of Holland carry the oldest working examples. The Henry Ford Museum has a lovely small hand driven frame that would have been the bandsaw of the 18th century. Early mechanical pit saws I have seen illustrated in books many times. Yet one of our leading names in furniture and a light in the Furniture History Society has a book that states: "From Tudor times specialist sawyers travelled the countryside in pairs, moving from one estate to the next. By manoeuvring the butts across a saw pit they could cut along the length of even the heaviest of trees with a long two-handled saw...since the beginning of the century (and you must assume this century) pit saws have been made redundant by the introduction of large band-saws" (The

Arthur Negus Guide to English Furniture, Hamlyn). I must say here that the doyen of English furniture, the late Arthur Negus, did not write the book! It does also state that many a faked piece has been discovered by the tell tale signs of the machine age. What on earth is the machine age? I suppose in this context we have hand work taken to a ludicrous degree.

In fact it was on Television that I saw this happen. A nice little mahogany chest of four drawers was being shown. A drawer was taken out and the back board of the drawer had the unmistakeable signs of a mechanical pit saw. Television has a remarkable ability to show the truth and it would have been impossible for anything but a mechanical pit or frame saw to have made such marks. Even from the comfort of my chair I would have laid odds that this little chest was right and came from the late 18th century! It was immediately said to be a fake. The crime was the saw marks. They were, according to the "expert", bandsaw marks and the piece a total fake! It was an amazing performance. I wish I could have been there. Bandsaws began serious work in around 1860 and this telecast was about ten years ago. How in Hell can something well over one hundred years old be a fake – a fake of what?

The thing that I could not understand about this eccentric performance was that he could have imagined that a faker would have been stupid enough to leave any machining evidence behind. I have to put myself in this category and know only too well this near paranoia where machines are concerned. This is more than anything the reason for this chapter. More importantly, though, the guy had no idea about the cost of making things. No one would fake a piece like this. It would just not be worth the time and trouble. Remember that. I shall be talking about it as we move along.

This attitude toward machines I can understand. But we are at the end of the 20th century. An antique piece of furniture is in the realms of 100 years old. Machines have been a fact for almost all our modern history and an understanding of them is now essential. My reason for saying this is that our reliance on machines is not a modern thing. I believe we have always had it. Until the days of reliable steam power, machines had been the servants of man. As steam power improved, machines followed and man became more and more the servant of the machine. I do not need me to say anything about electricity and the microchip.

When I first began, the workshop was small. It was not a factory by any means. It was just one of the small workshops that were all over the place. Out back was a circular sawbench, a small planer, a bandsaw, a morticer and whetstone. When I finally shut up shop I had a small bandsaw, a drill press, a couple of portables and a whetstone. When I had my last workshop, over the yard from me was a small cabinet shop with one young man and a boy. He designed furniture and said to me that it had to be designed around his machines. His shop was about six times the size of mine. He had two benches, both much smaller than mine. The rest of the space was mainly for machines. Including his portables, there were twenty-eight pieces of modern machinery in there. His rent, power bill and capital outlay must have been awesome. I suppose this must have been the case, because he had to close down and quit. That was sad because he did have some good ideas.

Memory banks are funny things. I remember an article that I took from our *Sunday Times* on the 6th of June 1993. They print a section for children. In it was a two page colour spread called "Building in Wood" and the date was the early 1600's. In the bottom left hand corner was a picture of a windmill and the text was about wind power. The text ends, "Some mills had wind powered saws. Six men could cut about eighty tree trunks a day into planks!" This was for building houses and the date, as I have said, was the early 1600's. It does make you wonder why the furniture industry did not think of using their services? I hope the television guy and the writer of the book reads the Sunday Times, or the "Funday Times" as the section was called.

The windmill in this article would have been

driving a mechanical frame saw, or mechanical pitsaw as it was later called. These saws were all powerful until the advent of steam.

The mechanical pitsaw however did have one drawback. It was only 50% efficient. This is really a contradiction in terms but it only cuts on its downwards stroke. So a saw that had a continous cut as it moved had to be the way ahead. The thinking revolved around a circular saw. Isambard Brunel took out a patent for a circular saw in 1806. This sort of date would work in very nicely when the evidence of the circular saw is there to be seen. The earliest I have seen is on Rosewood and Mahogany veneer from around 1810-1830. Having seen it once it was astounding how much other evidence of this most efficient saw began to be seen. Obviously this was because more and more furniture from the 19th century was coming on the market, being sought after and promoted.

The circular saw gave a new meaning to the preparation of wood. Steam and electricity made this sawing ability available to anyone who had a mind to use it. I have had experience of circular saws from my beginning of working with wood and have used many machines that were well over 80 years old. In fact, it is well in the realms of possibility that I have used a machine that started its working in the 1860's. Today circulars are in the province of everyone. The popularity of woodwork and do-it-yourself has made the screech of a circular saw commonplace. This is one of its drawbacks and many an older woodworker is today probably deafer than he should be. I know that I am. My advice to anyone using a high speed machine is to protect your ears. The speed necessary to make a circular efficient does mean that often the perimeter of the saw is travelling at about 350 plus miles an hour! This is with the modern small machine that used a saw of about twelve inches in diameter or less. The large saw of the mill, and the ones that sawed the early 19th century veneer used saws of a diameter that today we would find quite frightening and give the factory inspector nightmares. The sawing kerfs that I have seen on the back of some veneers and prepared wood from those early days show that saws of ten feet and above in diameter were used.

Since the making of steel was not really established commercially until the 1850's how these huge saws were made does support my idea of a casting with cutting teeth mounted on the perimeter. Because of this, I think a circular to just saw wood and not just a veneer would have coincided with the arrival of steel. My reason for saying this is a thing called a riving knife mounted behind the saw which stopped the wood closing on the saw as the cut was made. This was not needed with a veneer. It could be peeled away as it was cut and would have allowed a casting or even a wooden saw frame to be used.

The largest circular I have seen in use was four feet in diameter. It was almost silent when running. If the cutting edge of that had got near the speed of the smaller saws, that sawmill would not have seen me for dust!

The next (and possibly last) advance of the saw before portable power became a reality is the bandsaw. The success of such a saw was the ability to make a long narrow strip of flexible metal that could be shaped and sharpened into a saw. The strip was brazed or welded together to make an endless band of cutting teeth. It is fair to say that the making of such a band was the reason for the late appearance of such a saw. The steel industry again.

In the beginning these were mounted and tensioned over three wheels. Two wheels of the same diameter were on a frame one above the other. A third and larger one was mounted to the left of the vertical ones and a table set up between the two vertical wheels. The band of teeth was then tensioned around the three wheels. The larger of the wheels had a handle and some poor sod had the job of winding it to make the band revolve so a cut could be made. Obviously there were guides to stop the blade being pushed off the wheels as the pressure of the cut was made. In the beginning, no guards were put over the saw at all. It, as with many early machines, must have caused horrific accidents. It did not take long for it to be improved. Guards enclosed the saw. Two wheels were used, although three are favoured on some machines today. The continuous band idea was used to great effect. Very large machines made to run horizontally created a timber or lumber industry that exploited timber to a degree not thought about before.

Rightly or wrongly, I think one modern saw will become a scourge if it has not already done so. It had the power to decimate large areas of woodland or forest in hours. What is it? A chain saw. I am not a great believer in rules and restrictions. We have more than our fair share as it is. But the chainsaw is one machine, if it would be possible to do so that should have some control put upon it.

Machines have always been. And if an understanding of old furniture is to be acquired an understanding of them is helpful but not essential. If you do have the know how to recognise the evidence of machines and when they were used, so much the better.

In the days when I presented furniture for a television programme I had the misfortune to tell a lady that her treasured Queen Anne bureau bookcase was not from 1720 but a nice copy from the early days of this century. The colour was explained. This was not a faked up piece; it was a very good reproduction. I explained that the veneers were modern knife cut and that the feather inlays were machine-made. The drawers were looked at and they were lined in Oak but made in the way of the late 19th early 20th century, not as in the time of Queen Anne. Also, on the bottom of the drawer was the evidence of a circular saw kerf, a small area that the planer or the cabinet maker had missed (such a common thing to see). The lady was gracious and happily pleased when I told her that her mothers bureau was worth £1200-1500.

I got some fan mail from this one! One or two irate furniture buffs wrote, "What do you think you are doing talking about such a piece of rubbish? After all what cabinet maker worth his salt would even think of using machines, let alone leaving evidence of them behind?" Amazing, or at least I found it so, I did let the producer know what I thought in no uncertain terms. He rather wisely said that the Company would answer the letters for me!

Hands and machines work together well. I, as we know, come from a world that was predominately handwork. Now in my small workshop I have a small lathe, a mill, a small drill press and a grinding wheel. These machines do my bidding and my hands get to work and do the many things that these simple machines cannot do. A three-inch scale, traction engine has been built. It will be said that it has been built by hand. This is how it has always been for me and I am convinced it was just the same for all the men and women who made the things that I have spent my working life rebuilding, repairing and looking after so that their efforts can hopefully go on for another one or two hundred years.

Now that this has been put down as I have seen it and my involvement with my trade is not a practical one anymore, it has always remained a mystery to me that people from the world of antique furniture rarely ever bothered to visit or call into the workshop to see what was going on. Even when things worth a king's ransom were being worked on, any communication was on the telephone. Things were always left to me. I suppose you could say that it was a compliment. In all my years I doubt if I had more than thirty visits from my customers. Even stranger is that I have worked on pieces that are part of England's furniture history and yet have had only one fleeting visit from a furniture historian. I probably asked too many questions. In fact, I know that I did. So it has been very easy to safeguard my master's secrets and the mystery of the Trade!

Before our next chapter, The Workshop, I must put down something that may convince you, if you are not convinced already that this sort of thing is important or that my ideas about machines are even relevant.

We are leaving the cabinet trade for awhile.

For about a year before I went into the RAF I had the good fortune to work in the Great Western Railway works at Swindon, Wiltshire. A war can cause problems to the plans you might have had or the work you were doing. The Great Western Railway, or God's Wonderful Railway as it was known, was the work of my particular genius Isambard Brunel. This one ran from London to Bristol and was a going concern in the late 1830's – often a forgotten fact.

Isambard and a group of business men followed his idea that, as they were at Bristol, why not do the obvious and continue with an ocean-going, paddle steamer to carry passengers and freight to New York. Paddle steamers had been around for the past 25-30 years. So the decision was made to build an ocean-going ship to be driven by steam and wind, a decision then, almost akin to the Titanic about 75 years later.

She was named The Great Western, 236 feet long overall and built of wood. Building began in July, 1836, and the hull was launched in July, 1837. One hundred and eighty men did this and were paid £8,000 in wages. Simple division gives us an average weekly wage of seventeen shillings. (This was a surprise. You will see why when later on I shall be talking about the cost of making things.) She was first registered in 1837 and made her maiden voyage in April, 1838. She was in service for the next thirty years.

It is the time factor that I find unbelievable. Yet it is all on record and I doubt if such a thing would be possible today.

Your reaction is entitled to be, "What is the point of this?" It is this: to create her used a formidable amount of wood: Oak 16,592 cubic feet, Elm 3,340 cubic feet, Hard Pine 12,431 cubic feet and Soft Pine 4,339 cubic feet

This cubage of wood is as bulk. In simple terms it means a piece of wood one foot square that is 36,610 feet long, or just under seven miles, that had to be sawn up and shaped to create her (Brunels Great Western, Denis Griffith).

How advanced the machinery must have been to succeed in such a project in such a short time. To me, it speaks volumes for the ingenuity and invention that had gone on during the centuries before. Everything does seem to have been there ready for this and for our modern machine age to begin.

Chapter 5

THE
WORKSHOP

*S*EVENTY ODD YEARS IN HISTORY IS ALMOST NOTHING. For you and I, it will have been a working life and probably much more. The changes in history will be hardly noticeable; but our seventy odd years must have been the most dramatic anyone has lived through. I doubt if anyone could have predicted the development that has gone on during these years.

At the moment, we are in a small town called Quiberon. We come here regularly because the clock goes back thirty, forty years or more. Yet you still have the luxury of all mod-cons. It is in Brittany. Three days ago, we crossed to St. Malo by ferry. Our car and about 550 other cars and occupants drove off in about thirty minutes. The first time I crossed over was in 1950. A handful of cars were winched off one at a time using wheel nets. I am sure that the 550 cars and occupants that drove off the Bretagne three days ago took it all for granted. Just as we did.

In 1950, just 550 cars driving off and not one breaking down would have been a minor miracle!

It is much the same with everything. It is all taken for granted. A pocket calculator was amazing when we first got one. (I must admit that I still work out percentages in my head.) A customer gave me one of the first electric tuning fork watches. The hum of that kept us awake at nights. How many of us can remember with envy Telly Savalas and his digital watch? We can remember our first television, electric typewriter, computer. The first answering machine – and going out to a payphone to hear what it sounded like. The first plane ride with the family for a holiday in Malta. Saving up for months to pay for it. Instant credit. That one I do not and never will take for granted.

Yet all of it was paid for by a small workshop, working as it has always been – hands assisted by two or three small machines. My operation was always around two or three people including me. It never got any larger, just more busy. Often we would all be working on the same piece and I have found that this is something that people find hard to accept – or believe. It must be because when they look at the finished thing as they do, a slide at a lecture for example, there is just no evidence that more than one pair of hands has been at work. They find it hard to believe because of their rather cosy image of a workshop: very much two or three men working away, each making their own piece of furniture. Call it the bespoken image of one man making one piece. It existed; of course it did just as today. But, as today, I am sure that it was the exception rather than the rule.

History tells us of the fire in Thomas Chippendale's workshop and the tool chests of twenty-two workmen found in the ashes. If this was so, his operation was tiny when you compare it to that of Seddon, also of London who employed four hundred workers. He becomes small when Reisener of Paris in his heyday is said to have employed two thousand. It is these sort of facts that will show you my point about trade and understanding it. The success of any workshop no matter how large or small depended first and foremost on one thing: discipline. The discipline of the Trade.

This discipline enabled the workers to move about. Journeymen was not just a folksey name for the carpenters and cabinetmakers. Because of their training they could start work as soon as they began in a new workshop. Remember also that all workshops had apprentices. Imagine their problem if all the men they worked with went about their job in a different way. This is how it was, and it was much the same with me up until the early 1960's. After that time the decline in apprentices began. As far as I am concerned the decline in the basic understanding began at that time. You had to constantly explain, put mistakes right, check everything. It became ridiculous and because of that I did not take on one new man or give any work out since those days.

People do accuse me of being rather touchy when I talk about this subject. The problem is that I cannot for some reason get people to realise just how important it is. I use the Trade and what it can tell me when I have to decide if something is what it is said to be. That hack-

neyed phrase, "the buck stops here" – it really did with me. I had to be right. What follows will, I hope, show you how the workshop and its rules are used.

The year is 1775. You run a cabinet shop with one hundred men. It is well established and has a good clientele. You are approached by someone who today would be an interior designer. He or she shows you the design and plans for a pair of bookcases on commodes, highly decorated and expensive. It is, in fact, an important order for you. You go into the project, drawings put up, materials decided upon and a price given. This is accepted and the work can proceed. Unless you have actually done a job like this, how it is planned would not have been thought about. Why should you? As the customer, it is the end result that matters.

The plans come into the workshop. Your top hand, call him the foreman, will go over them. Any problems that he can see will usually be sorted out then. The materials will be gone into and a cutting list of the carcass woods drawn up, plus quite a good percentage for wastage. Because we have a high style pair of cases decorated with marquetry, the veneers will be selected.

You are a fair-sized concern and carry stocks of timbers, but not enough, or possibly not the correct ones for an important order like this. The timbers will be selected and bought in. These are then prepared so that we have all the materials on hand and the making can begin. The marking out of the component pieces will not be done individually. The bookcase tops for example have four sides. They will be marked out together. Also, let us say that they are carrying slots for shelves. Mark those individually and inaccuracies will happen. So it goes on. The carcass work is done and they move to the drawer and door makers. Hopefully in the time allowed the carcass work is completed and moved to the veneer and marquetry room, if you had one. If not, a marqueteurs shop elsewhere just as today would have made it up for you. It is delivered and the pieces veneered. The whole thing is cleaned up, locks and handles are fitted and the final, difficult and expensive thing begins, fitting the glass for the bookcase tops. Look at any piece of ordinary glass today. It will be clear and flat, rarely the case with common glass from those days.

My reason for writing such a mundane thing is to show how important this side of a piece of furniture can be. How many of you have heard the expression, "measure twice and cut one?" It originated here.

Right at the beginning I said that it was not my purpose to point a finger. But I was asked to tender for the repair and restoration of a pair of bookcases like these I have described. What they are does not matter. What matters is that they did not follow the rules:

1. They were not the same size. One-eighth inch or so across the grain is allowable for shrinkage, but, not in the length. These had differences of over half an inch in places and in an important pair that is unacceptable.

2. The carcass wood was quite different one to the other. In fact, they were so different it was obvious that one was 18th century and the other certainly not. Also, preparation. That is, wood thickness was different one to the other.

3. The construction work showed why the difference: one was 18th century construction, the other typical mid-19th century. Apart from the carcass work this was obvious in the drawers.

4. The other problem was that they were identically veneered! How could that happen with different carcass work? They had to have been veneered at the time of the later carcass.

One thing for sure: I did not want this job! I have had more than my share of fending off awkward questions. What I thought was a well-over-the-top estimate was tendered. That's right, I got the job. I found out later that another tender was three times more than mine, so I am quite sure that I was not the only one who did not like what they had seen.

These pieces are well known, or said to be, held up as examples of the finest from the time. Jolly good. The only problem as far as I could see was that nobody had ever really looked at them. Certainly no one had ever measured them. I can remember talking it over with one or two friends and a great mate in the Trade. The advice there was, "For God's sake, keep your mouth shut". What did I expect? Anyway, I did keep my mouth shut.

However, during the work I came up against a problem that pointed directly to the 19th century. The green colours in the veneer work had not faded at all! A piece of untouched, 18th century marquetry will, under all the dirt, French polish, wax or whatever, be faded – unless the surface has been scraped back time and again. These surfaces had not been treated to that indignity. The problem was such that I was sure the end result would be very garish. I did something I rarely do: I called the owners and asked them to come and look and tell me what they wanted. I knew exactly what the trade would want, but an unknown client was something else.

A workshop is a very different place to a long gallery in a mansion. When my clients were over, I explained the colour problem, and probably for the first time these bookcases were being seriously looked at. Being in a workshop, the difference between them was obvious. The questions began: why was this like this and that like that. I can remember a rule being picked up and measurements taken. The questions were very pointed. It was difficult. The end result was that a full photographic record was requested.

My next surprise was a telephone call from the historical side of furniture! The owners had obviously called him and he wanted to know what was the problem. I suggested, "As the work will not be finished for three weeks or so, why not come down and have a look?" He declined.

The job was finished. The green problem was toned down with some judicious bleaching work. I have never had to do that on original 18th century things before! They were delivered and I was paid. It was about six weeks later when I got another call from the historical gentleman. He had been to see the cabinets and really could not understand what all the fuss was about. "Obviously the maker of them had been so busy that he had made one in his workshop and had got someone else up the road to make the other one".

I discovered then what it was to be lost for words, or at least polite ones. To this day I do not think I have heard such a stupid explanation. I can understand someone being busy. I have had that problem many times in my life and surely if you have any common sense at all you give the whole job out. The thing that shook me more than anything was that the guy on the other end of the phone had not the remotest idea how a workshop operated. More than anything was the fact that I was expected to believe such a fatuous explanation.

The questions I will ask you now are the questions that should have been asked of him.

1. The carcass wood – is it from the same sawing? This will mean exactly the same. If it is not, ask why. Put it this way: would you buy a pair of shoes with different leather one to another? I cannot imagine a handmade pair of shoes not being cut from the same hide. Can you?

2. If veneered, is the veneer from the same sawing? Often when a pair is veneered the veneer will be turned over so that the pattern or grain will point to each other. This will change the colour. Make sure that the carcass or ground wood is the same just as if it was solid.

3. Are all measurements the same? I would expect sizes along the grain to be the same, but give and take a little across it.

4. If there are any fittings, locks, hinges or mounts, are they the same? Make allowances for damage. But be careful; it is not very difficult to alter metal and make things up.

5. If your pair has doors, are they handed? This means, does one open one way, one the other? They should.

6. The most important thing of all: is the cabinet making the same throughout? If one has different making than the other, I would not give them a second look.

When all this happened, I collected some flak. It was to be expected. But it was not as if I was some new boy in the game. Similar things had been found many times before. It is, I am afraid, the same old story of the man in the grubby apron not being credible because of his appearance. It is a pity; we could have learned a lot from each other. However, it was not to be. As all of this was years ago now and it still has never been talked over; I think that is rather sad. No it is not, it is downright stupid!

The thing that I have never understood about this tale is this. These pieces would have been expensive then and expensive today. If you order an identical pair from me today, I doubt if you would get much change from 160,000 pounds. If I delivered them to you and you find all the things that I have described wrong with them, would you accept them? You certainly would not. And I would not expect it. I am just as sure that the member of the gentry that they are supposed to have been made for would not have accepted them either. I have always been amazed that anyone could imagine that they would.

What we are talking about is something that happens all the time. It has happened to me on more than one occasion. A piece comes to me and I make up a pair for it. So a piece of 18th century furniture in mahogany was sent to a cabinet shop in about 1860 and they copied the 18th century one. The world of antique furniture as it is today did not exist. So it was copied and made as the trade of the 1850's. One look at the drawers was enough. They were then both veneered in sycamore or a Singhalese white wood (they are said to be veneered in Satinwood), inlaid with some commercial marquetry which was not even handed as it would surely have been in the 1770's.

They were never made together, for sure. The bookcase part carry shelves that run in grooves; the 18th century one has twenty-one, the other twenty-two. This is something that would never have been ordered and is a classic example of something that will happen when the discipline of a workshop, or rather when a break in that discipline, happens.

Understanding the workshop and how it works does make the story a fascinating one. With the way things are in the world of the decorative arts today (and if their provenance was seriously gone into), they could possibly prove more valuable than they are said to be – not from a monetary point of view; just the history part could have a valuable tale to tell.

One last thing – and a part of that history before we leave this rather sad and, in many ways, silly episode – they were glazed.

That glazing was at least mid-19th century glass. Today we would call it 3/16 inch plate. It was held in place with triangular strips, or battens, and pinned with needle points. How many of you have even heard of a needle point? Not many. They came out because of the problem of putting an eye in a needle. When they started to mass produce them in Redditch the failure rate was large and the needles without an eye were sold off and used for this sort of purpose. Years ago I could buy them and used them. You drove them in, bent them and broke them off under the surface.

I have never seen these points used in 18th century work, just as I have never seen 18th century glazing that was not set into putty. Then I suppose that is just me!

Pairs of anything when they were ordered were an important thing and warranted a little more attention than usual. Pairs of things in the world of old furniture are rare, usually expensive and can be famous. In this case, you did not need to know anything to see that they were not a pair. All that was needed was a look. It seems nobody took the time. And, as is so usual, they just took their history for granted.

You also did not need to know very much about things old to see that one had been made years after the other. I have a copy of the pho-tographs and also the negatives. About six or seven years ago, again quite by chance, I heard that they had been revalued and were now three times more than when they were insured in my workshop! Patience is an important part of my job. It can get worn a bit thin and this did not help very much. I broke the confidentiality that should be given to customers (I am not over proud of that) and showed just six photographs to five people. One knew nothing about the Trade at all. The other four I respected highly. Their understanding was as high as you can really get. You could not see from the pictures what the pieces were and yet all five opinions were exactly the same as mine.

The golden rule is to never let anything be something because you want it to be or it is said to be.

You will be entitled to say, "Why was the wood so different? Surely Mahogany is Mahogany". Well, it is not and you would be surprised how different the wood will be if you do not get a sufficiency at the time from the same stock at the merchants. Years ago I made up a set of six and two dining chairs for a customer. They were in Brazilian Rosewood. I never kept a stock of any size. Rosewood was just too expensive. Anyway, this customer about three years later wanted four more singles. Try as I might I could not find any timber that was a good match to the original eight. That stock had gone. This was explained and I advised them not to have the work done. I was not believed and the job was done. They never matched as they would have had I made the twelve at the same time. Just as with the bookcases you do not have to know very much about furniture to see that we have a set of twelve chairs with four added later. In this case it does not really matter. But imagine if this were a set of twelve from the Regency and you tried to sell them!

The development of the cabinet trade in the 18th century was, in my opinion, slow. How the workshop made things did rather just trundle along. We, the English, were more carpenters and joiners until a decade or so before that century.

However, emigrés from the continent were about to change all that.

Cabinet making obviously developed from carpentry and joinery. And when you get down to it, it is really quite a simple thing to do. As with most things, once the basics are understood the rest is practise, more practise, developing and improving, finding short cuts and, something rarely if ever talked about, being able to do the same thing time after time after time without getting bored out of your mind – discipline.

Tools and their use is not my purpose. They are very much personal things. And the basic hand tools have hardly changed at all. A cutting edge is a cutting edge and an example of this personal thing is how you sharpen that cutting edge. When I was at the Ford Museum I was asked how I got my cutting edges like a razor? This I had never thought about. They were simply worked on an oilstone then stropped on the palm of my hand. I showed them. Then I saw someone else try it. I was so horrified that I had to forbid them trying. The accident rate would have been awful. It was a very salutory lesson to me since no one ever got the cutting edge that I could, and for the first time in my life I realised how lucky I was to have started at fourteen years of age and not tried to pick it up as an adult. Tricks of the trade are vital.

How you use your tools does become your own thing. I was always frowned upon because I never used a mallet. Almost all my adult working life I used the side of a claw hammer. It never did any more damage to a chisel handle than a mallet. It never wore out like a mallet and is in my tool kit to this day.

Cabinet making can be said to be about five basic joints: mortice and tenon, dovetail, halflap, tongue and groove and a rebate, which is a groove with one side taken off.

Be able to produce these almost without

ILLUSTRATION 20: *Coffer, slabwood.*

thinking, make sure that your materials are prepared correctly and that everything is marked out correctly from your datum point, the facemark. Armed with that and these few basic joints and anything can be made.

I shall be accused of simplifying it all and most of the accusations will come from those who work in the field. But all the other sophistications that happened – mitered dovetails, rule joints, haunched tenons, angled mortices, double tenons, knuckle joints etc, etc – are all derived from these basics.

This simple illustration does show how it began. It is really just a box. ILL 20 I imagine all furniture began like that. Just a box nailed up, or if nails were not available nailed with wooden pegs, treenails. The next step would be to put a rebate on the cross board or the end. This will stop the end grain being so susceptible to damp and dust, also a good way to help stop insects and bugs getting in. The side was then nailed into that. It will be quite a long time before glue became the norm. As the box became bigger, nails were not enough and dovetails became common, these solving the first two methods in a much better, stronger, neat and decorative way.

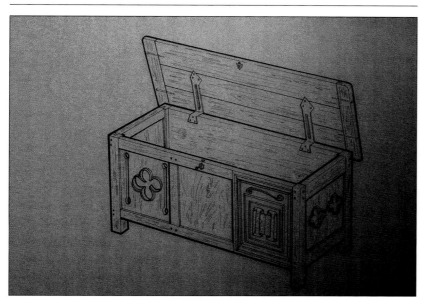

ILLUSTRATION 21: *Coffer, framed.*

The joints were pegged, not glued. These were set up so that the peghole in the tenon was a little closer to its shoulder than the hole in the mortice was to its top edge. The joint was put together and the peg, usually square and tapered, was driven into the hole. Being out of line, it would pull the tenon and its shoulder up tight to the frame. The tapered peg joint is really the most amazing and simple thing. As is usual with things like that, it is still in common use today.

Furniture from the 16th and 17th centuries would come into me – our boxes or coffers that we have been talking about, stools, early chairs, wainscots, armoires, bread hutches made from oak, elm, yew, sometimes a survivor in walnut or cherry – these were very rare and almost, if they had been left alone, built with the pegged tenon. ILL 22 is a walnut coffer dovetailed together, c1700 English and in excellent condition. That is very rare.

It did not seem to matter what nationality

The dovetail must be just about the oldest joint there is. I do not know how old it is, but a key-stone in an arch is a dovetail and the joint used in the context of woodwork is the strongest hanging and pulling joint there is. As our adverts today tell us that certain glues are "stronger than the wood itself", a dovetail most certainly is that.

Naturally as the boxes became bigger so did the wood needed to make them. Obviously the weight followed and became silly. So construction of the wood for the sides began and, for my money, the basis of the cabinet trade was born. Panelled frames were made up, just as the wainscot work for interior decoration. Small panels made to fit and the mortice and tenon came into its own in furniture. ILL 21 will show what is meant with the various ways and means of using these basic joints to hold things together. Air or ventilation was early on the scene and decorative ways of letting that air in was as early as painting to brighten everything up.

ILLUSTRATION 22: *Coffer walnut C1700.*

they were. Usually just a tap with a hammer on the peg and it would drift and the piece could be taken apart. It was, and still is, a wonderful system.

Few of you will have had my look at furniture. It is a bit difficult for you to hump something upside down and look at this and that as we were doing all the time. Usually, if it is old and has not been fiddled with, it does not tell you very much since the joints will often be covered. Sometimes if the piece has two center partitions, as a breakfront will have, you will be confronted with the end of their tenons. I would not like to see nails doing this job. The tenons should be wedged and it was common practise to put the wedge in diagonally. I would expect to see that on better work from the 18th century. Another way was to put a couple of wedges across the tenon.

Another thing of course is that you will often find the bottom of a piece painted out. This is a size wash made from thin glue and colour. It is not always the case on work from the first half of the 18th century but quite common from the 1760's onward and quite usual in the 19th century. You will find a pinkish colour for mahogany, black for rosewood, yellow ochre for satinwood. It should be completely matt in appearance, and if a wetted finger is pushed hard on it, some colour should come away.

One variety of furniture that will always be painted out will be ebony. Soot and glue was the recipe for that.

You can look inside the piece. My most important thing here is to remember what gravity does. Everything, no matter how light in weight, falls downward! So does dirt, so expect the horizontal surfaces to be much darker and dirtier than the vertical. You will be amazed how often a simple thing like this has not been thought about by the makers of the dodgy article.

So, with case furniture when you think about it, the only thing that can be seriously looked at, if it has them, will be the drawers, and these do have a story to tell you.

Again simplify it and think of a drawer as a box made to fit accurately into another box. When they were first made, they were mostly just nailed together, like the rebated side of our coffer. In fact, you will find drawers made like this right through the history of furniture. It is in the province of the goods usually dubbed country furniture. That I find a little sad. There are and always were the poor. And sadly this furniture is very much our heritage of a poverty I doubt if we could imagine. Comparatively little of it survives and something like a drawer that is well used and just nailed together will not stand the test of time. The dovetail, just as our keystone, does.

Look at one thousand drawers. Nine hundred-ninety-eight of them will be dovetailed together. However I think we will probably have to exclude some of our modern flat pack furniture from such a statement!

Go to any saleroom and watch the people looking at the furniture. I will bet you a fiver that most people looking will take a drawer out and look at it. I would love to ask somebody one day just what they are looking for.

When French furniture began to seriously appear in my workshop I had to rethink many of the things we did. Most unusual for me I made the time to read, mainly about the makers. I have never seen a piece of early English furniture signed; the French were sometimes signed using their name as a stamp, not always by any manner of means as a lot of people think. This is understandable as I have been told that the stamped ones have had tax paid on them. So I suppose the unstamped ones came out of the back door as it were. I will go along with that completely as, quite simply, I have seen far, far more authentic 18th century pieces unstamped than stamped ones! Times do not change very much do they?

What is a stamp anyway? It has amazed me, but I have known people who would not buy unless the piece was stamped! Many people who repaired things put their stamp on as well. When you think about it, a stamp is not a very difficult thing to fiddle about with is it.

Years ago I was asked to go and look at a pair

of small commodes in a sale at Banbury, Oxfordshire. They turned out to be a made up small pair from a large commode around 1775-80 vintage. The style of them was very much in the manner of Levasseur. I told my client so. They then appeared in the London rooms about twelve weeks later, now catalogued Levasseur. Complaints were lodged, apologies were made and someone paid about 5,000 pounds for them. They turned up again, this time in Paris. But now they are signed Levasseur! I did see them. The stamp was very good. The trouble was that whoever did it did not know that stamping a piece of wood in 1775 will not look remotely the same if you try to stamp the same wood 200 years later.

They were wrong for just the same reasons as the other pair ten years later.

Over the years I learned to recognise a maker's design and style, and it was surprising how often later research into the piece proved you were right. The rigidity of the trade or the guilds is well known. History tells us of famous names being fined, and heavily fined, for infringing the rules. This can be seen because the making of the furniture is almost without exception the same. This leads us very nicely to the drawer and the emigrés to this country around 1690.

The drawer when it appeared ran on its bottom board – not very satisfactory at all. One answer was to put a fillet of wood on the side of the piece, work a groove into the side of the drawer and run it on that, a very satisfactory way to get over a problem. It gradually disappeared and as far as I can see that happened with the appearance of veneering and the sophistication of furniture design around the end of the 17th century. I think I can say that I have never seen a veneered piece with the drawers set like that. It is, I consider, one of the best ways to hang a drawer. That will get me a few frowns and "Dear me's", but today it is favoured by a lot of modern furniture makers. The reason: quick and simple to fit and maintain.

With the advent of veneering the sophistication of the cabinet trade began and the drawer took up its pattern. The sides dovetailed into the front and backs so that they ran over the sides, or sailed through was our expression. The fronts sides and back board were rebated and the bottom board dropped in to make the flush bottom. When you think about that, it really was not a very practical thing to do was it? Also, they were nailed in place. The nails wore grooves as the wood wore down. I am sure that we have all experienced the struggles to shut some of these often irritating and frankly not very satisfactory types of drawers.

It has always surprised me that French furniture did seem to use this method of making drawers until at least the late 1770's. That was the discipline of the Trade with a vengeance. The strictness of their guild system is almost legendary and that sort of strictness would inhibit development severely. A few words about this is important.

The French cabinet maker was not the maker we envisage. He was really a veneerer, or I suppose a decorator of the carcass. The carcass was supplied by the menusier, the carpenter I suppose he would be, it does explain the complete difference between the inside and out of the furniture. I have heard it said that relations were often so strained that they would not even talk to each other. I wonder how they got paid?

I remember Roger, the rather gifted young man who did the bronze work for us, telling me once that it got to a stage at one time in the 18th century when his guild would not let the cabinet makers put the mounts on the furniture. That certainly does explain to me why on many occasions the fixing of the metal has gone on with no thought at all for the decoration underneath.

None of it was very useful. The problems it must have caused do not bear thinking about, and I am of an age to have experienced our milder 20th century version first hand.

ILL 23 is a French drawer from 1775. It is made in exactly the same way as one from a hundred years before.

When the emigrés arrived here in the 1690's,

ILLUSTRATION 23: *French drawer 1775.*

ILLUSTRATION 24: *Jensen piquet table. C1700.*

their work in case furniture followed much the same pattern. A short trip across the English Channel is not going to change that. I have worked on pieces of furniture from this time, and two in particular come to mind. They are attributed to Gerrit Jensen and are a rare and near pair of piquet tables in seaweed marquetry. ILL 24 is the rarest of them because of the lifting top. Also, during some repair years ago, when these things did not matter very much, they put the column back upside down. It is the wrong way up in the illustration! It is not now. The making, and that of the drawers, are identical to those of the continent. I would be happy to say that it was quite common to see drawers like this in furniture during the first ten years of the 18th century. I am sure that it was the design and style of English furniture that changed the path of our cabinet making.

ILL 25A/25B The front and back dovetails of the drawer from the Jensen table around 1700. Identical to any continental drawer, note how the top of the back dovetail runs over the side. ILL 26 shows the flush drawer bottoms, exactly as the French drawer from 1775.

This era of English furniture did not follow the, well lets face it, fussiness of seaweed marquetry. The English designs became simplified and lent themselves to veneering for veneerings sake. For the first time wood itself was used as decoration. We let the wood do the talking. Crotch, burr and curl veneers are the decoration. Also, these designs lend themselves to having the drawers mounted in banks with stiles in between instead of the drawer front overlapping, which is very much how the continental work developed. The stiles of the early English pieces, our chest of drawers or commode, our chest-on-chest or tallboy and the bureau, were all on this principle of drawer on drawer with stiles in between. The stile had to be veneered or decorated in some way. In the beginning a crossgrain moulding was in favour. This was set up across the stiles. The sides

ILLUSTRATION 25A: *Dovetails. Front dovetail of drawer. C1700.*

ILLUSTRATION 25B: *Back dovetail of drawer. C1700.*

for granted and something that, well, just happened.

You call at my shop, and the year is 1710. ILL 27 is a bureau, three feet wide with locums for the fall. Locums are the pieces of wood that pull out to support a bureau fall. It has four drawers. The area between the locums contains a well full of drawers and secret hidey holes. It is high style for the time and expensive. You buy it and, from that moment on, you are continuously calling me out to repair those vulnerable cross grain mouldings on the stiles. A flush bottom drawer dragging over them makes sure of that.

Anyone facing that problem, unless they are totally under the thumb of a guild or union, will, if they have any common or commercial sense at all, alter the cause of the problem. About this time, 1710, they did. They deepened the rebates on the front and sides, did away with the one on the back, dropped the bottom board in place, glued three small fillets

were treated in the same way and the cross pieces mitred in. This was followed by crossbanding with veneer – from a workshop point of view no problem. There was a very attractive end result. But from a practical point of view, and the way they made drawers, it meant trouble.

I am also convinced at this time that without the stifling rigidity of the guilds and the integration of the continental and British work people, a freedom of expression and ideas began. Pride in work began and by the Lord it showed. Just this fact of letting the wood do the decorating is very much the English way and is something that the designers and the cabinet trade in general have never been given the credit for. As with so many things it is just taken

ILLUSTRATION 26: *Flush drawer bottoms. C1700.*

ILLUSTRATION 27: *Bureau 1710.*

around the front and sides and nailed the back edge down. The English drawer was born. ILL 28 is a classic example of what I mean. The method is even used on a small drawer like this. It dates from about 1745-50.

ILLUSTRATION 28: *Small drawer 1745-50.*

This change happened fairly quickly. You will not see the flush bottom drawer very much after the 1710's. The sides were dovetailed into the

fronts and back boards as usual. But another obvious problem was the end grain of the side showing on the front of the drawer. When a piece was in the solid wood the end grain of the drawer side would usually be covered with a moulding or something similar. The veneered piece was easy; you veneered over it. Except veneer does not like being glued to end grain. The obvious thing here was to stop the dovetail short. The first way was to plant a small cross grain piece of wood all around the drawer front and work the edge into a quadrant that overlapped the drawer, a lot of work for a small result. You will see this on early English walnut ILL 38B.

It did not last very long, and by about 1750 the drawer was quickened up a little more, the side rebates were left the same, the rebate on the front was done away with and a groove was ploughed in. Because of that the bottom board could now be champhered, the front pushed into its groove, the back sprigged or nailed down and two runners glued in on either side. ILL 29 The fitting of the drawer to the carcass was now a much easier and accurate thing. Now, for my money, the style of English cabinet making coupled with Mahogany, Satinwood and Rosewood allowed the cabinet makers to blossom and interpret the designs they were given in a manner that was unique to them.

It is about here that I should try and answer a question that I am continuously asked: "Which way should the grain run in the wood of a drawer bottom?" Ideally it should run in the direction of the shortest distance. That will be the strongest and I would expect that in a drawer that is wider than its depth. However, although this is the general rule, it will be broken. Many reasons will cause it: convenience of the material, size of wood on hand, costs to join things up to make larger boards – all sorts of reasons. Do not let things like this put you off if all the other considerations are right. Also, you will see time out of number that the joints in the bottom

ILLUSTRATION 29: *Small drawer late 18th century. C1800.*

boards have gone or the wood is split. This is obviously caused by shrinkage and the habit of nailing the back edge and glueing the other three sides.

At about this time, or just before, that very English thing the cockbead begins to make its appearance. It has two uses: (1) it safeguards the edge of the drawer from damage and (2) when drawers are in place and do not have a cockbead they really do have to be flush. It is very noticeable if they are not. A cockbead gives you room to move around a little as it were.

As the 18th century moved on, and in the later stages of it the dovetailing of the drawers became smaller and smaller, they seemed almost to vie with each other to make the smallest. Time and again this is pointed out as a sign of quality. That coupled with thinner and thinner timber also being higher quality. It did become, for my money, a little bit, well, per-

nickity. I say that because you so often will find damage on this very fine work. It is a pig to repair. You cannot take it apart without doing more damage. However without doubt it was the apogee of the English cabinet trade. The way of the dovetails on the front and the back boards running over the sides remained as it had always been. ILL 30 is a typical drawer, around 1800, veneered with Partridge.

At about this time (the 1770-80's) the French copied the English and stopped their drawers running on the bottom board (ILL 11 in the chapter on Quality).

Here is a thought for you. In the 1770's, marquetry furniture gradually started to appear in quantity in this country – the Neo-Classical Revival. In France, marvellous mahogany furniture also started to appear and their Classical revival began.

I wonder if a few French marquetry cutters, or marqueteurs, were short of work and got on the boat to London where their skills were needed. Also, just suppose a few of our out-of-work cabinet makers took the boat the other way. You see, I have often wondered why French furniture with all the glitz and glitter never had the cabinet work to match it. Yet with the advent of

ILLUSTRATION 30: *Drawer Partridge wood table. C1800.*

ILLUSTRATION 31: *Back dovetail. C1820.*

mahogany, the making and style of making was suddenly as good as the finest English. I wonder.

Who am I to say!

The saga of the drawer was not over yet. Commerce, demand and speed were on the horizon. The 18th century had gone. The first years of the 19th century were turbulent to say the least. By 1840, Queen Victoria was on the throne. Steam had been going strong for almost the previous generation. Engineering had taken a serious hold. Raw materials could be produced much faster and the poor old cabinet trade had to change – and change it did, never to really return.

Repetition inlay work from the time of Bullock must have revolutionised the workshop. The thing that was long-winded was not anymore and the bench had problems catching up. So about 1820 the drawer changed again. The front dovetail was much the same. The groove in the front was the same but now it continued down the sides. Accuracy of machines was with us and the bottom board needed very little fitting to just slide in the grooves. The major difference, however, was the back dovetail. It was now shouldered. ILL 31 A much quicker way of doing it. This way of making a drawer remained the predominate way. You will see it almost without exception from furniture dating about the 1820's and throughout the 19th century. It was the way I was taught, and is an important point

in the world of old furniture.

The era of the split and cracked drawer bottom was over. The groove allowed the wood to move. This continued through the century.

When the Edwardian furniture began, the back of the bottom board was not nailed in place and it was often screwed and the hole for the screw made as a slot to allow the drawer bottom even more movement.

Machinery seriously developed. Wood preparation was now so fast it was almost a revolution – no, it was a revolution. Carving machines appeared, although I must say that I think their efforts were often monstrous. All sorts of mouldings could be run out and one of the first appeared on our friend the drawer.

It appeared as a half round moulding inside a drawer and was called a dust bead. This had a groove put in to carry the drawer bottom. It roughly coincided with the shouldered-back dovetail. The moulding could be glued to the drawer side. Another job, ploughing a groove for the drawer bottom, had gone.

The muntin, a piece of wood with two grooves in it, one on either side was fitted to the drawer bottom. The purpose was to be able to use two pieces of wood for the bottom board on the large drawers. This has been around since the last decade of the 18th century and was a rare thing to see. But now with the dust bead it became commonplace.

During the years that followed many groups and Societies tried to go back to the "old" ways and compete with the machine. None of them ever really were a success it seems to me. I do not know enough about them to comment except that today many of their efforts do command serious money. I have been lucky. Simply because of my job I have had to work as they did all those years ago. I have also been lucky enough to watch other people work like that.

Just making a drawer would be an eyeopener, because it is mostly made by eye. I have read and looked at how you make a drawer. All sorts of tools and gadgets are sold to make the task easier. I have never owned a dovetail gauge or any of these things. I just had marking gauges to set the various thickness of wood and depths of the joint onto the relevant pieces. Also I have read many times how you mark your dovetail onto its pins. Lord, they were all rather complicated. Some have let an error or two creep in. Everyone I have known, myself included, were taught as in ILL 32. It is called striking. The marks you leave are the sawcuts for the dovetails, or the pins as they are called. All you do when you saw the pins is to leave the mark from the striking. It guaranteed a good fit. Have a look. Have you ever seen a badly fitting dovetail? I doubt it. Also, and I doubt if I shall be believed (and if I am will be called a shoddy worker), when we sawed our drawer sides for the dovetails, it was always done by eye. I cannot remember seeing anyone measuring and drawing the dovetail in place before it was cut. But then when you do the same thing, sometimes hour after hour, day after day, you develop an accuracy that will not be understood unless you have actually done it. This will, I think, show again the difference between craft and trade.

Before we leave the workshop there are two more things. First is the bureau ILL 27 with all its secret drawers. I must apologise because it has been totally over-cleaned. An over-enthusiastic student did it – not his fault, mine. He came from a gilding shop where everything has to look brand new. I turned my back for longer than I should have. However, the piece is in America and I was told it was English. It is not; it is American. Why? The sides are made of Maple. The Walnut inside the fall is American Black Walnut. The drawers and the rest of the carcass are made of White or Snow Pine. We, in England, never had pine as huge as that. Also, it is said to be veneered in Burr Walnut; I reckon that is Mulberry.

Can you imagine an Englishman making it in those woods unless he was in America? It is a very rare piece of furniture indeed. So, as I have told you, persevere with trying to understand

ILLUSTRATION 32: *Striking a dovetail.*

and know the woods.

Secondly, why have I not gone into chairs? One easy answer is cabinet makers did not make chairs; it was a separate trade. I have made chairs, as we know, and wondered if they should be included – until I realised the huge field they can cover. They certainly are outside the scope of this effort. However I cannot leave the workshop without giving you a few tips about them.

Our poor old chair must be just about the most over-worked and abused piece of furniture there is. To find a chair from the days we are talking about that is in an untouched and perfect condition you are going to be lucky – very lucky.

A chair that has polished sides to its frame has more of a chance than an upholstered one. A chair like this, stripped out and ready to be re-upholstered, is often a horrible sight. Upholstery tacks are huge and leave quite a lot of damage. Rarely have chairs only been upholstered once. So ask how many times they have been done and do not be put off by re-railing, as long as the rest of the chair is all it should be. Re-railing is often caused by our good friend, that little sod, the furniture beetle, or woodworm. And as I have said, I would not give a wormy chair houseroom.

Having said that, worm in chairs is prevalent because of the timber – Beech. I hope we now know that it is the woodworm's favourite timber, unfortunately for the chairmaker. (Almost since chairs began it is without doubt the favourite wood to make a chairframe from.) The woodworm is a creature of habit. It emerges as an adult beetle late May to the end of July, does its thing and although it can fly it will often just lay its eggs in a corner of the place, in this case a chair frame that it came from. So if you see the peppery looking dusk or the holes, or if the holes produce the peppery dust when you give the chair a good tapping, call in the fumigators. I do not recommend the use of the liquid treatments on old furniture. A complete and total no-no is the use of paraffin.

I can remember a lovely set of Maple chairs in America. They had been treated with some liquid or other. Each hole had a dark brown mark around it the size of a cigarette's diameter. It was sad, and the chairs were ruined.

Hardwood chairs made of Mahogany, Rosewood and the very rare Satinwood will not be affected by the problem as long as they are all solid wood. Just remember that there can be rails that are veneered. These will almost without exception be made of beech or birch. Just be on the lookout and wash the non-showing part of the seat rails with the old-fashioned vinegar and water at the end of April. That was called spring cleaning. I wonder why!

Please never lean or tip back in a chair. Just the construction, after the mortices have been cut in, means that there is not a lot of wood left where you are putting all the weight. Apart from hurting yourself, the damage is often very severe.

And the cost of repairing it will often hurt more than your back.

Lastly, check your chairs now and again by wracking them. You do this by pushing down hard on the front and back rails. See if, when you try to twist or turn them, the joints move at all. If they do, keep an eye on them as they will need reglueing. Get them done before a joint does go.

An important point about chairs is how they are made. Several years ago I was asked to clean and tidy up a set of six and two Georgian chairs in mahogany. I had never met the people and as was usual in those days made an appointment to go and see them. They were just what they said they were – except they were not Georgian.

The weight of them and the type of mahogany discounted that straight away. I do not doubt that had I said anything I would have been told not to be silly – family history and all this sort of nonsense. You know what I mean. "I am 51 and they were my mother's and she was 82, and I know they were Granny's and she was 90". All this was added up and before you know it, we were back to 1780!

It was naught to do with me anyway. But family history aside, it was the wrong wood; the chairs weighed little. But if I was completely wrong about it all, one thing that was absolutely certain was that these chairs had been dowelled together and they never, never jointed a chair that way in the 18th century. They would always use the mortice and tenon to put a chair together. Workshop rules and the fact that they could not make dowells quickly and accurately enough are just two of the reasons.

How could I be so sure about the fact that they were dowelled? They needed tightening up. And it was quite possible to see the three beech dowells in this small gap between the leg and the side rail. This was a quite common way of jointing up chairs in the reproduction trade of the late 19th century.

Always check on this, for no other reason than if you are told the chair is 18th century. If it is dowelled, it ain't.

Finally, one important little tip. Years ago when there were lots of us it was often a struggle to get work. When you did, it had to be cheap. I could get fifteen shillings, or seventy-five pence, for glueing up a chair. Collecting and delivering was more than that (please, no tears). Corners were often cut. One way was to wiggle the joint open a little, put some glue in, pull it up tight and drive a couple of panel pins in about a 1/4 inch from the edge of the mortice. It was lovely and firm. Punch in the pins. Add a little bit of coloured heelball to hide up the holes. Lovely. The only problem with any bodge like that is that it will not last. ILL 33 is a classic example on the saddle of an early 18th century chair in Red Walnut. You tell me how, if you have to take that apart, you can do it without causing a lot of damage.

ILLUSTRATION 33: *Saddle of chair, nails, two of them on top edge of saddle.*

I know people who have refused to undertake that sort of problem. Needless to say that I have been one of them.

Another thing you will often come up against are chairs repaired by a blacksmith! This is perfectly true, and is something that I have never been able to explain. You will find chairs with metal angle brackets screwed in place between frame and leg. Usually these are modern and are just a bodge up. What I am talking about, and have seen on numerous occasions, are beautiful hand-made brackets rounded over and made with all the skill of the decorative black iron work of the smith.

On three occasions the work was so good and beautifully done the owners were persuaded to leave them in place since for me they were all part of the history of the chairs. I have never understood why this was done. Admittedly, there would have been thousands of blacksmiths; but then there would have been thousands of carpenters. But I did say that a chairmaker was a specialised trade didn't I?

When looking over chairs remember these sort of things. Also, when I have been presented with a chair that has got this sort of problem and you cannot see what it is. An X-ray machine will really come into its own.

Finally, if you can assimilate these few points and apply them to the furniture in all its various styles, shapes and dates, you will be astounded how correct these rules are. Ninety-nine point nine times out of a hundred they will not let you down.

However, just as I have said about the wood in the bureau, fully understand that sort of thing. As with age, get the feel of it, the sight of it and the smell of it. Get all this together with the workshop and its development and you will certainly not need me to hold your hand.

Chapter 6

VENEER

*"L*ADIES AND GENTLEMEN, WHY VENEER? What a damn silly thing to do. Make a piece of furniture and then glue another lot of wood all over it. That is basically what veneering is". So begin my talks on veneer and the decorated surface.

Placage – I must prefer this, the French name for it. "Commode en placage de bois de violette" – now that does have a ring to it, so much better than "a commode veneered in kingwood". Veneer – venereal – dear me, no wonder it is so often regarded as something rather cheap and cheerful. Even today the image is much like that, just a touch inferior, "not as good as the real thing in solid wood old boy". The number of times that has been said to me you would not imagine.

I will put it down now. Veneer is the most important thing that ever happened to furniture. And a thorough understanding of it and its history is vital when it comes down to the right or wrongness of a piece of old furniture.

When I was first asked to talk about this subject I soon found out that my ideas and understanding of it were at odds with what seemed to be the accepted history. I was often queried, had the embarrassment of being interrupted, and it got to the point where I seriously thought of quitting and staying where a lot of people thought that I should stay – in my workshop!

People from the workshop are rarely heard about. To be asked to talk to fine art courses, societies and this sort of audience is rare and, as far as people from my era are concerned, almost unheard of. Yet it was my views and understanding of veneer that caused it in the first place! I had been responsible for the repair of a piece of English, neo-classical marquetry furniture attributed to Thomas Chippendale that had been purchased by the Chippendale Society. It was in a shocking state. One or two sources said it was not repairable. That is not my attitude at all. We met. It was done. The Chippendale Society then asked me to explain how the miracle had been achieved. My name as a restorer, for the first time, was put to a restoration. In many ways I suppose I did that table a huge favour. Yet in its own way it did me a much larger one. It was the talk about its repair that was directly responsible for me being introduced and asked to talk to many Societies and groups about veneer and the cabinet trade in general.

I suppose you could say that fate took a hand. It then took another when a client of mine asked me to go to Christies and look over a Louis XIV commode. It had been catalogued as Boulle but not veneered in Boullework. Instead, the catalogue said it had been veneered in dyed pink Mahogany! That alone was enough to put me off and I told my client so. But I was asked to go (and you did get paid).

I found myself confronted with the remains of a superb early 18th century commode in Ebony that had lost all of its Boullework surface. It still had the inlaid and engraved brass that would have originally surrounded these panels of tortoiseshell and brass marquetry, or in this case very possibly Ebony and brass marquetry. Whatever they were, they had gone years ago as had the top and it had all been replaced with panels of English Walnut dyed this pinky colour.

I was not pleased. I had combined this with another job and driven a long way, diverting to London to look at this forlorn object. It did look rather sad. These things are magnificent when in good condition and for someone to have done this to it added to my niggles. I did something that is usually a waste of time. I wrote to King Street, Christies HQ in London and complained – plus a few remarks of my own! I got a reply, after the sale of course, telling me that the piece had sold for 34,000 pounds and that six independant experts had all agreed that it was veneered with dyed, pink Mahogany and said to be original. Sheila will tell you that I am not a very tolerant man when my trade is involved, or, I suppose queried. Out of it, yes, I am quite tolerant and lovable on occasions! However, I replied to the effect that I was delighted that thirty-four grand had been turned over. But what would the value be when it had been reveneered in Boullework, something that was bound to happen. Would people know and would Christies know? Also, I failed to see how six experts could make English Walnut into dyed, pink Mahogany.

The reply was a phone call and an invitation to lunch. Feeling rather apprehensive I accepted and went up to London. Nothing like this had ever happened to me before. It was after lunch that I was asked if I would talk to the students at the Christies' Fine Arts Course. My answer was

yes and the subject was to be veneer and the decorated surface. I have recently finished working with my 17th year of students and have accepted the invitation to talk to my 18th. I shall always be grateful to fate, in the shape of Hugh Roberts, for giving me that kind of opportunity.

Yes, we have a twist in the tale and the piece did turn up in all its new Boullework glory. It was about five years later in a New York saleroom. Enough to say that it was withdrawn!

Before we go on, in this day and age people will ask, "Why did they do such a thing to such an object?" The answer is simple: money and probably fashion. You must remember that furniture with highly decorated surfaces need constant attention and when things are left they reach a stage when they are just not worth repairing. It is only really in the last twenty-five years that values have escalated to a degree that the cost of radical restoration could be warranted. Years ago I can remember seeing a couple of early Mazarin desks being stripped of their red shell Boullework and being reveneered in Walnut. People find this hard to believe, but I can assure you it is true. I have done similar things myself on more than one occasion.

The usual idea of veneer is that it is for economy not just of wood but also of labour. The latter I have never understood. You make something and then glue another lot of wood all over it. How that can be cheaper is a mystery. But then history and often folklore would not be bothered with the fact that people got paid, no matter how little. Today the economic factor in machine veneering and in the saving of wood is incredible and for about the last 140-150 years has had a major impact in helping with the world of timber conservation. However, the economic factor has worked the other way with the hand veneering of my early days. The expense of that has caused a decline in that sort of fine furniture which I doubt will ever recover.

This economic factor has been brought about by the technology of creating veneers with a knife. Simply explained, it is the ability to slice wood down the length of a log with total accuracy to a thickness of 12-15,000th part of an inch which is roughly the average thickness of a knife-cut veneer – and to do this with the continuous accuracy of a bacon slicer. Also, technology allows us to mount a log and spin it against a knife rather like some gigantic pencil sharpener and produce peeled veneer. Before this technology, a veneer could only have been produced with the one available method of cutting up wood with some sort of accuracy: sawing. And sawing does have a problem – it produces sawdust. If the next paragraph is correct it means that at least 60-70% of the wood sawn to veneer would finish up on the floor as sawdust. So from the start, it was not at all economic – not to mention the other thing so rarely talked about, labour.

Veneer as a viable and commercial technique was established on the continent by the 1630's. Sawing, so it is written, was such that in the 17th century they could saw a veneer to 1/8 of an inch. As techniques improved in the 18th century, they could saw one to 1/16 of an inch. History unfortunately does not tell us what these techniques were. We are told that the only way it could have been produced was with hand sawing – a statement that does not make any sense to me at all. I consider that I am fairly skilled and have known many men with greater skills than I and would defy anyone to take a board of up to sixteen inches across and successfully cut a piece of wood off it 1/16 of an inch thick. Machinery would be very lucky to do that with some woods. Yet, they did it by hand? That is beyond my imagination. I say sixteen inches across since veneers of this width are not uncommon from the 1740's onward. And to do that repeatedly until the board was used up, now that does stretch my credibility a little. It might just have been possible if the log was about six inches or so in width; with a veneer, around 1/8 of an inch with a small log like this.

I doubt the possibility of 1/16 of an inch completely. And having read that the master of a workshop in the 18th century expected his workman to saw eight veneers from one inch of

wood, then I am grateful to have lived in the 20th century. Had I been around then I reckon I would have been unemployable. Where the writer of that got his information from I have no idea. I very much doubt if he has seen a piece of hardwood and its surface when it comes from a saw. If he had he would know that a saw, as efficient as it can be, has another problem, apart from sawdust. It leaves sawmarks behind. It always has and it always will. And these can often be deep and follow the character of the wood. No matter how much the techniques improved our saw marks or sawing kerfs, as they are called, will always be there. Now the one thing that is very rare to see on veneers from these days is the evidence of the sawing. The reason is simple; before a veneer can be successfully laid, it has to be flattened. In the doing of this, the sawing evidence will be taken away. This flattening was done by a process called toothing. This, when it is finished, leaves a random pattern of fine, shallow, parallel grooves on the back of the veneer.

I hope it is now becoming obvious that after the veneer has been laid the sawmarks have to be taken off the surface and that surface cleaned up to be polished. Cleaned up means the work that must go into the surface to create the lovely shine that you take for granted. That alone makes me wonder how they did that with a veneer that came from the saw at 1/16 of an inch thick! This is something that the writers of history, holders forth about furniture on television and experts should all have a little think about.

More importantly, when fully understood, this little fact is an invaluable aid in spotting the piece that has been reveneered.

Personally I am quite sure that veneers were very heavy indeed in the beginning, probably 3/16th of an inch or more. Now you must remember that we are talking about something that is surrounded with a mystery of how they could possibly have done that. Also the image of the solitary "craftsman" working away is the image created by hand work. With an image like that it is difficult to have machinery intruding into it. But when veneer began and the surge in its use happened, it would have been a very short time indeed before the sawmills of the day would have been rethought and rebuilt to have the capability of sawing veneer. I have never understood why we could have had sawmills in the 16th, 17th and 18th centuries capable of rendering trees down to lumber for houses, ships and for whatever else was needed, but to saw wood and veneer for furniture, dear me no, it was all done by hand.

ILL'S 34 A and B are both veneers from the last stages of the 18th century. These are after the workshop has finished with them. The one that I have removed is a good 1/8 inch in thickness.

From seeing so much old veneer it is the sheer size of some of it that does for me discount hand sawing. Unless the saws were held in jigs or guides, and if this was so we have human powered machines. The sheer quantity that was used must mean that machines made a very early appearance on the scene. This comes from the mind of someone who ran a small business, and time was money. To be successful, it must be that way. But it is also from someone who has been interested in early machinery for many years. I have seen working examples of saws from the 17th century and why they are not considered in the history of sawn veneer I fail to understand.

I can remember showing to a customer some veneer that had been taken off a piece of Dutch furniture from about 1730. We were doing a fairly radical repair job on it for him. It had all been caused by our friend the furniture beetle. The evidence of machine sawing was there to be seen on

ILLUSTRATION 34A&B: *Veneers: C1780's. The thickness is obvious.*

the veneer. It was just a small pocket about the size of a match box that the toothing plane had missed. It was a rare and for me an interesting thing to see. I honestly thought that he would be interested as well. When I showed him, he truly blew his stack. He had been sold a fake. I did not know what I was talking about. Machines from the time this thing was supposed to have come from? What absolute rubbish! He was going to get someone in who did know what they were talking about. It was an amazing performance.

He did come back with a young man who, when he came into the workshop, looked at me and by his expression showed that the one man he did not want to meet was me. Who he was I never found out – probably one of the young dealers from the area. Naturally, he went along with my client. He had to. He suggested that it was probably a later repair that had been put in. I have never really forgiven myself for going along with him and agreeing. "Yes, that is obviously what it is". This was many years ago and I just could not do what I should have done and told them to come into the real world. I had mouths to feed. It would be a very different story now and is probably why that on more than one occasion I have been told that I am not very diplomatic in my approach to antique furniture and its "experts!"

Over the years, I have often found evidence of machine sawing of 17th and 18th century veneer. People will say, "How is that possible?" The answer is simple. In my job veneer grounds have had to be replaced dozens of times. Worm, dry rot and damage were usually the cause. Time and again evidence of machine sawing has been found, albeit small – just small areas that the toothing iron had missed. Nevertheless it was evidence of the sawing and, almost without exception, the sawing was mechanical. When the evidence was manual, the veneer that had been sawn was always small, such as crossband work. When the veneer was large, it was always mechanical.

The difference of the saw marks left by a machine and by hand is obvious when it has been seen. The machine shows its mechanical power and ability to not get bored. Human hands cannot do exactly the same thing hour after hour. This is the difference and it will always show. The saw marks or kerfs from the machine will be parallel to each other and have a consistent accuracy between them. Quite simply, hand sawing will not. To be honest, this is some-

thing in the world of old veneer very, very few people will get to see. It has been put in here to show the problems that can be caused when you do speak out against the generally accepted ideas. An example must be when I was taken to task about it with the remark that I had not considered the obvious fact that the 18th century craftsmen were far more skilled than I and present day workmen knew how to be! (It is extraordinary how we in the 20th century are workmen, or "my little man around the corner!") There spoke someone who, as learned as he probably was, had never used a saw in his life nor had ever had to earn his bread with his hands. Hopefully he may see ILL'S 35A and 35B. Somehow I doubt if he would understand. It has also surprised me that people never seem to consider the huge cost that hand sawing would have been.

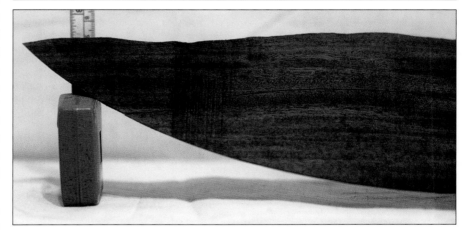

ILLUSTRATION 35A&B: *Veneer sawing marks. Mechanical.*

Much because of this and out of curiosity, I made up a frame saw and fixed a three foot blade from a mitre framing saw in it. This had ten teeth to the inch and was the kind of saw that would have left the evidence I have seen so many times. I sharpened and set it, set up a Yewtree log about five feet long and ten inches in diameter, got a reluctant mate on the other end of the frame and began sawing. After an hour, I had to sharpen again. In fact, we sharpened twice and set once more before we got the log in half, which was after about three hours!

The saw took out between 1/16 and 1/8th inch of wood. The cut was straight and one thing was sure there was no way could we have cut a 1/16th inch piece off it. I know what will be said: I used the wrong saw. I did not. You cannot use some huge powerful crosscut like a lumberjack for that sort of job.

However, to be fair, it must be said that the log of Yewtree was about 20 years felled and would have been much harder than when new. Being even fairer, inexperience with the saw would have caused problems. So let's cut the time in half, to be fair. Putting pen to paper and working out the time that it took the two of us at our hourly rate of those days, that piece of veneer would have cost twelve pounds-fifty pence to produce. And this does not even consider the preparation and laying of it.

It would have been about fifteen years before I did all this that I had stood and watched a beautiful machine working in Paris that would have taken a leaf of veneer off my log with total accuracy in about twelve minutes and reduced that log to a commercial bundle in about two and a half hours. Time is money; that machine must have earned a fortune.

The argument of hands or machine will go on as long as machines are not acceptable in the world of 18th century English furniture. There is no doubt that they abounded on the continent, but by 1790's things were about to change!

In an earlier chapter, we mentioned my particular hero, Isambard Kingdom Brunel – what a lovely name.

The first circular saw was invented in the very late 17th century. At that time there was just not enough power to run it and it became smaller and smaller until the small milling saw of the clock maker was born. That will cause a few screams of protest! Not just a logical thought, look up a man called Dr. Hook from about 1685. He invented the saw! Mr. Brunel in 1806 or thereabouts patented a circular saw for cutting very thin boards, or veneers. These saws were huge and around sixteen or seventeen feet in diameter is talked about. Although I have never seen one, I have seen the veneer they could produce. The advent of steam allowed these vast machines to be driven.

In the very early days of my working life we used to do some naughty things with Rosewood furniture. Time and again, veneer from the 1820'-30's was sawn off to maintain old colour. The last of the ground was pared away with a chisel to often be confronted with the evidence of a huge circular saw. By huge, I mean at least twelve to fourteen feet in diameter! A saw of that size must have been a casting with a cutting edge of teeth applied. It could even have been made of wood with teeth applied to the edge. After all, a veneer will not have to go past the saw. It will be thin enough to be guided away as soon as the cut begins. To explain, it would have been a circular saw with one flat side. The other side curved to the centre. This would give the saw some stability on the driving axle. Also, a saw of fifteen feet in diameter would not need to be driven at any speed at all. Sixty revolutions a minute would give a speed at the cutting edge of about three thousand feet per minute. A frightening thought. The early pioneers were very brave people indeed (a classic example of this veneer is shown in ILL 36).

The late and much missed Rupert Gentle was a great friend of Sheila and I. He was a dealer, bi-lingual and spoke French like a native. Me, I had trouble with English. We would go on the hunt for goods in France. On one visit we ran down a veneer merchant, madame, who ran the place, was at least eighty years old and we got to

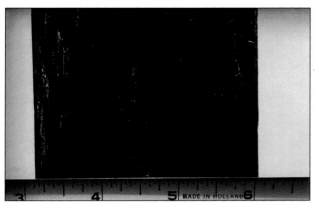

ILLUSTRATION 36: *Rosewood sawing 1830.*

ILLUSTRATION 37: *Kingwood bundle. Sawn C1890.*

know her well. I was always "M'sieur David, the pilot". On one visit she asked if I would like some sawn Tulip, Kingwood and Purple. I had to say yes and for the first time was taken down to the basement. It was an Aladdin's cave with full logs sawn through and through. I had never seen this before; it was magic. It had been laid down by her father in the 1890's. All of it was sawn. Rupert, God bless him, used his French and it was explained how it was sawn. But more incredibly we discovered that the saw still remained and was working.

It was set up in a garage and was the most hellish workshop I had ever been in. I thought the guy who produced pearl veneer and his workshop was bad enough. Dear God, this was something else. You could not see across it for sawdust. A handkerchief over your nose and mouth did not help a lot. But it was the saw that was beautiful. I do not know how you describe the wonderful cast iron work from the 1850's, but this saw frame was like that. It was a reciprocating horizontal saw about six feet across and was running at a speed that was amazing. The pawl and ratchet that drove the selfact to advance the wood on each stroke was about a millimetre and the veneer being sawn was some brown Ebony just over a millimetre thick. Time and again I have found veneer like this on furniture, mainly French and purporting to come from the 1850's onward. I had never really believed that it was that early, mainly because

the finish was so good that it had not been toothed. Now here I was looking at the saw that had sawn it. Even in the days of steam it was apparently just as fast.

To this day I have never understood how the guy who owned and operated it managed to work there without a face mask of any kind or even a vacumn to suck some of the dust away. To each his own I suppose. After all, he was in his sixties! ILL 37 is a full log of kingwood sawn by that machine. The accuracy and fineness of the sawing can be seen.

(I hope it is obvious that this is that beautiful machine I was watching in awe and envy all those years ago.)

When you see a bundle of veneer like that and there are forty-seven leaves in it, it does make one realise that the idea of doing something almost identical to that by hand is a little far fetched. It must also be explained that the log sawn was just over six inches in diameter including the sap wood and was flat when sawn. The curved shape happens by drying and possibly not very good storage by me. It makes no difference at all to its laying. Kingwood is very hard and is one of the veneers that the 18th century cabinet makers wanted more money for laying and working with.

Having put all this down, if it was not economic to do (and not very economic with timber), the question of why veneer must be gone

79

into. After all, why bother with something that can be a problem. I have asked the question and it has been asked of me many times. My answer is a simple one. The first veneered furniture appeared in the early days of the 17th century. It used Ebony, because, I firmly believe, it was the only way that this wood could be successfully used. Ebony is unstable; it will crack and split randomly. Also, it is a job to obtain large pieces of it. You can see pieces of furniture from the late 16th century made of solid Ebony. They are usually heavily repaired, cracked and held together with screws and dowell. They are not very satisfactory at all. The answer to its use appears in the early days of the 17th century when veneer was born. Look at any piece veneered with true ebony and the surface will be covered with lightly cupped cracks, called reams. Imagine what would have happened in solid wood. Also, look at the designs of these early pieces. They are always set up so that large pieces of veneer are not necessary.

The next widely used veneer would be Kingwood. You cannot get a large piece of that. A log of Kingwood wider than seven inches will be very rare and possibly unknown. The sawn bundle I have illustrated is about the largest that I have seen. This fact applies to many of the early exotic woods used in furniture. Almost without exception, they will be used as a veneer. This fact can be backed up by another early exotic wood, Padauk. This tree is huge and nearly all the early furniture made with it is in solid wood.

These are the parents of veneer. From my own experiences in the workshop and problems that have come up, the need to solve recurring problems has been the mother of invention. The problems that I have with these woods now are identical with the problems that they had then. Even today's machines will not successfully cope with these early hardwoods. They still have to be sawn. This is reflected in the price; some are on occasion fifteenfold more because of it.

A significant thought about Ebony is simply the trade of the cabinet maker. In France, as you probably all know, they are called Ebenistes, the Ebony workers.

I hope it is obvious that few of you will ever see the evidence of sawing. However, you will see at some time the evidence of its preparation, the toothing. The ground that the veneer is glued onto will also be prepared in this way. As it will be a very common occurrence for pieces of veneer to come off you will see this preparation as the ILL's 38A, B, C and D show. Now if you know what the toothing looked like up until around 1730, what the tools left behind up until around 1820, and what the later 19th and 20th century toothing planes left behind, then you are very much in the driving seat when you have to make up your mind. Did the veneer start its life on this piece of furniture? Has it been re-veneered? Is it all correct but just not as old as it is supposed to be? This sort of information is important and has been more than useful to me when serious authentication is needed. More than one argument has been settled because of it.

My ideas for toothing do not seem to be the ideas of the writers of furniture history. The late Christopher Gilbert, in his book "The Life and Work of Thomas Chippendale", states, "Where the veneer is missing you can see the heavy scoring to create a good key for the glue". I have always found that a smooth, close-fitting joint always produced the best bond. (We used the same sort of glue as Mr. Chippendale.) I must ask the question that if toothing was to produce a good key for the glue why is the greatest failure rate in old furniture the veneer?

Toothing was a simple and gentle way to remove the sawing kerfs from the veneer and to flatten the ground wood ready to be veneered. ILL 38, with the dates, will show what I mean and how the toothing irons developed. My own toothing plane is over ninety years old and carries two irons. One is very fine indeed, so fine I hardly ever had need to use it. It is original to the plane. The other has been replaced at least three times. Again, so much for old tools.

It is the glue. And we must go into just what a miraculous substance it is. Pieces of furniture came into my workshop that were 250-300

ILLUSTRATION 38A: *Toothing, late 17th century*

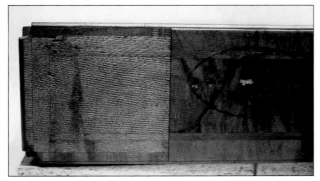

ILLUSTRATION 38B: *1720 – 1730*

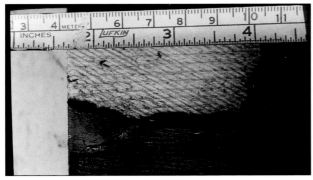

ILLUSTRATION 38C: *1770*

ILLUSTRATION 38D: *1860*

years old and still in fair condition and the glue was still as sound as the day it had been made. I often wonder if some of our modern miracles will last like that.

Today we are surrounded by a bewildering display of glues for this and glues for that. We have glues that will bond immediately, glues that are waterproof and glues that will withstand being boiled. Some can be frozen. Some are chemical two part ones – mix the two parts together and they will glue aeroplanes together. We have glues for glueing plastics together, some of these giving off fumes that can cause addiction. Some glues will stick you together instantly. You can buy a huge array, but you will have problems buying the one glue that I have used all my life – the old fashioned hoof and horn or hide glue, the one that was always simmering away on the stove in any woodwork shop when I began on the bench. Why it is hard to come by is understandable. It has to be constantly looked after. It does not smell very nice unless it is kept clean. Yet this glue carries properties that not one of these modern ones carry. It can be easily and quickly reversed. And, with the use of heat, it is just as quickly and easily reconstituted. Without that property veneering would more than likely not have been possible, or, it certainly would not have become a commercial success.

The easily reconstituted property must be explained. I have seen these glues explained as a sort of jello that had to be used hot and must have been impossible to use during the winter months. It is gelatine. And we have all heard of poor old horses and the racehorse that did not win as being only fit for the nackers yard or the glue factory.

The rendering down of the "hoof, horn and hide" came from the glue factory as hard slabs of brown material about half an inch thick and about a foot square. This you broke up with a hammer – it was that hard. Later on, it was sold in "pearl" form, pieces about the size of a barley grain and as tins full of a very tough jelly. These pieces, the pearls or jelly, were put into a pot covered with water and usually left overnight. In the morning you had a pot full of a pale brown but firm jelly. This pot was put into another one with water and heated until all was simmering. The workshop's porridge maker I suppose. When the glue was at about 150 degrees Fahrenheit, it was runny enough that when a brush full was lifted up from the surface it would run in a stream back into the pot. When that stream broke up into drops, usually at a height of about 6 inches, the glue was ready. Crude but effective.

One hundred-fifty degrees Fahrenheit is not very hot and the glue will quickly cool when taken from the pot. Once it began to cool, or chill as we called it, it was not a glue anymore, just a rubbery jelly that would not stick anything. Ways and means of getting over the problem were many. The first was speed when putting a joint together. Warming the work up a little was done. Also, the workshop was kept nicely snug during the colder days. It is this property of the glue chilling quickly that allowed veneering to be successful. That success came from the ability it has to be easily reconstituted by the simple application of heat.

To explain, the year is 1750 and you want to veneer a piece of wood three feet long by one foot wide. Your veneer is a heavy one from that time. All is prepared. You brush the glue onto the ground wood and also the veneer. With an area like this, it is obvious that the glue will chill by the time you are finished. This chilling is used to make it the success it is, because, quite simply, YOU ARE GIVEN TIME.

To veneer our board it is laid on a firm flat surface, something like a table or bench. Another thick board is prepared the same size as the piece to be veneered. This is named a caul. Also, in the veneering room from 1750 is a large hearth and fire. The veneer and the ground with their chilled glue are put together and set up so that the veneer does not move during the process. The caul is heated in front of the fire and made hot – a temperature of about 190-200 degrees Fahrenheit. This is then laid onto the veneer and pressure applied. The heat reconsti-

tutes the glue. The pressure makes the glue run out. And this fine joint, called the glue line, between the veneer and its ground is achieved. You take the rush out of it. The work is left for as long as possible under this pressure for a minimum of 24 hours.

That was in 1750. I was still veneering like that in 1993. The only difference was, I did not have an open hearth. Why? My insurers would have gone spare. Thomas Chippendale's shop was burnt down. I wonder.

I do not know how long this glue has been around – probably as long as man has needed glue. But the basic idea of using these animal products were many. Rabbit skin glue was developed for the making of gesso for gilding and panel preparation for painting. Transparent glues were developed from fish skin and bone. This used when cowhorn became a product in the often extraordinary techniques of Boulle, when transparent horn needed a glue to fix this onto the decorative paintings so often used in that technique. Glue could be coloured and then used to create the under colours needed for coloured shell.

If it has a failing, it has to be the property that made it a success. It is not waterproof and damage from this can be tragic. Also, allow it to get too dry and it will fail. It likes to live in a humidity of about 45%. For me this is nothing when you look at its other side. And it is quite simply that it can be, once you know how, reversed. Joints can be taken apart. Without this property many pieces of furniture good and bad could never have been successfully repaired!

What veneer allowed to happen is vast. The decorative surface of marquetry and parquetry are examples, and for the first time we could see the natural beauty of wood. I have been amazed that people do not understand that these highly decorative woods carry little if any structural strength. After all, they did not just appear when veneer happened; they simply were not used before veneering began. So now the burrs and crotch areas of wood could be used. The extraordinary woods from the root structures of trees were used. The use of wood as a veneer grew so fast it is astounding to me. Yet more astounding is this insistence that it all had to be sawn by hand. Time and time again you will see this sort of thing written: "Machines, mechanical saws, abounded, especially on the continent and from the earliest days in America". But England, they say, did not because we preferred the traditional way of by hand. This is such an extraordinary statement and makes me wonder how we produced what we did produce. As an island it seems we were thought to be isolated. It makes me (and I hope you) wonder how we produced the largest navy and merchant fleet that the world had known! Who knows, maybe when it comes down to furniture and veneer we imported most of it, just as we seem to these days.

One final point about the decorative woods not carrying any structural strength. Possibly one of the best ways to illustrate what I mean is this. We will, I am sure, all be familiar with flame or curl Mahogany. It will almost without exception be in a veneered form. However, you will occa-sionally find the top of a sideboard or a small table with a top in solid curl mahogany. Ninety-nine times out of a hundred, the wood will have cracks running right through it. It will be repaired to hold it all together. Also, these boards are often thin or thinner than you would expect and when on a sideboard often no more than 3/8 inch. I have never seen one, when found on a sideboard, that does not suffer from the problem. They are in fact a veneer flitch, the piece of wood left when the log was too thin to saw anymore veneer off it. You will also see these cracks all over a veneered surface as well. Now, without veneering I am convinced that not much furniture made from these decorative woods in the solid would have survived.

Just the invention of veneering, that is glueing these decorative and often fragile woods onto a firm and stable groundwork that does frankly hold them all together is a facet of veneer that the trade has not been given any credit for. Hopefully it may fall to my lot to change all that and give it all the status that it so rightly deserves.

Chapter 7

VENEER
AND THE
PITFALLS

*A*PART FROM UNDERSTANDING AND KNOWING THE DIFFER-
ENCE between an 18th century and 19th century veneer, it must also
be assumed that you know the different woods and when they were
used. Many a mistake has been made here. It is a continuous learning
process and putting things into memory banks.

The first and most important thing to ask is,
"Did the veneer start its life on this piece of furniture?" If you are satisfied that it did, check out
the condition. The best way is to have a kind of
check list like this:

1. Is the ground wood hard or soft?

2. If hard, which is always a better bet, check
the joins in the ground. Almost always when
a veneered piece has a crack in the surface
you will find that it is caused by the failure of
a join. Rarely will you find a ground made
from one piece. The way was to join smaller
pieces together. The reason was to try and
lessen the shrinkage and movement that
must go on. In the finest quality, the tops
were made up as flush panelling, the panels
themselves small, sometimes as small as five
inches square. When you see this method
used rarely will there be any problems, as

early as 1688 the system was used ILL 39. All
things considered, and what must have happened to that panel over the years. I reckon
the idea works!

3. If soft, the problems can be many. Check for
warping. This can be concave and convex.
Remember that wood shrinks in two direc-
tions, in its width and thickness. Just as in
hardwood but to a much greater degree, the
shrinkage in thickness of soft wood is much
larger than in hardwood. Also, faults in the
ground will show on the surface, often quite
dramatically – especially in late 19th century
work with the very thin veneers of that time.
I once saw a name written on the ground
clearly showing through the veneer.
Naturally everyone said that it had been
caused by someone writing on paper on the
top. We will all know and probably seen what

ILLUSTRATION 39: *Back of Petworth panel. C1688.*

a ballpoint pen can do. It was on a piece of Edwardian furniture that I had as a breaker. So the veneer was taken off and there it was Jones & Thomas No 14. Just the indentation of probably a cabbies pencil and the glue shrinkage was enough – extraordinary.

The difference between a hard and soft-wood ground can be illustrated. We have a long case clock from about that favourite antique date 1790-95! It is Scottish and we inherited it. ILL 40 shows most of the front. The door is veneered with Mahogany and is in perfect condition. Below is a panel veneered with a curl of Satin Birch. ILL 41 is the door open, and you can see that it is made of mahogany. The panel

below is veneered on pine. The faults can be seen. Usually the knot that caused the problem would have been cut out and replaced with a sound piece of wood that followed the grain. The coloured crossband is rare; the wood is Abura. Look at the escutcheon. That dark mark across it was caused by oil. My father-in-law thought the lock had rusted. It was and still is stiff from a strong spring. Anyway he oiled it! That mark will very possibly always be there. If I have said this already it will do no harm to say it again: never put oil anywhere near a piece of furniture.

4. Veneered table tops, sofa tables and tables with flapped tops are a culprit. The shrinkage is often such that the flaps will not hang down correctly. The flaps can be warped or pulled, usually convexly. My advice with this last one is to leave it alone. The books on restoration will give you all sorts of ways and means to straighten them up. You will be very lucky if they work. And if you do get someone to take it on, get him or her to guarantee it for at least a year. There is no way that I would do that! So have a think: firstly, why has the thing warped like that? Wood is a very obstinate material, and it will usually take up the shape it wants to be. Once it has done so, there is not an awful lot anybody can do about it.

Years ago there was an old-time dealer in the Fulham Road area. When anyone new went in touting for work, he would give them a tripod table with a warped top and ask them if they could straighten it up. If they said yes he would most impolitely tell them to go away.

The reasons for this are twofold. One is the annular ring structure of the ground wood. If the rings curve toward the veneer the warp will be concave. Rings that curve away from the veneer mean that the warp will be convex but not as severe as the other. The culprit that causes it all to happen is the glue. This problem was known from the beginning. On the finest work you will often find that a veneered surface that is not fixed – flaps, doors – will be veneered on both

ILLUSTRATION 40:
Clock front. C1795.

ILLUSTRATION 41:
Clock front door open. C1795.

most people; I will be called a Philistine for suggesting such a thing. However I have done this in various ways to numerous tables over the years. They have all been for the trade or dealers who have sold them. I wonder how many people knew it had happened. One private client tried to sell her table with flaps that did not hang at right angles to the top. The reaction was as usual: "What a shame about the flaps". She was offered very little,

sides. As veneer production became cheaper around the 1810's, it gradually became common practise to veneer both sides, called compensators. We can thank Mr. Brunel's saw for this. It is normal with veneered boards today.

5. A tip here, if you are faced with the problem of the flaps not hanging correctly, caused by the top shrinking across the width (and it does look horrible). Do not do what I saw recently. It was in a house open to the public. They had this problem with a sofa table and had added about a quarter of an inch to one side of the top. It stood out like a sore thumb. It is very easy with a sofa table's construction to lose an eighth of an inch from each side of the drawer frame or top carcass. It will do no harm to the piece and more importantly keeps it looking cosmetically nice. I doubt if this will be agreed with by

came to me and I did it. We all made money! OK, money is not everything, but I would have hated to live with the one that had had the 1/4 inch added.

6. Often on a veneered surface the veneer will be smothered with what appear to be small cracks. They will be lipped, or cupped as we call it. This will usually be on the very hard exotic woods such as Ebony and Kingwood. This is normal and is of no concern. It cannot be laid, or rather it can be but is a waste of time. The problem is a part of their character and because of that will reappear. It is called reaming.

7. With any veneered surface, tap it lightly with a finger nail. If you find areas that sound hollow have it looked at as this will mean a loose or unglued area of the veneer. Have it repaired. It is not a difficult thing to do at all

and should present no problems. If there are problems and you get the shaken head or the sucked hollow tooth syndrome, take it somewhere else.

8. Untouched veneers will be very thick until around the 1810's. After this time, they can be thin and, after 1860, very thin indeed. If these very thin ones have damage, be careful; repair can be difficult.

ILLUSTRATION 42: *Veneer pine ground one inch. The veneer has pulled a ground this thick. C1800.*

Just because a piece of furniture is without any doubt from, say, the early 18th century, it can have veneers on it that are like paper. This is the consequence of workshops over the years scraping the surfaces back to restore the colour of the wood. This problem applies more to continental work than English, and I have seen surfaces scraped back to such a degree that you could see the toothing in small areas. I would not touch a piece like that with a bargepole and advise you not to.

Another reason for my saying how important old colour is.

9. Re-veneering must always be looked for. Before the days of prices the size of telephone numbers we would be asked to veneer things up. A common practise was to veneer an oak bureau with walnut. We would use veneers called double knifecut, simply thicker veneers. One simple thing here is that they will always be very parallel in their thickness. The period veneer because of its way of production and toothing will not be. Look at veneer edges of something genuine that was veneered in the 18th century then something from our 1860's, and all will be understood. This side of it is very difficult to explain. Even illustrations and photographs will not really help. However, ILL 42 is a cross section of wood from 1800. The wood is one inch

thick overall and will show just how thick the veneer is. Also it is nowhere near parallel in its thickness. Note how the glue of the veneer has pulled the ground.

10. Re-veneering was rarely done to seriously deceive. When this was attempted, old veneers with their old colour were used. I bought wrecks of antique furniture that were not worth repairing. They carried superb veneers, and we used them. I have been presented with many pieces that have carried lovely colour and were the owners' pride and joy. But one look was enough to know that the veneer was wrong. The surface was not smooth, you ran your hand over it and it felt very slightly rippled, you bent down and reflected daylight over it and you could see this slight rippling. If the veneer is original to the piece, when you do this, it will appear as smooth as a calm water surface.

The reason for this was that the veneer had to be taken off one piece and laid on the other. If the veneer was taken off with water and heat, the object of the exercise, the old colour, will obviously be lost.

The best way was to remove the ground wood from the veneer! Sounds like an impossible task, but it was not. And with modern machinery, well-sharpened paring chisels, self-adhesive tapes to protect the surface and some skill and experience, it became very simple indeed. So why was it not successful? The answer is that I did not scrape up the surface after the veneer was first laid, and I cannot scrape it up now. No matter how well I tooth up the new ground or even the back of the old veneer, that initial scraping and cleaning up will always show. That is the rippling that I talked about. It was caused by the new glueing of the veneer.

One way of getting over the problem was to leave some of the original ground on, ideally about an eighth of an inch. This has been used very successfully on many occasions in serious repair work, usually to replace a seriously worm-eaten surface or seriously warped top. You are entitled to ask how did we cope with worm-eaten wood. The answer is with great difficulty until modern inventions came to our aid in the form of resins and modern glues which enabled us to inject the wood. We could stabilise it sufficiently to do the job. I do not doubt that today it can be done and the top or whatever it is made so firm that the old wood will almost become plastic. But I am talking of the days when the sight of a seriously worm-eaten top would be the kiss of death to a piece of furniture. So should you see a piece of veneered furniture and on the back edge or somewhere else there is evidence of this, take care. I am ashamed to say that many ways and means have been used to hide that evidence up!

This way of taking a veneer off was obviously expensive. You are entitled to ask, "Wasn't there a cheaper way?" There was. I learned it from the old boys like me. A warm flat iron and beeswax will lift a veneer and keep all the old colour and even the glue underneath it. This was the way of Jimmy Little and all of them before him. I can remember asking why it worked so successfully without harming the colour. The answer was, "You polish with beeswax; that doesn't hurt the surface, does it?" If it is not simple, it cannot be successfully done.

Happily, this cannot be done with a large veneered surface.

11. That little bastard the furniture beetle, woodworm, can cause damage that is often tragic. The favourite wood of the creature has got to be Beech. In fact, any nut or fruit-wood will be suspect. It does not like alien hardwoods such as Ebony, Mahogany and Rosewood. Because of this, you will rarely see the exit holes on the veneered surfaces of these woods. With any piece of veneered furniture be extra careful about the worm problem. If you are not sure, get advice. There is not an awful lot that can be done after the event. I have heard people say, "Oh yes, it has a touch of woodworm". There is no such thing as a touch of woodworm. I have seen just four holes in a chair rail; inside it was completely riddled and the rail just disintegrated. I make no apologies for repeating myself about the problems throughout this book.

12. When I first went to America someone said to me, "My veneer keeps on popping". I had no idea what was meant until I was told it was the old, old problem of veneer falling off. Time and again I have gone to a customer to collect a piece of furniture and have been given an envelope or a box with all the bits and pieces that have fallen off.

It helps, but usually they have dried out, warped and are just a niggling problem to put back. And I can tell you now that most times you need not have bothered because we replaced them!

I have never understood why, when a piece of veneer falls off, you do not just glue it back straight away. Amazing, but it was not until I began running study days in the subject that I found out people seemed to think that there was some huge secret about it.

The most vulnerable thing must be the veneer that makes up a crossband on a piece of furniture. It falls off very often because of cleaning. A duster will catch a slightly lifted corner and flick it off. The reason it is so easy to come away is because the glue has failed. Now that is like telling you how to suck eggs, but the glue fails because it has completely dried out. Look at the back of the veneer and you will nine times out of ten see some dried glue. Also you will see some glue where the veneer had been. It has only fallen off because the glue has completely dried.

Dampen the back of the veneer and the glue on the piece – I say dampen – just enough that, after about five or ten minutes of keeping it just damp, it will feel sticky and the veneer will not fall off your finger. Then just put the veneer back in place and hold it down with a small piece of masking tape. Never use Cellotape or Scotch tape.

This will nine times out of ten work. If it does not, it is usually because there is not enough old glue. Just glue the piece back with a little PVA glue, wipe off any surplus and tape it as before. I can remember showing this to John; he did not believe it either.

Never, never but never glue these things back with any of our modern miracle glues. One of the most important things in a restorers armoury is to be able to reverse his glue quickly and easily.

Chapter 8

THE
DECORATED
SURFACE

HE DECORATING OF WOODEN SURFACES has been around for centuries before veneer entered our known furniture history. Veneering was certainly known by ancient civilisations; the treasures of the pharoahs show us that.

Furniture has been carved, plain painted, decoratively painted, gilded, gilded and painted. You can mention any combination you like, and it will probably have been done. Painting is said to be the earliest form of decorating there is. However I would say that inlaying, if not running alongside it, runs a very close second.

Intarsia, the scholastic name, is simply the process of physically insetting something into the surface of something else. In our context it is for decoration. In our subject – furniture – the materials used for the insetting or inlaying are diverse.

Right at the beginning I told you that I can only put it down as I have seen it, so I will list the materials that I have seen and worked with. It came as a surprise when I started to make such a list just how many there were. Also, the number of times I was confronted with a material that I had no experience of were many. An aspect pos-

sibly not considered is that very often we had to learn as we went along! I was so lucky that I knew people like me. They would tell you how, if they knew, just as I in later years have tried to do the same. Nothing infuriates me more than someone who stupidly talks about Trade secrets. I have to say that they usually seem to be young and would not have any secrets anyway. I must assure you that is not an old man being rather sour.

It starts with almost every sort of wood that you can think of. Many of them I do not know the name of, even now.

Metals begin with gold and end with zinc. In between you have silver, copper, brass, pewter, lead, aluminum, cut and engraved steel and on one occasion blued steel. This was quite beautiful, such a soft blue for such a hard material. It fell to my good luck to know someone who showed me how to create it. The blue we are talking about is the blue that you will see on the finest decorated swords. It always astounded me that the method was just like sand burning, except brass dust was used instead of sand.

The sea and its creatures provide us with Turtle, whalebone or balleen – the ivory of it and that of the walrus – pearl, mother of pearl in huge diversity, from the rainbows of the abalone to the subtle pinks of clams. I have used coral on just two occasions. One of these was on a small box veneered with sharkskin and inlaid with coral.

I have worked with hardstone and soft, marbles of every variety and colour. These were not just pietra dura but used separately and inlaid into surfaces. There was slate, soapstone, agates in colours from blue to crystal and on one memorable occasion a small table decorated with silver and amber. (You should not covet your neighbours goods; by God I did covet that one!) We must not forget malachite; I once had a chair through my hands veneered with this, mounted with gilt bronze and Russian – an amazing thing.

The animals of the world made their contribution: ivory (the quantities used make me wonder how elephants were not wiped out years ago), bone in all shapes and sizes. As with ivory, the bone was often dyed to all colours of the rainbow. We had cowhorn and antlers. Humans are also animals of this world and on one horrible occasion I was presented with a small box veneered in shell and inlaid around the top with what turned out to be fingernails. The date was the 1790's, which predates the horrors of Belsen by a few years. Whatever happened to that charming antiquity I do not know. The owners of it were as disgusted as I when we realised what it was. I hope that it was destroyed. Somehow I doubt it.

The early inlay of wood predates our 17th century veneering by centuries. The inlays themselves were usually about the thickness of the earliest veneers and were small enough to have been sawn by hand. This certainly could be one reason why veneers are always said to be handsawn in furniture history. This is my opinion and being from a workshop is an obvious answer to the question.

Early inlay with English work is usually into oak, the predominant wood of England. It is not the easiest of woods to work with. Very often, you will find the inlay missing, but when it is still in place, it does follow a very simple pattern and style of rarely more than two woods – a light and a dark. The continent was more adventurous than we, pictorial and armorial work being made with great success. To my mind, the greatest work and peak of the technique has got to be the work from Augsburg. Walnut was the predominant wood used as a ground for the technique.

A tip for you. Dutch marquetry work abounds, especially in mahogany furniture. You will find bureaus, armoires, bookcases, card tables sets of chairs – almost anything – made of mahogany or veneered with it. It is all inlaid with marquetry but predominantly laid into the solid wood. Not a lot of it started life like that. Fashion decreed the popularity of it so almost anything was inlaid up into solid mahogany. The genuine will mostly be laid as marquetry, that is, as a veneer with the designs in the veneer before the laying began. However the popularity was such that veneered mahogany pieces did not escape.

How can we possibly know things like this? It can be difficult I will agree. But this sort of inlay work, just because of its nature, will often appear crude. You will see evidence of the knife that cut around the shapes. The work will also be rather crudely engraved, and the wood of the inlay will be of one colour, more often than not. The most important thing of all however is down to our old friend the glue. It shrinks. So no matter how good our later inlayer was at his job, when he had finished the job, the surfaces had to be smoothed down. The glue however would continue to shrink for months and possibly years to come. The shrinkage will possibly be imperceptible to your eyes but not to your sense of feel. Run your hands over one of these pieces and you will feel that every piece of inlay is just a little below the surface of the mahogany it has been laid into. This is an infallible rule and will apply to the solid as well as the veneered piece.

This sort of inlay work appears crude for another reason. The mahogany they inlaid into was not new. A lot of it was on pieces sixty or seventy years old. The mahogany would by then be far, far harder than when it was first worked. It must have been a very tedious and often difficult job. It is no surprise to me that the work is so often crude, and it must have been the most boring job you can imagine.

When inlaying was combined with marquetry (by this I mean a surface veneered and then a design inlaid into it), the work is always of the best. For my money, the reason is a very simple one. Look at the ground veneer of these pieces and almost without exception that veneer will be of an easily-cut and easily-worked wood. Sycamore and Harewood are classic examples from the late 18th century.

The later inlaying of furniture has gone on no matter from which time and place. The reasons are many. Fashion is the most likely one in days gone by. However, that has not got an awful lot to do with it. Tarting up was our name for it. And I am ashamed to say that in the last seventy or eighty years it was done for one reason only: to make something more saleable and more valuable. The simplest one of these was to put a crossband around a piece that did not have one. An original crossband will always for some reason look exactly right. Having said that I do not quite know how to explain it! You just do not have to look twice. Also, it feels right to the touch.

Where the band meets the main surface, it will always be completely level and smooth. There will be small lifts at the joins in the crossband veneer. Often the later added band will have shrinkage as well as quite large lifts caused by the lifts being put in artificially. It is the old problem of trying to recreate age. The usual give away is more often than not our old friend colour. More about this later.

Inlaying and marquetry have been classed together from the beginning. This is understandable, and there is no doubt in my mind why. It is quite simply because the English called the mar-quetry workshops the inlayers. It has caused me a few problems during my lectures. Also, I have seen a few quite genuine pieces of 18th century furniture condemned as being inlaid later quite simply because there was evidence of a knife around the decoration.

Inlaying, marquetry and how it is made and animated has already been gone into in depth in my book, "Techniques of Wood Surface Decoration", published in 1987 by Batsford. I may of said in that one that life in a workshop is a continuous time of learning, and if I did not say it then, I have said it now!

The maker and breaker of marquetry is the animation of it. This can be the engraving of it which began in the 1770's. Penwork began in the early 1800's, simply because it was cheaper than engraving. However, right from the start in the 1650's, one method of animation has not changed; sand burning and heat scorching.

This was put down in my other book. The tray of hot sand was shown with the pieces of veneer having their edges toasted up. It showed how to do most of it. The only thing it could not do was give you the experience of doing it. I also put in and illustrated how you can put a sand scorch in the centre of a piece of veneer.

It was something that I had never done, and I just put it down as I thought it must have been done. In fact, I did exactly what I have been complaining about – putting it down as I thought instead of as I knew. Confession time.

This is what it was. How do you put a sand burn mark around the edge of a piece of marquetry but set it in a 1/4 inch from that edge? ILL 43 is a nice little urn table from 1780; it is even nicer because it also has a makers label. ILL 44 But how do you put those sand burn marks so neatly away from the edge of the pieces that make up the shell? In the book I said that you simply pour hot sand into a heap around the shape you need – an obvious answer. The publishers did not query it. Why should they; I was the author and expert! (p. 87, diagram 46)

It is right that things like this should catch

probably read my book! They had done the only thing they could – the usual thing – and tried to paint the burning in.

John obviously wanted it repaired; and I must confess that I did put it off as long as I could. However things do catch up with you. I said, "Yes, I will give it a try". (In fact, I was on my way home from doing the job that gave me my memorable ride on the 747's flight deck.) I tried heaped sand as the expert said in his book – rubbish! I tried a template of hot metal – useless. I tried very hot brass dust; that did not hold its heat as well as silver sand. Eventually, I was almost in a panic (brought on by having to tell John that I did not know how to do it). (Pride I suppose.) Anyway, I thought, "How on earth can you paint with heat?" Because this is what was needed.

ILLUSTRATION 43: *Urn table 1785.*

My brush was a very gentle, tiny, blowlamp flame. I practised for quite a few hours until I could do it and feel comfortable while I did it. I found that I could reproduce the 18th century work exactly and that has to be exactly how they did it in the 1770's or 1780's. ILL 45 It will be said here, "But you have a modern miniature blowlamp".

ILLUSTRATION 44: *Makers label.*

So I have; and my friend from 1780 would have had something similar. In fact, I had a mouth blow lamp donkeys years ago when very delicate solder work was needed. They would have had something much like that. It was simply an alcohol flame. I had a blow pipe that directed a jet of air at the flame. This produced a fine pointed flame that could be directed where needed just like my small gas one today.

up with me, and hopefully here I can put it right.

I found a superb eliptical Pembroke table veneered in Harewood decorated in classical marquetry with a huge shell in the centre identical to the one in the little urn table. I contacted John, and he bought it, which was good because he also owns the urn table. There was some damage to the shell. The repairers, like me, did not know how to do this particular type of sand burn. They

ILLUSTRATION 45: *Blowlamp. Painting heat!*

An important point here is the specialist workshop that these superb shells came from, something rarely if ever talked about. We have them today. And when you think about it, I suppose that I had one. I have now seen at least 9 pieces of furniture from this era that carry these shells. They come from an Italian pattern book (by Pattrenello? I think that is the name, I suppose I should check). Whatever the designers name there is no doubt whatsoever that all the shells I have seen were cut by the same hand.

Years ago I can remember talking to John about reading veneer: being able to know just from the character of the wood that all the veneer came from the same sawing or all the wood in a piece came from the same sawing. He was sceptical. He is not now. Using this has answered many an unanswered query that surrounds so much old furniture. The same thing applies to these shells. Look at the illustration and you will see a small piece of boxwood that looks like a fingernail paring. It is amazing how

they are almost identical one to the other. This appears in all the other shells like this that I have seen. That will only come from someone who has cut so many that they can do it with their eyes shut – a specialist.

This will also apply to the sand burning. It has been done by someone completely familiar with the method, in fact someone far more familiar than me. I practised on and off for over a week before I went to America. Doug and I practised again when I arrived. And I am not in the least ashamed to admit that there were a lot of cock-ups on the workshop floor by the time we were ready for polishing.

The specialist workshops abounded; they had to. Just look at the furniture and you will see how often these designs repeat themselves. This is what it is really all about. I have been far more fortunate than most. This sand burning thing is just one classic example; no one can know it all.

The later decorating of furniture will always happen. And it will happen as long as a piece with a crossband is worth more than one without.

I have said that the original one will feel right. Confused? Of course you are. Once again, the reason is down to these simple rules of colour and glue shrinkage.

We are making a new table. We fit the crossband and glue them into place, let it all dry, clean it all up, polish it and away we go. Now try to do that without cleaning anything up and disturbing any of the surface colours. That is what has to be done if the band is to appear original to the piece.

What had to be attempted was to use old veneer that carried its old colour, then fit the banding so that the old surface of the top and the old surface of the band were level – not difficult, just fiddly. Fine. Glue it in place and the glue now shrinks. Ninety-nine times out of a hundred when you run your hand over these bands that did not start their life on the piece you will feel the odd place where this shrinkage has happened, and you will feel this slight difference between the main surface and the band. It is a

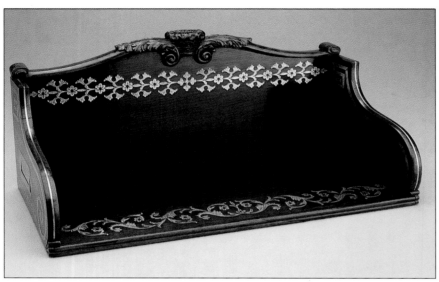

ILLUSTRATION 46: *Book caddy. C1815.*

difficult thing to explain. I suppose one way to explain it is that in the finest cosmetic surgery there will always be one place, no matter how small that will give it away.

The best tip of all is to close your eyes and run your fingertips over the banding. If it is original you should hardly feel that there is a banding there at all.

When I was involved with rosewood, a plain round breakfast table was worth hardly anything compared to one crossbanded. One with some brass string work or a little brass marquetry or inlay was worth a whole lot more. I have seen a whole lot of these that were performed on, and I am ashamed to say that they looked pretty good. Admittedly, forty-odd years ago is not exactly yesterday. Even if I had not known what had happened, I would have given them a closer look. The reason: accuracy.

The accuracy of the brass inlay line is usually the give away. The brass was an extruded 1/8 inch or 1/16 inch square. They just did not have that in the first half of the 19th century. Also, when they made one of these in, let us say, 1820, they had the job of cleaning everything up and getting it ready for the polisher. After all, it was brand new. So the metal inlays were also cleaned up. Because of that, they will not be accurate in their thickness. All I can say here is that these brass lines are often lifted, especially in the original ones. This inaccuracy will always show.

I did not have the luxury of cleaning everything up so my inlay line was put into place by making the groove for it slightly deeper than was needed. It was then very easy to gently press the line flush to the old surface. The area of veneer outside the line was taken off and usually an old veneer was then fitted up to the brass line.

Human nature being what it is, you did not have to be quite so accurate. For some reason they expected to feel the brass line. This always surprised me, strange but true. It also made the job far easier.

It has to be said that the brightening up of this rather dowdy rosewood furniture went on apace. Also, in those days, the price things were sold for did not really hurt anybody. The only thing that may have hurt a little could well have been pride, considering that they had not bought what they thought it was. A little knowledge can be a dangerous thing.

A couple of years ago in a catalogue a William IV library table in nice, faded Rosewood was estimated at £2000-3000. Also, in this catalogue was another rosewood table dated 1810-1815, leather-topped, brass-inlaid with four, nice, hair paw, lions feet – £12,000-15,000. It makes you think. That would cheer the people up who may have paid around 200 pounds for a dodgy one forty or more years ago.

If I had been a few years younger, here was a classic case for treatment. And at £2,000-3,000, the price differential is tempting. No, forget it, I sold my last set of paw feet years ago.

The accuracy thing is important in this embellishing game. Modern strings and inlays carry, just like the brass, an accuracy not possible

ILLUSTRATION 47: *Box on front cover.*

stringwork was. It was made by pulling that fine piece of wood under a scraper – not very conducive to producing an accurate string. That dark mark across the escutcheon still annoys me.

One final thing. Brass inlaid furniture was, for me, the beginning of the end of the hand workshop. The reason was stamped brass inlay. ILL 46 shows a superior, small, book caddy from those days. Just look at the accuracy of the work. Only a machine can do that. One thing for sure I could not possibly saw it by hand to that sort of accuracy. And no way in this world will the piece stand the cost of making up the die stamps that were used then.

So the clock has gone full circle. The thing that made the furniture valuable in the 1810-15's – the cost of doing it by hand – has gone. ILL 47 shows a survivor if ever there was one. It is from roughly the same date as the caddy, but all the work has been pierced by hand. As clever as the mechanical way is, it can never produce work like that.

The mechanical way is here and I have to say this: it becomes boring and within the pocket of an awful lot more people. In the next 150 years, the how and why of it all was in the understanding of less and less people. It really did seem to become what it has always been called: a mystery.

in the 18th century. In fact, the accuracy was not possible until small and fast circular saws driven by a treadle became fairly common.

In the illustration that shows the front of our clock case you can see just how inaccurate the

Chapter 9

BOULLEWORK, OR BOULLE MARQUETRY

A FEW YEARS AGO I was invited to go down to our west country and give a talk to a small society whose interests were antique furniture in general. It was a longish drive from our home. I accepted because we both liked that part of the world and Sheila's Granny lived there during World War II. The talk was accepted because it meant a two to three day break with most of it paid for!

It took place in a lovely little village hall, and we have been back to them a few times since. However, it is the first one we will remember for two reasons. The first was that the poor guy working the projector dropped all my slides just before I began. The other, and the purpose of this, was my introduction: "I would like to introduce David Hawkins who is going to talk to us this evening about Boullework, whatever that is!"

Right. If any of you have that problem, Boullework can be described as the practise of veneering something with materials other than wood. These materials are odd to say the least. They can be brass, pewter, copper, silver. Animal products come into it: tortoiseshell, pearl, cowhorn, ivory, bone. On rare occasions, I have seen semi-precious stone from marbles, malachite,

agates, bluejohn and on one occasion amber. The list is quite extraordinary, and people are often surprised when I come out with a list like this because Boullework is always, or seems to be, just thought of as brass and tortoiseshell as a marquetry design with the latter usually coloured red.

To be fair, this is what is usually seen and is a technique not thought of as very English. It is understandable; the name alone is enough. It is named after the brothers Boulle. The younger, Andre Charles Boulle, was born in 1642 and died in 1732. His name has come down through the centuries. I saw it written years ago that he invented the technique. Today, however, it is said that he perfected it. I do find it very difficult to understand a statement like that, mainly because friend Charles was not the only Boulle cutter by any manner of means.

My own ideas are rather cynical I am afraid. A.C. Boulle was cabinet maker to Louis XIV, or l'ebineste royale. To be even more cynical, I reckon that if I had been unfortunate enough to have held that position and my workshop had produced the work that he did, the technique could well be called Hawkinswork!

However, unlike the majority of people who hold forth about this subject, I am fortunate enough not only to be a Boullecutter in all its styles and complications but have also had the advantage (sometimes the misfortune and often the privilege), to work on some of the finest pieces of Boullework that have survived from the 17th, 18th, and 19th centuries. It is because of that I am convinced that some time in the latter stages of the 17th Century someone found a way of plasticising the glue.

Working on period pieces of the technique, a technique I call Boulle marquetry, very often a lot of the original glue was on the surface when an area was removed for repair or when an area was missing. This glue was often thick. I would remove it with warm water. It was not like the usual glue. It was rubbery and could be pulled and stretched, quite unlike the usual glue.

Why? The answer is simple and one that I have never seen put down before. If someone had perfected the technique it would have been this elastic-like quality of the glue. The reason is that wood shrinks when it gets warm. Metal in the same situation will expand. The animal and mineral products will stay, to all intent and purpose, inert. So if you have a glue that cannot move when the surfaces are in conflict with each other that joint will fail. But if the glue can move with this tiny expansion and contradiction then the failure rate will not be eliminated, but it will be very much reduced. So I will say again, if someone did perfect the technique, I reckon that that was what he or she discovered.

I know what I did about the problem; but I did not know what they did in those early days.

I enquired about what this could be and did

not get very far. Eventually, I was told that garlic was added. This came from a young Hungarian (I suppose it figured; vampires, Transylvania, Bela Lugosi and all that). I did try it. Dear God, no wonder it kept the vampires away – it got everywhere. A Polish guy said that urine was used – he never told me whose! However, for what it is worth, I have always put some Venice turps in my glue; that seems to work. Why Venice turps? Quite simply that was what I was told to do when I was young. I never asked why. But when Jimmy Little came to work with me and we were making up this dodgy Regency gear, doing the brass inlay thing, he asked me what I put in my glue. I, being me, said, "What would you do?" The answer was, "Have you got any Venice turps!" There is a lot to be said for knowing people like Jimmy who began his working life in 1884. Venice turps is the stuff you put onto a leather grip to keep it tacky so that you can get a good grip. It never seems to completely dry out. Makes sense.

Having just written this last paragraph, it does appear that I should have had the glue analysed. Frankly, it never entered my head to do such a thing. More than likely, I did not imagine that it was possible! It was a very different world in those days. We were very much the tiny workshop scene, and I can still remember the shock I got when I first did a small repair job in the conservation lab at a museum. The first thing I was given was a pair of white gloves. I had a large suction pipe arranged over me, not only to take any dust away but the fumes of some methylated spirits I used to break a joint! To me it was just unreal. To this day, I have never figured out the white cotton gloves.

I know little of history research, but if Andre Charles Boulle did perfect the technique, he is the man who found out a way of plasticising the glue.

Today there are many other names known of people who made the highly decorated work that is Boulle, and the research into them goes on. However, the technique and how it was supposedly done does not seem to have changed. No one has ever asked me how I created it. It does not matter I suppose unless you want to try. It is said that the French horse, or the marquetry cutters donkey as it is commonly called, was used for its making. I find that very difficult to accept for many reasons. The three most important are:

1. I have used the French horse. A parcel of wood veneers to be sawn are held vertically in the vise. They can often be heavy and awkward. How you are supposed to manage when that parcel is made up of brass, tortoiseshell and possibly pewter I would like explained. Maybe they were much stronger than me. Somehow I doubt it. Also, I have learned over the years that when the practical side of something is discussed by people who do not actually do it, they will not know some of the very simple things that can go wrong and often making it that way almost impossible. Anyone earning their living in a practical way will always find the easiest and quickest way of doing it. Explain to someone how to thread a needle, then watch them try. Then see a tailor do it.

2. The saw being used is not cutting wood, it is cutting metal. Then just as now, it is called a piercing saw. Because of that, it is much finer than a wood saw. Because it is in metal, the design and the scrollwork of Boullework can be very fine, far finer than a design in wood can ever be. Because of this, the saw has to be able to turn almost upon itself. How you can do that when the work is being held vertically in a vise with the saw cutting horizontally is difficult to understand. Also, and more importantly, it is not a practical thing to do.

I have been told that because I do not, or cannot, do it that way does not mean that they did not. Fair enough. My answer has been, "Go and look at a silversmith piercing a silver fret. After all, Boullework can be and is often as fine as that. The silversmith uses the saw vertically. They cut down onto the metal which is on a firm base. This way you do get some use from a saw blade. Used horizontally and without firm support all around the work the breakage of sawblades would be ludicrous. That breakage is no small thing

today. Have you ever heard anyone talk about that side of it all? Of course not; they have not had the problem of continuously breaking saws, even if it has ever been thought about. The blades are not cheap, even in our world of incredible mass production, Lord knows what the problem would have been in the late 17th century.

3. I have been cutting the metal inlays for Boulle and brass inlay work for forty-five years. The work has ranged from simple repair to radical repair work. Replacing complete Boullework tops in contra Boulle and horn, areas of pewter inlaid with brass and shell and brass and ebony, and on one occasion an Ebony top inlaid with brass marquetry so fine I doubt if I could possibly manage such a thing today.

The complication of some of this work has been a challenge, often a worry. The value of most of the pieces has been incredible. More importantly though, they have all been successful. The work sits in collections and museums all over. I will be arrogant enough to say that I have to look to see where I have been! From the beginning and during all these years I have always used my saw vertically. This is why, although I do not discount the cutters donkey, I do wish that some of these points could be talked about. Maybe it does not matter until you have to undertake it. But then I suppose it is far more romantic to see a print from the 18th century and a guy with his hair in a pigtail sitting astride his horse cutting his marquetry with a saw like a coarse coping frame – far better than me sitting at my vee plate, piercing saw in hand with a flat cap on my head!

When I have read of the donkey being used it always seems to be in places where time does not matter, and the turning of a profit is the least of their worries!

I said this was to be a book about the workshop. And it is things like this that are important. We think that because it is nearly the year 2000 we cannot do what was done three hundred or more years ago. Well, we can. And it will be difficult

101

indeed to see where the experienced man has been. My reason for saying that, especially in the world of Boulle, are the materials. Simply put, the materials used will be identical today as those of three hundred and more years ago.

Tortoise shell, if you can get hold of it, will be the same creature as the one from the 17th, 18th, and 19th centuries. The colours it is made into are made the same way as then. Coloured glue is used under the shell. This then is usually glued onto rag or linen paper. The colours can be natural: vermillion, yellow, umber. They can have gold or silver dust sprinkled in them, which produces a startling effect. This is usually on Dutch and German work. The technique is not just French.

The turtle is now happily being protected. The favourite was and is without doubt the hawksbill. The greenback is being bred in the Cayman Islands, where my last supply came from. You have to get a licence to import it. Thirty or forty years ago, it was not like that at all. I had two sources in London and one in Paris. The Paris one also sold ivory, bone and hair. He was a couple of doors away from a workshop that made some very frightening "Prisoner-of-War" work, such as ships made of bone. I have always wondered why those Napoleonic POW's were all so good at making things and made such a huge quantity as well!

Cowhorn is cowhorn. When cut and flattened with heat and pressure, it is not the transparent thing that is imagined. It has to be split, thinned down and then cleared. It is cleared in exactly the same way as always. It is pressed between hot metal after being coated with tallow. It is a revolting, dirty and often smelly job. It then has to be finally finished and buffed to a polish. The end result however is amazing, a piece of horn that is as transparent almost as glass that protects the often wonderful paintings that are glued upon it.

Today, ivory is supposed to be protected. The greed of man, however, just as with wood, is not really allowing it to happen as well as it should. Ivory is still ivory and just discolours with age.

There are different jumbos from different continents. Their ivory is obviously different, just as the ivory from whales and walruses is different. For our exercise, ivory is ivory.

Pearl or mother of pearl is the same as all the others, and it will be just a question of choosing the sort and colour you want. It will be the same with hardstone, finding some to match or one that you fancy to be inlaid.

It will be the same with the metals. Out of all the things in the world of old furniture Boullework is the only one that positively benefits from looking brand new! These facts can make the authentication of Boulle difficult. Often, scientific analysis of the materials will have to be called in! Be careful. I know what I have done!

One thing about the work is that it is always engraved. I will go as far as to say that the engraving is the maker or breaker of it. Also, it is fair to say that the finer the piece the finer the engraving.

Poor restoration and over-zealous cleaning is usually done because fine emery cloth has been used on the brass. I went to see a table once and the Boullework had been metal polished for years! This had often destroyed the engraving completely; sometimes just faint traces of it are left, and I would not touch a piece like that or advise a client to buy. To find a piece with all the engraving intact and original will be a fortunate find. Also, with experience, you will learn to recognise 19th-century engraving to its earlier cousins from the 17th and 18th centuries. The reason is the difference in technology from the tool steels and the making and alloying of the brass. This makes the cutting easier and will give the hands that do it more confidence. It shows.

One way to describe what I mean is this. When I began, the blade in the circular saw had to be continuously sharpened. Today, the blade is tungsten tipped and seems to last forever. And the cut it leaves behind is totally different from the one from my early days.

When this work is explained it is always as one-part and two-part Boulle, or Boulle and contra Boulle. The Boulle, or first part, has the background, or as we call it the ground in shell inlaid with the brass. ILL48 The contra, or second part, is the brass as the ground inlaid with the shell. ILL 49

It is said that the materials are prepared so that we have a sheet of shell and a sheet of brass. The two are put together with the shell on top and fixed together. The design pattern is put on the shell and sawn out. You then, just as with marquetry, change one with the other and – bingo! – one- and two-part Boulle. How I wish it was as easy as that.

Of all the techniques that go into the world of old furniture I would say that Boullework is the most expensive by far of any of them. It goes back to my point about breaking sawblades. The technique has not really been thought about.

Let me try to explain. Today you want a sheet of soft brass. This in the late 17th century would be called yellow copper. I doubt very much if you could have called up a merchant and ordered a four by two foot sheet of 70-30 soft brass and had it delivered (70-30 means 70% copper 30% zinc). From what I have seen of the metal used in the early days, it had been hand- or water hammer-beaten into a sheet with all the problems and time that would need. Also, a fact about all brass in this sort of inlay work is that it must be soft and pliable. This is called annealing. Bringing the metal up to a cherry red heat and allowing it to cool is how that is done. Also, the brass has a problem. The moment you hit or beat it, it will harden again. So the annealing process has to be continuously done. It would have been a pretty arduous and costly job to prepare the smooth sheet of brass that you see on a Boulle surface. This is point one. Point two, the sheet of shell also has its problems. A turtle has thirteen main plates on its shell called scutes. Also, they can get very large indeed. I have had a single scute eighteen by twelve inches that was a quarter inch thick in places. It is also the shape of a turtle! This has to be flattened and prepared down to a thickness near to that of the

ILLUSTRATION 48: *Boulle the first part.*

ILLUSTRATION 49: *Boulle second part.*

brass. It means boiling in salt water, using pressure to flatten it and a lot of hard work scraping it down to a consistent thickness. It is, in fact, tedious and often just downright boring. I cannot remember ever hearing or reading anything about this side of it.

A design is needed. I always had to copy designs that already existed. You can talk about tracing or needle pricking, which would have been the way in the beginning. Then an engraving, let us say for a top, would be produced. One designer, Berain, comes to mind. A print from that engraving comes to the workshop and the age-old method of needle pricking would be used to keep the master pattern, the earliest form of carbon paper I suppose. It was the only way of keeping that master pattern. These are important points. The Boston Museum of Fine Art has one of these early engravings.

I never found those ways accurate enough. You somehow lost the character of the guy who cut it in the first place. It was only human nature to try and improve a little bit, straighten up a line, make a symetrical thing accurate that was not – that sort of thing. Because of that, it was very easy indeed to see a repair! Frankly it was not good enough for me or my customers. In a month I became a photographer, a developer, printer and enlarger! The workshop eventually had the ability to copy exactly. We could now achieve that elusive thing – copying the character of the hand that cut it in the first place. You will all have heard of the artist restoring a painting and practising for hours to get the brush stroke right. We cheated, or rather I did, and used a photograph. If there was a reason for the success of our radical work in this field, it was the day I began using photography for the cutting patterns. The results were startling.

In my workshop, we always made the parcel up for cutting in one way, different to that often described. The brass was always on top of the shell. There is a practical reason for that, brass will cut much more slowly than the shell, if the shell is on top, the saw, because of the slow progress forward, will not produce a clean cut on the shell. It will have a lot of saw strokes for a very small amount of forward progress which will leave a ragged looking cut in a soft material like shell. Also, when period Boulle is taken apart you will always find quite a lot of brass dust in the saw cut of the shell, another indication of vertical sawing. The pattern is fixed, usually with glue size (thinned glue) to the brass. It then has to be cut into pieces of a manageable size. That

is something not often thought about and is an important point when pairs are being looked over. The pattern is sawn out. You now interchange one with the other, and we have our first part Boulle and our second part Boulle.

Fine. The only problem with that is, as far as I am concerned, they have got it the wrong way around. I have always called the one with the brass ground the first part, quite simply because that is the one being cut. I have been told that I am splitting hairs.

To back this up you must put yourself in a workshop with me. I do not believe that they cut a paper pattern, or find it very difficult to accept. It has all to do with us – dirty hands, perspiration, dust and being in a workshop. I do not believe that the pattern would have lasted five minutes. Okay, they could have varnished it. I doubt it. In my case, a photo could be handled but you would be surprised at the mess they were in by the time we had finished. There is another and very practical way if the brass is on top. The engraving of the design would be a copper etching. So suppose they waxed the sheet of brass. The design is now needle pricked from the master through the wax and the brass is acid-etched. They have a permanent pattern. The golden rule of any successful technique has been followed: simplicity. The pattern will not be lost through accident – or the surest way with a paper pattern, dirt grime and sweat of a workshop.

Another thought: they have an etched design; this could possibly be fully engraved before the cutting began. However, with this one I think that I am getting fanciful. I have never found any evidence of that having happened. Any evidence found has always been that the engraving was put in after laying. I have done small areas that way, but then I had the luxury of modern rolled brass.

Have the hairs joined together yet? Not quite? Well, does this story help?

In a collection in London there is a superb three door cabinet in contra Boulle. The gilt bronze is so good it is from another dimension. It

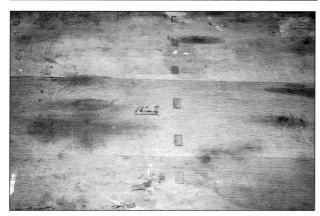

ILLUSTRATION 50: *Top Joseph No. 2.*

must be about fifteen years ago that I got a phone call from London. Huge excitement: "Maestro, I have bought the pair to the Joseph in the Wallace collection". I went up to town and could not believe what I was looking at, mainly because it was untouched and in quite remarkable condition. Also, and even more remarkable, it had all its original documentation from a sale in Paris when it was sold with its pair in 1772. A door was taken to the London collection and the Boullework compared. All the sawcuts from the piercing lined up and without any doubt whatsoever it was the pair. So my customer had made a major discovery. So did I. The one I handled was veneered in first-part Boulle. I wonder why in typical Indian ink from the time, written on the top was No 2! ILL 50

Sadly, and sods law I suppose, the one in the collection had been fiddled with in the 19th century and the top under the marble had been painted black. I have got a few quid or dollars to say that if that black was gently removed you will find No 1 written in ink just like its pair. As I said, this one was in contra Boulle. Maybe I am splitting hairs but most things in this world do have a reason.

How the work is made, engraved and all the rest was put together in my other book. But what follows was not. And I want to take this opportunity to add my own little piece to the history and often controversy that surrounds Boulle and

ILLUSTRATION 51: *3 part Boulle.*

things old generally. It is all very understandable when the people who made it did not leave a lot of information behind. Blame the masters for safeguarding the mysteries of their Trade.

One- and two-part Boulle is one thing. But over the years, many pieces have come into the workshop that were not as simple as that. ILL 51 is an example from a piece of Dutch or North German origins from the late 17th century. It is, as you can see, red shell, brass and pewter. Follow the rules of cutting and, as far as I am concerned, you will get three surfaces.

One of the finest pieces that ever came my way was a small Piquet table, veneered this way in pewter, brass and brilliant red hawksbill turtle. It was in one hell of a mess, but when restored, it was quite simply a piece of jewellry. Of all the things that I have been responsible for, this was

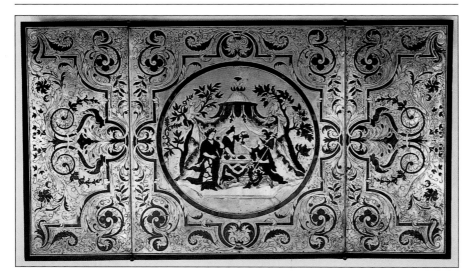

ILLUSTRATION 52: *Inside of Golle table when opened.*

the finest, and the one that gave me complete satisfaction. I got very well paid indeed for doing it. But, in all honesty, I would have done it for nothing – well not quite nothing! You can see how much I reckoned this incredible little table.

It is a royal piece and has a pair in the Victoria and Albert Museum that belongs to the Royal Collection. They were made in Paris around 1685 and are attributed to Pierre Golle. I will happily go along with that as I have worked on one other piece by him and can tell that the work on them both was identical. The little table is tiny, the top was only about sixteen by fourteen inches. The flaps opened to reveal an amazing sight of a central scene. On each flap was a pair of Royal Dolphins. ILL 52 It is now in the Getty Museum, and Sheila and I were invited to visit. I was to describe how the repair of the piece was done and run a small seminar on general repair. We went, and I did my thing.

It was at a small reception afterward that the question of the Royal Collection table came up. Someone said, "Would it not be nice if it could be possible for that table to come on loan so that a true pair of Boulle tables could be exhibited?" I had probably had that one glass of wine too many and said, "Why not start to really look around and find the third one and exhibit the three!" Dear

God, you would think that by now I would have learned to keep my mouth shut. You can imagine; they had never heard of such a thing. What did I mean three-part Boulle? All I could do was say that it is simply the technique, and a third one would have happened automatically.

To me it made complete sense. I had repaired a table that had a pewter ground inlaid with brass and red shell. The table that belongs to the Royal Collection has a natural shell ground inlaid with pewter and brass. The way the work was done and how I repaired it was to make a parcel of brass, pewter and shell, just as Pierre Golle did, and sawed the pattern out. Automatically, apart from one with a shell ground, a third one with a brass ground inlaid with pewter and shell will be produced. It will happen. It is a fact, no matter what history, one and two part Boulle or anything says. And absolutely no one will make me believe that that surface would just be discarded and not used. This was explained but it was to no avail, and I was put down in no uncertain terms. It was, I am afraid as usual, by people who had never cut the damn stuff in their lives.

Unhappily or maybe happily, I am me. I did not let it drop and asked to have a close look at the table in the Royal Collection. This was granted, and there was no doubt whatsoever the work had been cut at the same time. As was expected the thought of a third one was dismissed, even when I said that I will cut a sample. That was rejected with the remark, "That simply means that you can do it, and certainly does not mean that Pierre Golle did or could". If any remark over the years got to me that one did. I could not and still do not understand the stupidity of it.

I came home not in the best frame of mind and tried to forget about it.

ILLUSTRATION 53A, B, C & D: *Three part sawing.*

ILLUSTRATION 54: *Three part Gollework.*

It is about nine years ago that my talks about Boullework began. It was in the question time after one of them that I had occasion to bring this subject up. The questioner said why not cut it, photograph it and put it in the lecture. I did. It is amazing why you do not think about these things yourself. ILL'S 53A, B, C & D will show what I mean.

Happily there is some justice in this world, because very shortly after this small example from the stem of the table was pierced, quite by chance, I discovered that the third Piquet table with the brass ground does exist, and I know where it is. So ILL 54 showing my three small panels is, as far as I am concerned, one-, two- and three-part Boulle – or better yet one-, two- and three-part GOLLEWORK!

I have said it many times before, and I will say it again. Understand how these things were made, and everything else will fall into place.

These panels and how they were made are now all part of my talk about this extraordinary technique. I am not introduced as I was all those years ago anymore. Boulle and what it is all about is not the mystery it was. I finish my talks about it like this: "If I know anything about the world of art, one of these days the table with the brass ground will come on the market. I doubt if I shall be around. But if any of you are and you see it, I hope you will say, "My God, look at that. That silly old sod was right".

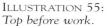

ILLUSTRATION 55:
Top before work.

ILLUSTRATION 56:
Top after work.

I have heard that people are now talking about three-part cutting. Some of them are from the world of the decorative arts, and I must admit that that does make the time and trouble that has gone into it all very worthwhile indeed.

The last chapter in this story is to be about the care and attention of furniture. Mainly it is some of the simple ways of looking after things. After all, my job has really been to put it all in order so that you can look after it. I thought it would be appropriate to show you how these simple ideas produced an amazing result on the top of this magical little table.

The Getty museum that the table now appears in states that the top was completely black when it was found. ILL 55 So it was. Also, the marquetry was severely lifted, had a few pieces missing and, worst of all, was suffering from various degrees of pewter rot. When I first saw it, I was, well, shocked. I had not seen anything quite so discoloured. The problem is caused by the fact that the groundwood was Oak and the acid content of it. However, I was even more shocked when I first went up to London to see it and the ways and means of how to do the job were being talked about. It was vaguely suggested that the pewter be stripped off and new pewter over-pierced around the existing brass and red shell. That for my money was not on. Just the thought of that put the fear of God up me.

The table was brought down to the workshop for restoration, and here is a classic example of, "If it is not simple, you cannot do it".

To overpierce with new pewter would have been well nigh impossible and not very responsible. Instead, you go back to this wonderful property of the glue, the ability of it to be reconstituted with damp heat. The flaps were taken off. The hinges still had their original nails. That, in itself, is so rare it is almost impossible! The flaps were washed a couple of times and allowed to dry. A sixteen-gauge, copper plate just over half the size of a flap was made up. Glue was then washed and worked over the surface so that it was worked under all the lifts in an area to the size of the plate. Three pieces of writing paper were cut to the size of the plate. Pressure blocks of the same size to go top and bottom were made. The plate was put into boiling water. When it was at that heat, it was put on the paper, the blocks put on and pressure applied. The whole thing was left for twenty-four hours.

This was done to the other three areas. Repairs were put in, and the whole top cleaned with weak citric acid and a mild abrasive called rotten stone. The end result is shown in ILL 56. If I remember correctly, the whole job on the top took about nine hours. That is experience and following the golden rule of simplicity. (I did charge for a little more than nine hours!)

108

Before we leave this chapter I must put in a thought or two from my, or rather the workshop's point of view. The idea of veneering something to make it look like gold or silver is not new, the tombs of the Pharoahs have shown us that, as has the extraordinary silver furniture that has survived from the 17th century.

I have oftened wondered what the guys in a workshop during the 1650's must have thought when a designer, or whoever, presented them with the design for a piece and said that they wanted it veneered in the materials we have been talking about. I can well remember the hollow feeling in the pit of my stomach when things, similar to this, happened to me. The Historical side is well documented, the workshop side is not, and frankly why should it, and how could it have been?

We, or rather I, did not know it all. I was expected to. It was often a worry, and interesting for me to find out just how to do the job. I was also more than lucky to often have their efforts in front of me during that finding out. They did not have that good fortune, and I wonder how many people have ever considered something like that? It must have been a nightmare for some of them in those workshops of three hundred and fifty years ago, and as I have just said, a side to it that I doubt has ever been thought about.

More power to the elbows of the people in the workshops of those days, their efforts have never been surpassed.

An extraordinary technique that has more than stood the test of time, often in an incredible way as this little Picquet table shows us. It is still being practised, happily plastic does now usually replace the poor old turtle. That can be no bad thing in this day and age.

An afterthought
I have said that I did no research, happily someone else did and it involves Pierre Golle.

At the beginning of Chapter six I mention a Chippendale table from C1772, a table that quite frankly changed my life! ILL 62 is that table after the workshop had performed. The colour of the frame and legs are something very rare indeed, because that colour is original to C1772.

The reason is that the table was made for a circular dressing room in one of our stately homes, this room was removed in 1844 and the table, surplus to requirements, was put into the vaults. It surfaced again in the early 1970's in one hell of a mess. ILL 91 will show you a marquetry top seriously in need of attention.

The table is illustrated in *The Life and Work of Thomas Chippendale*, by Christopher Gilbert, Studio Vista, Christies, London, 1978.

I have mentioned many times that these things were really no big deal when they were made. Look at ILL 62 again, the left rear back leg is painted a nasty brown colour, the whole frame was when it came to me, who knows what happened to it during its sojourn in the vaults! This was all removed, very cleverly by Simon Redburn who left one leg to show what it had been. I believe that leg has now been treated. However, my reason for this paragraph is that when I removed the top, there for all to see was the painters had used the top of the frame for their pallette, it was no big deal, just another job to get out of the way as quickly as possible! Disheartening, not really, I have seen this sort of thing far too many times before.

You may well ask what has this got to do with Pierre Golle, boullework and all the rest of it, well, quite a lot really.

This is the place for some thoughts about Pierre Golle and three part sawing. This, three part sawing was practised in the wood marquetry trade from the beginning. I have never seen more than three woods or three veneers used in the technique until the advent of modern veneers, the reason, just the thickness of early veneers ruled it out. To explain, put three early veneers together and you have a package a quarter to three eighths of an inch thick, not very condusive to sawing out a complicated shape with a fine saw is it?

The veneers on the Chippendale table had never been touched and were all a bare one eight inch in thickness.

Because of some publicity about this table, out of the blue, I got a phone call. "Was I the David Hawkins that could repair marquetry?" Just like that. I said yes and was asked to go and look at a marquetry panel that this gentleman owned. I asked what it was and was told that it was large, six foot high and four foot wide, the subject was birds, insects and foliage. I was more than intrigued and asked how he had come by it, and was told that he had found it under his bathroom carpet. That was enough, and I asked where he lived to be told Petworth, and he believed that this panel had been in Petworth House in 1688, removed in 1705 and had disappeared until he had found it. That sort of thing could only happen in England.

Petworth was about twenty five miles from my home in those days and my journey there was rapid to say the least. I found myself looking at a late 17th century marquetry panel that for all the world looked like a Savonerie tapestry executed in wood. It was superb and in a mess, bits missing, there had to be, and I asked if he could possibly lay his hands on some of the loss. I went up into the attics of this very old house, at least mid 16th Century if not before, and miraculously found the remnants of its pair.

This is not the time or place to go into a job like that, it would be a book in itself, enough to say that it was one of the most absorbing jobs I ever got involved in. They are also the rarest things I have ever seen or am likely to see and this will apply to you because they are in a private house.

The pair of panels with their birds of three part sawing and Pierre Golle and the three part sawing of the piquet tables, it can now all come together in a most intriguing way.

I give talks to the students at Christies Education in London and I have on occasion talked and illustrated how this job on the Petworth panels, my pet name for them, was tackled. Deborah Lambert is now a senior tutor

and it is hard to believe that I have known her and been giving talks for her for 19 years. She was the only person to see them during the repair and was impressed to say the least. Permission was obtained for some research which she did and an article by her, titled the Petworth Panels was published in *Christies International Review*, September–October, 1984.

It was discovered that in the early 1680's Daniel Marot, the designer and architect, was working at Petworth House and who was his father-in-law? Pierre Golle, and he worked at the Gobelin in Paris. I had always said that these panels had the Gobelin workshops written all over them!

This does round out this chapter very nicely because I have also always reckoned that there would have been more than two of these panels, at least three and very possibly six! This was received with some raised eyebrows and "oh dear, he is off again" but, just think about it. In the birds we have the classic three part sawing from the time, when you look at them, they each carry three identical woods this taking the place of the brass, pewter, and shell in the Piquet tables, elsewhere in the foliage and insects two identical woods take the place of the brass and shell of one and two part Boulle. The technique for all of it is identical. Just in the making of the bird with their three woods, automatically a third one of each was produced, it happened to me, and would have happened to them.

I cannot go back to Petworth and tear up all of my customer's carpets, but one day I must take the time and seriously visit Petworth House and see if there is a small room or cabinet where these panels could of been. Who knows, but I have found that it is extraordinary how techniques, dates and history do have a funny habit of running together.

It must be at least twenty five years ago that I worked on a spectacular split top desk from C1680-5. It was veneered with pewter, brass and ebony over the top, front, legs and stretcher, the sides and back were veneered in three part wood marquetry. A few years ago it was attributed to

Pierre Golle. It is illustrated in my last book on page 109. Look at that one day and you will see what I mean about dates, history, techniques, etc?

Part of my fee was to be allowed to talk about and illustrate the complications of a job like this. I am more than grateful to the owner for the opportunity to show you just about the rarest things I have ever seen.

ILL'S A, B, C, D

The next four pages are the Petworth panels, before and after. They are not exactly "Book" pictures. More just mugshots from the workshop and I make no apologies for the lighting flare and obvious amateurism of them, mainly because they are mine and are also the only negatives that exist!

ILL A is the panel exactly as it was found under the owner's bathroom carpet. The photograph was taken in the workshop and the panel has been braced on a frame so that we can move it around.

ILL B is the remnant that was found in the attics, this is also braced on a frame, the loss here is severe. The bottom third is missing as are the top left and right corners. The panelled ground is made of French Oak. The background wood of the marquetry is French Walnut, the birds are made of Sabecu, Boxwood and a Green dyed Sycamore that has now faded, the foliage is made from Sabecu and Boxwood. The black dots that are the acanthus berries are Ebony as are the black lines that surround it all. To repair and rebuild such a thing was quite a challenge and just to cheer us up it had also been sawn in half!

ILL C is ILL A after repair. The dove and cockatoo that were missing proved to be rather difficult. The making of them is no problem once you know how, in fact the technique is very simple. You just need the thing that takes the time, experience! The problem was to recreate the animation. Look at the two pheasants at the top of the panel, the bird on the left has almost got an expression of greed in its eye as it sees the moth or butterfly coming toward it. The bird on the right has its wings half opened and the beak is ready to try and catch the moth that has just settled below it. It looks just as a bird does when it takes off.

The dove that was missing bottom left, you can see the outline of it, that did cause some problems, it has what appears to be a large hornet like insect coming toward it. I think that we got what we were after, the bird has a look that is almost complete surprise. The cockatoo on the right, just from the body shape we had it seemed to have feet but no legs, it took quite a while before it was realised that it was roosting and asleep.

ILL D is the remnant after the rebuild, the bottom third is brand new. It does not matter. These are a pair of Savonnerie tapestries executed in wood. In this day and age it will probably sound rather old fashioned, but it was an honour to do a job such as this.

ILLUSTRATION A

ILLUSTRATION B

ILLUSTRATION C

ILLUSTRATION D

Chapter 10

METALWORK

WHEN YOU LOOK AT A PIECE OF FURNITURE I wonder how many of you consider the metalwork side of it.

The Roentgen desk with that amazing lock is mounted with gilt bronze. This can sometimes make furniture so flamboyant, and on occasion almost vulgar and people have said to me, "How on earth could they live with that"? The answer, "18th-century aristocracy, and you do not live in a palace or grand chateau, do you?" Rightly, I suppose, that does caused a frown or two.

To get back to you and me, many of us will

own a little piece like the davenport shown in ILL 57. How many of you will have ever considered the other quite large industry that was needed for the five locks, the four socket castors, the cast brass gallery around the top the nine cast and inset escutcheons and three cast brass hinges. Not many I will wager, and even less will even consider the nails, screws and one powerful spring to operate the quill and ink drawer.

It was because of this that I had a lot of misgivings about including a chapter like this. It is, and can be very technical on occasions. I asked advice and was pleased to be told that, "you seem to have explained other technical things in fairly simple language". That did decide me to try with this. Here goes.

In my youth, there was this old man still making the large-headed, black iron, upholstery tack by hand. He would take a tapered sliver of black iron, put it in a fly press and give it a thump to form the head. He was still making them one at a time. That was sixty-five years ago, and it was not unusual to see places like that.

Going back to the davenport, all the brass had to be cast. The days of extruding

ILLUSTRATION 57: *Davenport.C1820-30.*

117

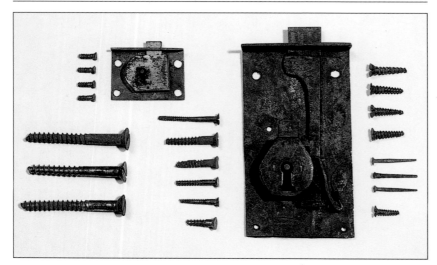

ILLUSTRATION 58: *Screws, English on left, French on right.*

doubt if they thought that it would help someone a couple of hundred years later. It has to be said that almost without exception this was found on the better work.

The image of the screw is again this thing of "hand made". The only thing hand made is the thing you see, the slot in the top. Rarely is the slot in the centre. The thread bit, I have been told, was put on by hand. I have asked how and had many answers. The strangest idea has to be, "Well, I imagine it was filed in!" That is hard to understand when you add up the screws in the davenport. They come to forty-four. Imagine the time it would take if filed by hand. Time is never considered – strange. The threads were put on with a die. As with our tack and cut nail maker, there would have been the screwcutter or

and rolling large quantities of that metal are in the future. Iron and brass are used together and the smith and locksmiths had an art very much their own. Nails are these tapered slivers of black iron. The bottom of any drawer from this time will show you what I mean, The screws need more explanation, and since I was told off for my remark about no brass screws before around 1860, I had better explain. Few people will have seen a screw from these times. There is little reason why you should. Also, do not try to take one out. Rust will often make this difficult and on occasion well nigh impossible. Unless you know the tricks and dodges in removing old screws, damage can result.

We used to have a tallow or grease pot on the bench to help in driving screws. One of the dodges to remove an old screw was to tighten it up a half turn or so, to break the rust. I used to do this automatically. Occasionally, there was no effort needed at all; the screw would come away almost as if it had gone in yesterday. The screw would have a faint greenish look, almost like verdigris. I reckon it was the tallow from all those years ago. I

ILLUSTRATION 59: *Inside drawer from 1790.*

ILLUSTRATION 60: *Handle 1790.*

maker as well, and, although I do not know this for sure. I will lay odds that the screws came into the shop, and the cabinet maker filed the head and cut the slot in it.

Just from the job they do, I doubt that few, if any of you, have ever seen screws and nails from these days. So here is a highly exciting picture for you: late 18th and early 19th century on the left; three early 19th-century iron nails and some 18th-century French screws on the right. Note that the old screws do not have a point and are almost parallel. This means that the hole for them must be the correct depth and size. The French are more tapered and are usually threaded to the head, isn't that exciting! ILL 58

Another side of this is the cost. This is rarely if ever mentioned or considered. My faithful price guide[5] has page 265 devoted to putting on brassware. ILL 59 shows the inside of a drawer from those days. The fitting of a lock was three pence, or about 1 1/4 hours work. Notice how they scrimped. Two screws only have been put in and the other holes not countersunk. The handle ILL 60 and escutcheon was twenty minutes of time. To put the nuts in flush was even charged – one farthing per nut. The nuts themselves were cast, as were the pommels of the handles. It was fifty or sixty years before hexagon nuts became the norm. They were usually round like this or square and carried a slot for a two-prong turnscrew.

Our fifty or sixty years in the future coincides with the extruded brass, giving the metal the shearing strength not present in cast brass. Now, brass screws begin to make their appearance. All this coincides with machinery and the first tentative years of mass production.

[5]The Cabinet Makers London Book of Prices 1793.

ILLUSTRATION 61: *Joseph. C1772.*

ILLUSTRATION 62: *Chippendale table. C1772.*

The metalwork side of the trade was fairly low key on this side of the English channel. We did on occasion show off a little in the first years of the 19th century. But in the 18th century, we were positively drab when compared to the continent.

ILL 61 shows the Boullework piece by Joseph. ILL 62 shows a piece attributed to Chippendale from the same date. In the latter, the contribution of metalwork is just eight, fairly hefty screws to hold the top on. With the former I would bet a few pounds that the mounting of this piece cost far

ILLUSTRATION 63: *Foot from Joseph.*

more than the rest of the piece and would not hazard a guess at the cost of such a thing in 1772. Even if it could be successfully done today the price does not bear thinking about.

This is the world of gilt bronze, or ormoulu (usually spelt ormolu). These mountings were always called gilt bronze by me and my associates. Ormoulu is I believe the bastardisation of the French "d'ore moulu", meaning "to grind gold". On its short journey across the English Channel, it became ormoulu as similarly Boulle became Buhl in this country.

Of all the techniques in furniture for its decoration this must be the most exotic, expensive, certainly the most highly skilled and without doubt the most dangerous. Apart from that, and what I have seen happen to it, it is one that is often not fully understood!

The fact of its cost can be shown here, or maybe not that, just the cost of the gold can be shown. ILL 63 is one of the feet from the Joseph. Where it does not show, it has not been gilded. This is not unusual, and I have seen it many times on original work. This I have shown to audiences, and the reaction is always the same.

First, they find it hard to believe. Second, "What shoddy work" and "Typical of workmen to do that". My reaction is, "Well, if they were like that, why bother to finish the foot all round? Why bother if no one is going to see it?" The answer is the same then as it is now – to save gold. Go around a gold beaters shop today, and you will see the extraordinary measures gone into to salvage every piece of gold there is after the days work is over.

Being involved with this sort of furniture, it fell to my lot to have to try to understand gilt bronze. Not only to repair it, I had to find people who could recreate it. I had to make the models to cast from. But more importantly, I had to learn how it was made in the first place, how it was chased or sculpted, and also how it was gilded. I had to learn to recognise the copy, or fake as it will be called. Also, I have been talking to students about gilt bronze and how it was made. That is not difficult. The difficulty has been trying to explain the subtle difference between the old way of gilding and the gilding of the last 150 years.

First, I must explain the making. Whether it is cast in bronze or brass does not really matter although bronze will usually be the case in gilded work. Sometimes, when a mount was being cleaned and the quality was exceptional, we would accidently knock it, and it would ring like a bell. Only one bronze will do that, which, for my money, is the best: BELL metal. And what can be done with that needs no explanation from me. Of course, we have two sorts of casting that have been used from the beginning. The beginning goes back into antiquity.

The first sort of casting is to put the object to be cast, or a model of it, into sand and leave an impression. Then, the molten metal is poured into that. It obviously is not as simple as that, but this is not the place to go into all the technicalities of what is a highly skilled job.

The second method is that of lost wax. This seems to have been around since casting began. It is the method used by the greatest sculptors of history. Again, lost wax is self-explanatory! The object to be cast is carved in wax. This is put into a mould, molten metal poured in, the wax melts and is burned off, and the metal takes its place. Simple.

There is rather more to it than that, though. First, we have the wax carver or sculptor – highly skilled people and their material, beeswax.

Look at the pair of commodes illustrated in the chapter on Boullework. You cannot just melt the model and absorb the cost of carving another. Because of this, mounts do tend to repeat themselves. There was obviously a way of keeping the original, or the patron as it was called.

Apart from wax, clay would be a good medium for carving or sculpting a mount to the piece. These mounts are often complicated and three dimensional. They would have to be modelled on the piece or a copy of it. As with a sculptor, the clay or wax models would have a plaster cast made from them and this used to pour the wax models that go to the foundry.

This is going to be expensive when compared to the sand cast. With this, a model would be carved, usually in walnut. Once you have that, you can cast as many as you wish from it. However, wood is wood and not very durable. Having been in workshops that created these mounts, I can tell you that the way it was done – especially when an object was to be created many, many times – was by making a casting model in bronze. This, for my money, was the best and most economical way of ensuring an accurate reproduction. Also, in the long run, it was the cheapest and simplest way. I know that this was the method at the turn of this century and in a workshop that I knew in the 1960's. When you consider the repetition of the 18th century, this would have been the obvious method then.

The result from a lost wax casting is much cleaner than one from sand. However, no matter how accurate the casting is, it will never be the same as the model for the quite simple reason of shrinkage when it cools. So when a piece of metal is missing such as, for example, the Joseph is missing a foot, you can use an existing foot and

ILLUSTRATION 64: *Mount from Joseph 1772.*

copy it. However, because of the shrinkage, it will not be very difficult to find the replacement. Just measurement is usually enough. Because of this on one memorable occasion there was one foot missing on a fine piece of Louis XVI furniture. Rightly or wrongly, I got a colleague in Paris to make up four new feet. It is surprising how one new foot would have devalued the thing. It has never ceased to amaze me that we had to go to this sort of trouble. No wonder the thought is that nothing can be done today. I doubt if anyone was told!

Right. We now have our casting, and it has just come from the casting mould. The second real skill begins. It has to be chased, the art of the ciseleur. This is done with tiny chisels, punches and little tools called fettlers. It brings a fairly rough looking thing to life. I have done a little of it, not very well. Whoever did the work on this, ILL 64 was for me a near genius. Workman indeed! The piece is quite beautiful.

ILLUSTRATION 65: *Back of Illustration 64.*

The next stage is the gilding and the thing that makes it so lethal. We are of course, talking about fire or mercury gilding. Mercury is just about one of the most toxic things there is. The method was to mix gold dust of near purity, and 23 carat is talked about, with mercury. It becomes an amalgam that is a silver colour. I expect we all know how mercury will almost eat gold. (Nurses take gold rings off in case a clinical thermometer breaks and the mercury gets on their jewellery). The mount, when it is chased and fettled, is degreased and the amalgam is pounded over the finished surface. None is allowed anywhere else. The mount is then put on a charcoal fire and heated until the mercury is fired off and the gold remains. Naturally, everyone breathed in the vapour of that. I doubt if there was such a thing as an old gilder!

The gold left on the surface is then worked, brushed and burnished giving the effect of ILL 64. The gold here is original; nobody has had a

go at it over the years. The number of times I have seen this work crucified by the ignorance of people using metal polish on it you would not believe. All it will ever need is a very gentle wash with soap and water. I must ask you to remember that gold does not tarnish.

I am continuously asked, "How do you know original gilding when you see it?" I am afraid that the answer has got to be, "See enough that is original, and you will know". ILL 65 shows the back of that lovely mount. That is original. The first giveaway is the colour of the bronze. I have never seen that faked successfully. The other is the little overrun of the amalgam, or dross as it was called in the workshop. This overrun is completely unintentional. Because of that, the phoney one will not be. Remember that fire gilding is illegal – not that that will stop it being done! However, it is very expensive to do. One of the dodges is to electro-plate most of the mount and just put in a few little bits of fire gilding.

ILL 66 shows a 19th-century mount electroplated. ILL 67 shows the back. It has been painted out with a varnish, not to try and imitate the gold overrun but to just save gold. There is about ninety years between these two pieces. The technical advance of the 19th century is there to be seen. Learn this and the difference between the two will be easy to see. The most important thing here is that no heating is apparent on the back of the casting.

One thing that must be explained and is often not understood is called overcasting. It has quite simply happened because of the demand for 18th-century gilt bronze outstripping the amount that was made – the story of antique furniture and a book like this I suppose. So it was just copied. People were not overconcerned that it was new in those early days.

Because of the techniques of the 17th and 18th centuries, many faults are apparent on the backs of the castings from those days. Blowholes are plugged, holes are put in purposely to hold the pattern in place (these have to be plugged), cracks happen and have to be repaired. All sorts of things like this will be seen on the backs of mounts that are original. You learn to expect them. So, when they copied these things and cast from the original, all this sort of thing would automatically be cast in. To me, it is a completely obvious thing to happen, and I have been amazed that people who should fully understand things like this do not. I will say it again: understand the technique and the rest will be so much easier. In fact I would not buy or allow a customer to buy until we had had a really good look at the back. Again, I will stress how important the colour and faults are.

ILLUSTRATION 66:
19th Century mount 1860-70.

ILLUSTRATION 67:
19th Century mount behind. 1860-70.

Another reason for not using the word Ormoulu must be explained, there are two sorts of mounts: bronze d'ore and bronze verni – gilt bronze and lacquered bronze.

My reason for trying to explain this is that you do not want to buy something as gilt and find out that it is lacquer. The problem is how to go about it!

The first thing is again because of the gold. The gilt bronze piece will ninety nine times out of a hundred be of a much finer quality than the cheaper finish of lacquer, especially the chasing.

Lacquer today seems to have one purpose – to stop tarnishing. It is my belief from seeing late 17th-century and early, 18th-century lacquer, that they had a recipe that could be called COLD GILDING. I have no photographs, but the first time I saw it was on a chandelier. It was in the workshop for some repair before going to be lacquered. I kept finding areas that had been covered and parts that cleaning had missed over

the years. As far as I was concerned, I was looking at gilding. I called my customer and told him. Consternation all around. I took it to London, and yes, it looked like gold. The piece certainly could not carry the cost of a re-gild. I can remember my total surprise when we checked it out. I used a cotton bud and alcohol. Had it been gold it would have stayed there. This gradually softened and came off. It was as far as I am concerned a lacquer that was the closest thing to gold I have ever seen. As is usual with things like this having seen it once I have found it on several occasions, I have tried to find out what it was with no success, as with so many of these things.

Many, many tricks, dodges, recipes and ways and means have just, well, gone over the years. I am convinced to this day that they had a lacquer that to all intent and purpose looked like gold. And like all lacquers, they had a short life and would probably have needed a refurbish every three or four years. Just the soot from candles and heating would make sure of that. Gilding

ILLUSTRATION 68: *1730's French commode.*

became more and more the norm for the up market piece.

This is such a piece. ILL 68 It is from those days. The mounts are lacquered and appear to all intent and purpose gold. My money says that this is the lacquer I have been talking about, ILL 69 are survivors! It does happen. I certainly have never seen a modern lacquer that looks like that. Just look at the backs. ILL 70 No overruns and the colour is quite different.

Finally, can you see that the figures have got two navels! One is a navel; the other is a stamp. It is the crowned c or c coronet. ILL 71 shows it on another mount for you to see it clearly. Thirty or more years ago it was thought to denote a Royal piece. Research has found that it is really a tax stamp, put on to say that the mount contains copper. I have no idea what the tax was, how much or how it was gathered. It was in operation from 1745-1749, and began at least 10-15 years after ILL 69 was made. I probably should not say this but tax gatherers do not seem to change much do they? Fancy banging that stamp in where they did. They probably enjoyed it. I must apologise for being negative about the history of these things. I am sure that if you have further interest you can look it up and find out all there

is to know about it.

The range and scope of the metalwork in the furniture industry has never ceased to amaze me. Gradually over the years we could undertake and make almost anything. It is a side to it all not really understood even today. The bewildering array of locks that we are faced with today is one thing. The cost of them is almost nothing when you see their complexity. You can get a new key cut in almost seconds for your front door. How very, very different it was two hundred or more years ago.

With the huge difference in the style and shape of things continental to things English, the way of locking things was also very different.

See the tiny locks of the davenport? One is shown and is at the left in ILL 58. Locks like this are really the classic drawer lock in English furniture until this time. A larger drawer had a larger lock. You put a key in, turned it once and that was it. We did start to get clever as time went on. Patent locks of many shapes and sizes appear. They did not seem to have much of a success rate. I say this because I have rarely found one that worked! They had often been altered to make way for a simpler key! The continental lock was different because you turned it twice to throw the lock. The reason is the shape of things. Often because of this the spigot of a lock would have to move up more than 1/4 of an inch. Now suppose it has to move up 1/2 an inch or more. You either have to make the key twice the size or do it the continental way and turn the key twice, which, like a ratchet, winds the locking bar or spigot up. In ILL 58, the large black iron lock is typical. Also, it is original and was the lock from the drawer fronts (ILL 1 & 2 in chapter one). You can imagine how we became key makers of all shapes and sizes.

This side of it all has never been given the credit it deserves. The cleverness of some of it has always amazed me. Also, it saddens me at the

ILLUSTRATION 69: *Mounts with two navels. One is the C Coronet.*

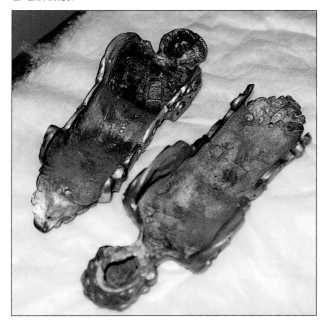

ILLUSTRATION 70: *Mounts behind.*

ILLUSTRATION 71: C Coronet. *The mark roughly in the center.*

been put upon so many things today.

I have just written about wards. These are the little half circles of metal that a key has to pass so that it can turn and throw the lock. It is a simple system that makes it almost impossible to unlock a lock without its key. You will need a locksmith – or be a burglar and simply smash it.

Who would have believed, least of all me, that I made up a key that when I told John about it he said, "Jeez that's a thousand dollar key". So we will finish with a key that will I hope show you just what an important industry it was.

It was the usual phone call. "Maestro, you know the Reisener armoire. It has just come back from New York without its key". This was bad news because the lock here was about five feet long and apart from locking at the centre it also threw bars top and bottom and was also

vandalism that went on in the workshops. Time and time again you would go to make up a key for a piece and find that the lock had been stripped of its wards, just to save some time in cutting a key to fit. Understandable, I suppose. No one could have imagined the value that has

ILLUSTRATION 72: *Lock Reisener.*

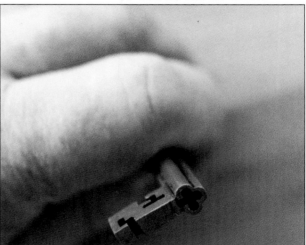

ILLUSTRATION 73A&B: *Key.*

spring-loaded on the handle. Another problem was that the pin the key was located on was in the shape of a clover leaf.

The piece of furniture came from around 1780-5. Reisener was a Royal cabinet maker. One little fact of the time is that Louis XVI was a keen locksmith. I will let you imagine just how complicated locks became in those days. In this day and age when something like this happens you will look to modern technology to see if it will help. I went to a small engineering firm to see if they could help in the making of this clover leaf stem I needed. "No problem. A spark eroder will do that. Then we can put a broach through. Leave it with us, and we will call around". I got a call about a week later. "£350 to set up the machine. How many do you want?" When I said that I wanted one, I will let you imagine what happened. So it was as usual. Back to the bench, the forge, the drills, files and saws. ILL 72 is the lock and ILL 73AB the inside of the lock and the head of the key. When I sat down and thought about how, it turned out to be surprisingly easy. The wards in the lock can be clearly seen as can the slots on the key that enable it to pass. I have to be honest; I really did enjoy making that one.

This is hopefully to be a book about age.

ILLUSTRATION 74: *Handle mark 1720. Original colour under the handle.*

The next chapter is about fakes and fiddles. Metalwork can help enormously if certain things about it are understood. When I first began talking about the Trade, I told you that I was often interrupted and queried. The most memorable was the first time that it happened. I showed ILL 74 and was trying to explain old colour and new colour. I was instantly told by a "gentleman", to coin a phrase, that I was talking absolute rubbish and everybody surely knew that those handle marks were caused by the alloying of the brass.

This really threw me. It was only my fifth performance, and I honestly did not know what to do or say. I know what I would like to have done, but that would have been impolite and painful! However I asked him how he knew that and was told that he had read it somewhere. Enough said.

Had it been now, he would have been told not to be silly, and how could brass alloying have caused what is shown in ILL 75. It was a shame, but I did not have this picture then. It is a wonderful example of old colour and new. The piece is from 1775 and has never been touched. The drawer has just been left half open, probably to show off the backgammon board it contains.

So, here is another one for your armoury. This is a nice, little piece of honest, 1770's furniture. ILL 76 Take the framing mount off the fall, and it will look like ILL 77. A classic, old colour-new colour thing for you. If it does not, it means that the mounts did not start their life on the piece. This is a fairly common occurrence and should always be checked. Because of that, the rules are simple: ask to have a look; and if permission is refused, do not buy it. I certainly would not.

By the way, you cannot fake ILL'S 74 and 77. Or at least I could not, and believe me, I have tried many times. (I am a little ashamed about that.) It was never successful. To bring all the colour back to our mint condition look is something that I could very easily do. Now that could make life a little different and difficult for you and me.

In this age we live in the technology of working with metals is vast. The progress over the

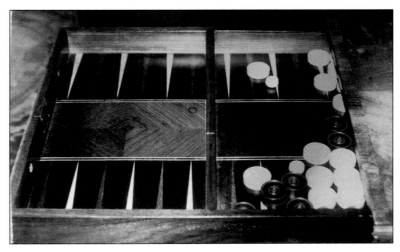

ILLUSTRATION 75: *Drawer Nostell Priory C1775.*

ILLUSTRATION 76: *Joseph secretary C1770.*

ILLUSTRATION 77: *Joseph mount removed, new colour underneath.*

years has been far greater than that. By comparison, the 17th and 18th centuries were almost primitive. Yet their achievements have and will never cease to amaze me. It will possibly sound silly, but some difficult problems have had to be solved. Just the nature of the job makes sure of that. One of the major satisfactions of the job was in the solving. The doing could and did

often become a bore. Self-discipline was needed to not find ways and means of cutting corners. This never happened to me with the metal work. Obviously, one reason was because it was not continuous. But it was more than that. It was, I am sure, the often obstinacy of metal and the continuous learning process – and the fact that it was all seriously handmade. Also, as I have said, that satisfying click when something mechanical works correctly, now that really does take a lot of beating, and a lot of the tedium out of it as well.

I began the first chapter by saying that I would never write a book like this. Having changed my mind, one of the reasons was in part to do with the last few words of this chapter.

Do it yourself has become one of the biggest boons of the last fifty years. The problem with most of it is that a little experience and understanding helps. Books to help that understanding are many and good. Do-it-yourself in antique restoration also has its books. I have one or two, and they are blacklisted, or are, if you like, in my Black Museum.

One in particular has been around for a long time and I feel that I must, at the end of a chapter like this quote part of a paragraph from it. It is about the cleaning of ormolu (that word again!). It states, "Remove the mounts and clean them with a stiff wire brush to remove the worst of the dirt and old lacquer. Hang them on a wire hook and immerse them in a mixture of half nitric and half sulphuric acid. After a few seconds it will start to bubble. They can now be removed and rinsed with water. If they are not clean enough the process is repeated. When clean enough, they are rinsed in water to which a little soda has been added. They are then dried".

Dear me, this extraordinary paragraph breaks all the basic rules of workshop practice: safety and just plain, old-fashioned, common sense. One thing is certain. Never, never do anything like that.

The rules are simple. Learn to recognise the difference between gold and lacquer. Never use any sort of metal polish on mounts. I have cleaned gilt and lacquer bronze for years and it has always been done with soap and water. Sometimes a mild detergent and a short soak in water no hotter than your bath will suffice. When they are clean and rinsed, dry them as fast as you can. A hair dryer is good. I often just put them in an oven that is warm to my hand.

Acids have no place anywhere unless they are fully understood, and you have the correct facilities for their use.

Chapter 11

FAKES (MOST ARE WISHFUL THINKING!)

*J*UST AS LONG AS SOMETHING OLD IS SOUGHT AFTER and regarded as better and more valuable than the same thing new, there will be someone who will try to supply that need. I tried, and in the trying I learned all sorts of tricks and dodges that have served me well. But I soon learned that I was wasting my time. It was just not possible to recreate age as it naturally develops. Because of that, one thing a fake will not stand up to, is a workshop that was like mine having a close look at it.

I once made the remark that I doubted if a fake would get past me. Arrogant? Yes. And I was seriously and embarassingly put down as being stupid. Understandable, I suppose. It was very off-putting at the time. But the world of top furniture and its collectors is surprisingly small. And a piece came to me for repair. One look was enough to suspect that it was not the expensive early 18th century thing it was supposed to be. Quite simply, the techniques of the surface decoration were of the late 19th century. A quick going over confirmed that this was not what it was supposed to be.

This was unfortunate to say the least because the owner or buyer of it was the one who put me down. I agonised about telling him. Usually you keep very quiet when this happens. It has nothing to do with us if the piece is wrong. It was also a sure-fire way of losing your customers if you did open your mouth. After all, you go out and spend a small fortune on something, and the last thing you want is someone in a grubby apron telling you that you have made a bit of a Charlie of yourself!

This piece was expensive – very expensive for those days. Possibly, I was still a little miffed

– no, I was still very miffed – by the rather public putting down I had received. So I told him. Dear God, the tirade was something else. It was such that it was almost funny had it not been so sad. People will say that I prostituted my art because I did the repair job. Money is money, I am afraid. The story ends as this chapter began. Eighteen years later, it turned up in the London rooms, was catalogued as 18th century with colour photographs, given a two-page provenance and sold. It went to be tidied up in another restoration workshop and was shot down as a fake. I will stand by my remark that no fake will stand up to a serious look by a workshop.

The ironic thing about this is that I was called in by these rooms for my opinion. The first thing that I saw on the workshop's report was that the surfaces were late 19th century. It is a funny old world.

The area of restoration that I worked in during my last thirty years became such that the furniture was valuable. Always thousands or even hundreds of thousands of pounds. As far as I was concerned, it started to become ludicrous. A standing joke in the workshop when a piece of veneer or something fell off was, "Don't lose it for ***** sake; it could be worth a couple of grand". Thank heaven I never had to insure any of it. It could not last. We all know how bad it was when the bubble did burst. It is so sad that so many established names have gone.

One of the nicest perks of my job has been this opportunity to talk to groups of people. It must now run into hundreds of groups and many, many thousands of people who have a deep interest in furniture and the things that go with it. They are from all walks of life and are young and old. I have the opportunity of working with students, trying to introduce them to the Trade, wood and furniture from my side of the fence.

Some have a profound interest in the subject. Some are very knowledgable. Yet the workshop seems to be a mystery. Some genuinely do not know what treasures they have. And it has been nice on occasions to be able to tell them.

Some have had real strops that they have been stitched up with. Some want advice on how to look after it or advice on the repair of it. You would be surprised just how many really gifted amateurs there are. Some are in the Trade, on the bench, and want to know how to get over a problem. Two heads are often better than one. Yet the all-pervading questions are about the cabinet trade, about the old days, why they did this, why they did that. The questions were such that I would have to say, "Whoa, I am not an encyclopedia". I was surprised and flattered to be told, "Well, if you do not know, who does!"

One question was put to me about fakes and had to do with money. The gist of it was that with the huge escalation of prices over the years, surely the faker will be tempted more and more. My answer was as usual. No matter what the money, it could not be done from scratch. There are too many problems to get over. The questioner would not accept this. He said that he was sure anything could be made and faked up to fool people. He claimed to have seen this and that. The old wives tales about using old wood and old tools came up. The chat went on, and it was obvious that what was involved was not understood. I finished by saying that most things, if you tried to do it, even at todays prices, would just be too expensive to do. This was greeted with complete disbelief. It was this that made me realise that the time it takes to make something would not be understood unless you have to earn your bread doing it. It was a thoughtful drive home.

Within a week I was invited back to Somerset, this time to explain why I did not think it could be done. I accepted and put this to them six months later.

ILL 78 is a rather nice Harlequin table from about 1780-1790. It sold for £5,000 in the rooms. I was the underbidder for an American client. It needs at least £1,000 spending on it to put it into acceptable order. Someone had cut the socket castors off the legs. This was probably done when one of them broke, and it was not worth the expense of repair or replacement.

ILLUSTRATION 78: *Harlequin piece. 1780-1790*

It was cheaper to just cut them all off. (This little fact did really surprise them.) How things have changed.

Using these figures, when the repair cost is added plus the buyer's premium from the sale, we have a price of 6,500 pounds.

Using this as an example for our fake, the faker has to sell this somewhere, and the rooms are probably the most anonymous place for that. This is a minor part of the operation. The problems of creating such a thing are these:

1. Getting all the necessary materials that have come from the 18th century. They must be such that you do not have to do anything to them that will show tools have been recently at work. This must apply to the inside of the piece as much as to the old colour outside.

2. Finding all the necessary fittings. These, or at least some of them, must come from the 18th century.

3. Sawing and preparing the wood. This one is veneered in West Indian Satinwood. If you can find it, it will have to have been sawn and prepared in the 18th century way.

4. Achieving the correct, aged effect on the inside of the piece. The inside must have the dryness of colour and the touch that a piece from around 1780-1790 will always have.

5. Constructing the piece in the correct way. The construction and making must be as the Trade from the 1780's. If by chance a joint is taken apart that must show no evidence that it has been recently cut. How do you get over that?

6. Creating the necessary effect in the veneer. The strings, or inlay lines, must be hand-pulled as they would have been in the 1780's. The Tulipwood crossbands must be built on the piece. The ready made ones that have been available for the past 130-140 years must not be used. This alone has been the downfall of many a reveneered article.

7. Achieving the correct, aged effect on the outside of the piece. The outside colour must be the rich, deep, golden colour of old Satinwood. Apart from possible repair work the piece must not show any evidence at all that it was not created two hundred years ago.

8. Creating the correct smell that an old piece will have. People think I am joking when I say that the smell alone will be a huge problem.

These few points alone will discount it. There are many, many more that will show just how many problems are involved. But let us suppose that the good fairy came along, waved her magic wand and all these problems were solved. How much will it cost?

We are told that little is really known about wages, costs and the expenses of the 18th century. I know little about them. Understandable unless you actually lived then. Our children used to look amazed when we talked about prices and wages, but I do not doubt that if you know where to look all the information could be found. I have no intention of doing that. It is far better to do some sorting out for ourselves. I know what people were paid for their labours during the last 120 years. I also know what I was paid and what I have paid out during the last sixty years. So we are more than half way – not a bad basis to begin.

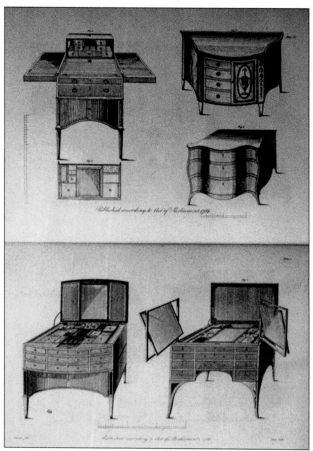

ILLUSTRATION 79: *Print book of prices. Harlequin table top left. Plate 10.*

I continually mention the "London Cabinet Makers Book of Prices from 1793". This book is a list of prices that the cabinet makers would charge the workshop master for their labours and is a quite fascinating record of the times. However, for me, it is the birth pangs of one of the Trade's big mistakes – piecework. This is a thought that could probably cause a few raised eyebrows.

Plate 10 in this book illustrates our Harlequin table. The workmen wanted three pounds-six shillings to make it in Mahogany. ILL 79 By the way, the Harlequin is the name given to the nest of drawers that rise up at the back of the piece. The list of extras they have is amazing. They want extra for veneering it, extra for making the harlequin rise with weights, extra for veneering in Satinwood because it is so hard. In

fact, the extras go on for a page and a half. Because of this you can work out exactly how much they would have charged the workshop for making the table that I bid £4,500 for. This comes to three pounds-fifteen shillings.

So it was three pounds-fifteen shillings in 1793; two hundred years later, it was £6,500. There is a fortune to be made. I wonder. You must remember here that you will not get six and a half grand from the rooms. But for our exercise let us say that we will.

I know that a marquetry cutter in 1793 was one of the top earners, being paid one guinea per week. A journeyman cabinet maker was on fifteen shillings, or seventy-five pence. The hours worked were twelve hours a day, six days a week. A working week was seventy-two hours! History tells us that they went on strike about this time when the masters wanted to put the working day up to thirteen hours. Small wonder.

Their work was priced, as it is today, by the hour – or part of one. This does appear to cover most trades and a lot of professions. Using a calculator (or as they would, arithmetic), our man on the bench was paid fifteen shillings for a seventy-two hour week. So he was earning two and a half pence per hour. Using this very simple idea, the time needed to make our Harlequin in Satinwood is 360 hours. This is just to make it and does not include the materials, workshop costs and profit. If we say that this doubles the price, our table would be sold for seven pounds-ten shillings. The extraordinary thing about this is that contemporary accounts show that a Harlequin like this was sold to one of our stately homes in Yorkshire for seven guineas, or seven pounds-seven shillings.

Talking about old money, it does occur to me that there could well be many people who will not be very sure or even know what old money is, and how it worked. If it ever came back, a pocket calculator would be essential! It has been over thirty years since we in this country decimalised our currency. Before that, our pound was divided up into 240 pence, or pennies. Each penny was divided into four; these were farthings. Two farthings made one halfpenny, so two of these made one penny. Six of these made a sixpence, or tanner. Two tanners, or twelve pence, made a shilling. Two shillings made a florin. We then put sixpence to that and had a half crown. Two half crowns made a crown, or five shillings. Four crowns made a pound. So two crowns made a half pound, or ten shillings, which was in note form as was a pound (which was twenty shillings). Slang for a dollar is a buck; slang for a pound is a quid. If you are confused, we then added one shilling to the pound and called it a guinea. Also, we had a three penny coin to add to your confusion. It really was an incredible system and a problem for people not used to it. People of my age however do, I am afraid, still tend to think in old money terms. I remember the huge weight of the coinage that you humped around in your pockets. I do not think that I have had to have any trousers re-pocketed since we went decimal!

Understand? Right. Back to the Harlequin for seven guineas. Coincidence? I wonder. Personally, I would say that we are on the right track.

Because of my old mate, Jimmy Little, I know that in 1902 he was paid five pence old money per hour. Also, to copy the piece made in 1793, it has to be made in the same way. If you use some of the twentieth century's technology, I can guarantee that it will show somewhere. It must be made in the old way if it is not to be tripped up at the first hurdle – which is someone with a bit of understanding giving it the once over.

So in 1793, at two and a half pence (two pennies and one halfpenny) per hour, one harlequin table, veneered in Satinwood. The harlequin to rise with weights: £3-15-00 (three pounds-fifteen shillings). It was likely sold for £7-10-00.

In 1903, at five pence per hour, £7-10-00; sold for £15-00-00

In 1937, at one shilling per hour, £18-00-00; sold for £36-00-00

In 1952, at six shillings per hour, £108-00-00; sold for £216-00-00

In 1988, the cost of the harlequin, charged in at my workshops cost when the Gobelin desk from Chapter 1 was restored, comes to £9000!

If the ideas applied to the other years are put to work and we halve the selling on cost, we get a price of £4,500. This little flight of fancy is peculiar because if we now add the cost of modern materials to making this, say £200, we get a price of £4,700 – not far short of my bid at the rooms in the mid-1990's. All this was a complete surprise to me.

The surprise was such that I applied this thinking to another well known and majestic piece of furniture, the Minerva Commode from Harewood House. It is known that this cost £86 in 1777. When I applied all the same rules to it, I finished up with a price of £230,000. This is a lot of money. But when you see the price asked for some one off pieces of furniture made today, it is not an unrealistic price for a piece of furniture like that. I would not even hazard a guess at the price for the real one if it ever came onto the market.

The figures that came up during this exercise were surprising. I cannot help but wonder that if one was put up today, using modern materials and machinery, whether it could be sold. Machinery could take a lot of the cost out of the operation, but it would take most of the character out of the piece as well. The charm of pieces from these times is the hand work that goes into them. This always shows. Hands have quite a job doing exactly the same thing twice. In fact, I will say that they cannot unless aided by jigs and guides, something that comes as a surprise to a lot of people. It is often not believed. My answer to the sceptics is quite simple: "Try it, and you will see what I mean".

Personally I am sure the one from 1903 would have sold. The one from 1937 would have been a little more difficult. You would have to have been very lucky indeed during 1952. And it would have called for a miracle in 1988. Who knows? I know one thing: I am not about to try because there are much naughtier ways.

ILLUSTRATION 80A: *1904 Carlton house desk.*

ILLUSTRATION 80B: *Early 20th century making, Brazilian Mahogany.*

sible to put something up that would fool everybody there would be no such thing as antique furniture. So before we go into what can be done, I have a thought for you. It revolves around what might be done.

The year 2000 looms ever nearer. Goods from the beginning of this century will enter the magic kingdom of one hundred years and the antique club. I have already said that some Edwardian Satinwood furniture is starting to make serious money. A Carlton house desk from those days made £12,500 about four years ago. One turned up on an "Antiques Roadshow" programme and was valued at £10,000. A friend of mine owns a beauty that he was told to insure for at least the same figure. He was shattered. His father had bought a house near Newport in Wales during 1948. It was fully furnished and included this desk. The whole shebang was £4,650. It makes you think. It certainly makes me think, because I bought a nest of four tables from a secondhand shop over thirty five years ago for twelve pounds, tightened them up, cleaned them and sold them on for twenty-five pounds. They were from the same era of 1900 and in Satinwood. I only did this because a customer asked me to. I would not have touched them as they were regarded as just some secondhand furniture. I hate to think what they would be worth today. In fact, I do not want to think about it. I still had the customer when I retired, and she still has the tables. It makes you sick.

This fact of making costs will apply almost across the board with goods that are within the scope of similar articles. Quite frankly, if you see an article like this, which is charming but not very practical, you can usually be pretty certain that it will be right. However, it is not quite as simple as that!

The first, important thing is that if it was pos-

It is better that I give you something to think

about. A Carlton house desk ILL 80A and 80B, c. 1904. It is veneered with knife-cut, East Indian Satinwood, inlaid with African black lines, banded with Tulipwood lined with black and white strings, on castors with a leathered writing pull-out. It is veneered onto a Brazilian Mahogany ground. As I have said, my friend was told to cover it, for insurance purposes, for £10,000.

Now, this piece has been made using 20th century technology by the likes of Jimmy Little. The era of his making is almost identical to that of my workshop when I designed and built new pieces. The last time that I did that was in 1990. So you can expect to see the evidence of machines. You can expect to see the total accuracy that machines produce. But the most important thing is that you can buy the identical Brazilian Mahogany. You can obtain the same genus of East Indian Satinwood, knife cut in exactly the same way as 1904. You can also buy the identical string and inlay work that Jimmy would have been supplied with. And this could well be still produced by the same company. Some of these desks are marquetry inlaid, and you can still buy these inlays! After all this, it is possible to visit a furniture hardware founder and pick up the identical fittings, castors, handles and locks. Even the screws will be identical.

The thing that made the Harlequin impossible has been solved. Even the toning down of the Satinwood would not be a serious problem. It is East Indian Satinwood, which responds well enough to the judicious use of bichromate of potash. The polishing will be twentieth century French polish. The introduction of ninety years of living with us would not be very difficult to solve. I am saying this because I have spent a few hours of serious looking at the one that came from Newport in 1948. With the fact that these prices can only go up and, as more and more of it is sold and it becomes harder to find and therefore rarer, surely someone will be tempted to fake it. Whether or not they already have been tempted I do not know. What I do know is that it would not cost anyway near the £10,000 of the one that stands in my friends lounge. If you got away with

it, it would be a nice little earner. Just a thought.

Another thought for you has to do with something that I call the small cabinet trade. It is the art of the box maker.

In some of my study days, people are invited to bring in small pieces of furniture. At least half of the things brought in are in this category – caddies, knife boxes, toilet boxes, sewing boxes, glove boxes, jewel boxes, writing slopes. The diversity of this side of the game has always surprised me. Some were in perfect condition and ran from solid wood to others beautifully veneered, often in the most exotic woods. Decorated ones from brass inlay to Boullework, paper scrollwork and Ivory veneered ones. The skill needed to make these things is much higher than usual and was, I am sure, a very specialised part of it all. Also, of course, we have Tunbridge ware and treen. This was usually in the form of tea caddies turned in the shape of fruit, such as apples and pears.

The important point of this is that the boxes were not worth a lot of money. In fact, it would not be possible to make any of them for their market value. Even repairing the damaged ones would often cost more than their current value. The few that I did repair was always for the sentimental reasons of the owners. However, a more important point about this is that they were always honest. I never saw one box that was not honest. Obviously, some had been altered. Knife boxes and caddies were gutted for other uses, usually stationery in the former and a useful box in the latter. But they were all quite simply honest. However treen was different. Here we are talking about the fruit-shaped tea caddies, the ones turned to look like apples, pears, melons etc. I handled many of these, and out of them only three were truly honest.

Money really does rear its ugly head where these are concerned.

ILL 81 shows a small sarcophagus caddy in Kingwood from about 1805. It sits on our mantlepiece and was a gift from John. It is original, apart from an outside repolish and the brass

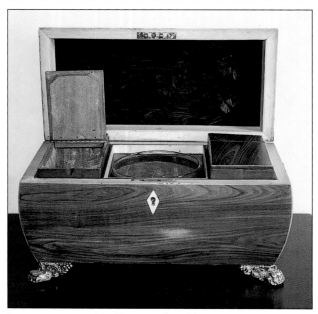

ILLUSTRATION 81: *Kingwood caddy.*

ILLUSTRATION 82: *Kingwood caddy glass.*

feet that were added about forty years ago. When new in 1805, it would have retailed for about one pound-twenty-five pence, or two dollars. Applying the book of prices to this it would cost around £1,400 to make today. The important thing with this caddy is the glass bowl ILL 82. It is original, and I am as sure of that as you can ever be about these things. That does not really matter because I want to put something about the history of these things right.

Whenever tea caddies are talked about, this bowl is called the mixing bowl. It is said that one canister is for black tea and the other for green and the bowl was used to mix the tea. The number of times that I have heard experts, furniture buffs and articles about tea generally telling us this, I have lost count. The almost reverential way that tea and its cost is talked about does make it almost a tea ceremony.

They are wrong! The bowl is a sugar basin. I was told this by my father who was a grocer and tea blender. Even old Jimmy used to laugh about it. No one has ever believed me. But page 235 from my faithful Book of Prices, 1793 states, "A cover, with a hole cut to receive the sugar bason 0-0-5 (five pence)...making a case for the sugar bason to lift out, the inside of ditto shaped to the circle, top part veneered and mitred, the inside lined with cloth, 0-1-0 (one shilling)".

I have always wondered why this book has not been consulted before. As far as I am concerned, if the people who made them did not know what the glass bowl was used for, who in hell would.

It is safe to say that I have never seen a faked piece from this era that is as complete as this. By this I mean that I have seen faked boxes that have the appearance of the inside being stripped out. It is understandable when people seem to be prepared to pay £200-300 for things like that! However, when you get down to our treen or fruitwood caddies, I have seen an awful lot of them, and, as far as I am concerned, only nine or ten of them were right!

The reason is simple, and I quote from an auction catalogue dated 23rd February 1990:

"Lot 5, An apple-shaped fruitwood tea caddy, early 19th century, with wood stalk and iron hinge and escutcheon, 12 cm high (4 3/4 in), 1,600-2,000 pounds".

I must confess that I have made one or two of these over the years, and at that sort of money proportioned over those years, do you blame me?

ILL 83 shows a real one. ILL 84 is the inside.

ILLUSTRATION 83: *Real apple caddy. C1840.*

ILLUSTRATION 85: *Real apple caddy. C1840.*

ILLUSTRATION 84: *Real apple caddy. C1840.*

ILLUSTRATION 86: *Fake. 1988!*

ILL 85 also shows a real one. They both came from the first half of the 19th century. ILL 86 was made in 1988. Be careful.

George Bernard Shaw, in Pygmallion, has Eliza Doolittle saying something like, "In Hampshire, Hertford and Hereford, hurricanes hardly ever happen". Well, in October 1987, Hampshire and all points East and West were hit by a hurricane of tragic proportions. We were without all the things we take for granted. For a little while, roads were blocked. The worst and long term sadness was the destruction of millions of trees that were uprooted.

We used to sail. Making a landfall from the south to Chichester harbour, if the visibility was good, a small copse of trees on the South Downs above the town was lined up with the drop in the coast. There was the entrance. All of that copse went. However it also twisted out of the ground, almost like a weed, a very large cherry tree.

At the foot of the Downs, there works a very good turner. Early in 1988, apple- and pear-shaped caddies started to appear. ILL 87 For awhile it was quite an industry. ILL 86 This one I faked up and used for a talk on fakery.

It is said that the real ones were not usually painted. I find that very difficult to agree with.

<small>ILLUSTRATION 87: *Lots of caddies*</small>

<small>ILLUSTRATION 88: *Squash.*</small>

<small>ILLUSTRATION 88A: *Pear caddy.*</small>

Tea was almost a ceremony in those days and the more unusual the caddy the better. Imagine a hostess taking her tea out of what was to all intent and purpose an apple. Also, why make up something like our caddy just for tea? This was a long, long time before the tea bag. However, whatever your views, the only real ones I have ever seen were all painted. Half of them had silver or plated escutcheons. Apples looked like apples, pears like pears. Melons were beautiful and often carved. On two occasions I have seen a carved gourd and a squash. They were lovely and looked exactly like the real thing – in fact, like ILL 88, which is a real squash, just to show what I mean. When I first showed this at a lec-

ture, it was incredible but people thought it was wooden! Wishful thinking. It happens.

It is sad that these things were never photographed, but then who could have imagined the turn of events that happened to me. The last one to imagine that was me and who would of believed that I would work with Television. It was at a Roadshow recording that I had my most memorable sighting, if that is the word. It was in early 1985 that I was presented with nine! We have a weird expression these days, "gob smacked", I imagine that is when you are presented with two apples, two pears and five melons, all original, four still had their original keys and naturally they were all painted.

I should have kept diaries, of that there is no doubt, as memory is not what it was; this one does remain very clear, probably because I put a value of £14,000-00 on them. How much today? I would not hazard a guess.

The date 1988 is after hurricane time, and I

took a pear from the group that I have shown you and painted it as best I could and my memory of the television collection allowed.

It is amazing how you just forget so many of the things that you have done. Just recently we flew over to Michigan, met up with friends and visited with Doug and his family. He, Doug, is a man of many parts, one is to create Nantucket baskets. Sheila has one he made, it is a love-ly small evening version, ivory whale inlaid on the base. I had forgotten that I had swapped it with the painted pear and it was quite a shock when I saw ILL 88A standing on a side table at his home.

I hope this will help to show why I reckon that they were mostly painted.

A right caddy of this type will have a threaded hole in the bottom, usually filled up. But you will see where it was. It is where the block of wood was screwed onto the face plate of the lathe when it was turned. The inside will be lined with either tin, lead or pewter foil. The better ones will have a brass stop hinge with four screws, just as the hinge in our own Kingwood one in ILL 81.

ILLUSTRATION 89: *Tea in fake*

ILLUSTRATION 90: *No black marks in fake.*

The bottom will usually be covered with hopsack, velvet or thin leather. It must be said that this has usually gone. Also, surprise surprise, they will smell of tea. The number of times that they do not you would not believe.

These things are difficult for the unwary. One golden rule is this: look again at ILL'S 84 and 85. On the top edge of the base and the bot-tom edge of the top are three black marks. These are the iron stain marks from three small nails put in to locate the top onto the bottom after the insides have been turned out. If a caddy does not have these, do not buy it. If you do, buy it cheaply. Learn to recognise the real marks; they are not easy to fake. Why? The wood was not fully dry when they were made and that little mark would not show up and be black for quite a while, possibly a few years or more. A faker does not want to wait.

I was an honest faker of this one. We did put some Lapsang tea in this one to take away the smell of the weak nitric acid used to create the colour. You cannot see a nail mark can you? I used some of our instant miracle glue instead. ILL 89 and 90 Also, I have just remembered something. One of the furniture people on television was handling an apple caddy and telling the owner that an old one will always be perfectly round. He explained this by saying that the makers would always use perfectly seasoned wood. Surprising how they know things like that. For what it is worth, if I feel one and it feels nice and round, it usually proves to be a wrong one. The most important point about this is that if the wood was perfectly seasoned it is more than probable that the black mark would not have developed. That iron stain only happens because of moisture. It is rust or iron oxide.

By the way, this only took ten to eleven hours to make. £1,600-2,000. Dear me, that really would be an earner. Be very, very careful indeed.

This side of it, the money, is a side not often thought about. It is probably the best side there is when looking at old furniture.

The naughtier ways are many and varied. One is to make something already old into something more valuable, and not necessarily that, just more saleable. This sort of thing, I am sure you will know about. Few of us live in large homes anymore, so the demand for small things that were old far outstripped the supply. The workshop's job was called cutting and shutting. Because of this, anything that is small and an odd size needs a much closer scrutiny or going over than its bigger brother. This will apply to furniture that is in common use: sideboards, sidetables, bureaus, small tripod tables and one of the favourites, our common

or garden chest of drawers.

Look in one of our price guides and find a three foot chest of four graduated drawers. Find one in good condition. Then find a serpentine one of the same size and proportion. They come from around 1780. I will wager that the latter will be two to three times the price of the former.

So how about changing the former into the latter?

It will take a skilled man no time at all to render your flat chest down into its component pieces with no damage at all. The serpentine shape is decided upon and four drawer fronts are made up to size using the brickwall method. This is exactly that; your bricks are made of wood and the drawer front is made just as if you were making a serpentine brick wall in your garden.

If the drawer fronts of the flat chest are veneered, that veneer will be taken off. If they are solid, a veneer will be sawn off them. The drawer stiles will have the same treatment. The drawers can be made up into the new serpentine fronts using the old joints from the sides. The only new ones will be the dovetail pins of the front. The drawers will be reveneered with the old faces, the inside of the drawers coloured out as they did at that time. (ILL 59 from the previous chapter) Reshape the stiles and veneer them with the original veneers. Shape the edge of the top and the plinth. New front feet and cockbeads not very much of a problem and feet are often repaired or replaced anyway.

Easy. A flat one is £850, a serpentine at least £2,500. When do we start? Slow down; there is a problem. Making a flat shape to a serpentine will cause the drawers to be about 1/2 inch to 3/4 inch less in width. The serpentine will become a fractional size. What all this book is about is here, making things easy. You just do not set out to make something in an odd size. They very rarely made things to the odd inch. It would be 3', 3'3", 2'9" not 2'11 1/4". At least, I never did. Remember what I said: if you do that mistakes will happen. They were practical men, and any practical man will tell you the same.

So if it is a funny size, give it a better looking over than usual. I shall be accused of and have been told this is a fairy tale. I can assure you that it was done. I was shown how by an old timer who made a regular habit of it. He knew, as I, about the size problem. His attitude was, "Who would notice or care?" And I am afraid he was right.

Tripod tables are always suspect. However, pole screens were very plentiful. They are not today, are they? Most of them are the bases for desirable, small tripod tables.

Enhancement. My own contribution was the decorating up of the rather dowdy Rosewood from the 1840's that I have talked about.

Walnut furniture. I would always treat Walnut with suspicion, the small pieces in particular.

Even this, if you follow the hidebound rules and traditions of my Trade, will not be difficult. But it has been a long working life. The things I take for granted I have found were often difficult to put onto paper. Talking about it is far easier.

I had cataract surgery about eight months ago and decided to also retire from the talking side of my life. I resigned from the various societies and organisations that employed me. But no, my phone still rings. Happily, the surgery has been a complete success. Vision and colour are once again the miracle they are. The greater miracle must be the modern technology that enables it to be done.

Last week, a call asked me to fill in at the last minute. I did and got the usual questions. This time, I got a very different one. The questioner had read a newspaper article doing yet another "expose" of the antique trade. Two bright sparks were writing about a Walnut bureau c. 1730 that had been made up by the "chop shops" (a new one on me that was). It had sold for 5,500 pounds. She wanted to know how she could buy something like that and not get caught. I could not believe such a question.

All I could think to say was that a real one from that time would cost her at least £25,000 and that she should go out and see if she could get a bureau like that made for £5,500. She was not a very happy lady.

How to wind things up is difficult. Hopefully, if the lady reads and understands all this, I could just possibly have succeeded.

As I have said, it has been no easy task to turn my tongue into a pen just like that. I have had a little go at history and the writers of it, and I apologise for that. My one sadness is that for some reason we never got together. It was more than likely me. However, I am quite sure that dear old Jimmy Little and his mates could well be pleased with me.

One thing that I am totally sure of is, when you think you really understand this business, that will surely be the time to QUIT.

Chapter 12

THE CARE AND ATTENTION OF FURNITURE

When I was first asked to run a short course on this subject, I refused. In fact, I refused on and off for about seven years! For the life of me, I could not see what good three or four hours with me would be to anybody. Eventually, I agreed to run just one day for a society who had been more than kind to me when the talking side of my life began. The success of that day has never ceased to amaze me, mainly because, as far as I was concerned, I did nothing but go into some of the simple things that I take for granted. The shock was to discover that what I took for granted was practically unheard of by the majority of people who attended. A greater surprise was the fun it turned out to be!

It was a surprise to discover during that first day that at least nine people in the audience polished their furniture with wax at least once a week. I could not believe that one of them did it more than that. She was blaming the polish because her furniture was always smearing and showing fingermarks. The more she did it, the worse it got! In fact, most of them were complaining about that sort of problem. Anyway, she wanted me to give her the name of a polish that

would not do that. I think she was a little hurt — and I expect embarrassed — when I told her that it was she and not the polish that was the cause.

It was amazing how often a simple thing like that came up. Use one of the good, old-fashioned furniture or paste wax. Follow the instructions. Use it once and no more than twice a year. This has helped to make me popular, as you can imagine, especially in this day and age where help in the house is an exception rather than the rule. I tell them how in the workshop we put the wax polish on, smooth it out, then leave it for at least a couple of hours. It is usually much longer before we buff the surface up, but a couple of hours is the minimum. This could be difficult for the householder, I know. But if the waxing is only an occasional thing, try it. You will be surprised how much easier it is. It is the buffing up that is important. Do it long enough and what do you get – a patina. By the way, we put or scrub our wax on with a soft brush before smoothing it out.

I am getting ahead of myself.

A lot of people imagined that I was going to wave a magic wand and give them miracle cures for this and that. I am sure that there were many people upset when I told them that most of the problems they had were their fault.

As a repairer, almost all the damage that has occured on furniture, especially old furniture, seems to stem from this century. There is no doubt at all that an awful lot of it comes from the last forty or fifty years. Why, apart from accidental damage, most of it is caused by central heating and insulation generally. It is lovely to live in our warm house where almost the only thing you have to do is to pay the bill for the luxury. No more cleaning out the grate and building a fire, getting the coal or wood from a cold, often grubby store. But, like all things that have a disadvantage, there is an advantage. Likewise, this will be reversed.

Burn a ton of coal; it will give off heat, and about a ton of moisture will also be released. The same with wood. But heat up a lot of water, pump it around pipes so that it will heat up large areas of metal that give off heat and that is all that will be given off. The heat is dry and that dry heat will absorb moisture from the atmosphere of our homes – and to a degree you – until there is very little left. It will then turn its attention to other things that have moisture. It starts with containers that hold water and then anything that contains water. And the thing you have all got standing around is wood. So your furniture is asked to give up the one thing that

keeps it stable, the moisture content. Then one day, there is a loud bang, and your lovely old table that had belonged to Granny and her Granny before her has got a nasty crack across it. It does not discriminate. It does not have to be old; it could happen to anything, old or new.

Even now, I find it surprising that this is quite often not fully understood.

The rule is simple. Keep a humidity level of at least 45-50%. The rule may be simple, but to implement it can be very difficult indeed. My advice here is that if you do have the problem and have difficulty, call in the specialists.

So rule one: get everything feeling comfy from a humidity and temperature point of view, and you will be amazed how chairs stay firm. Bits of veneer will stop falling off. One thing for sure is that things that creak and go bump in the night, if they do not stop, will more than likely be a whole lot less.

There are many humidifiers on the market. They can be expensive and will need attention. There are going to be many who cannot go into something like this. One way is to devise a way so that water can be evaporated by the dry heating. Bowls of flowers, containers that hang on the radiators (you will need several of those). The vogue today is to have potted plants that sit in their own bowl of stones and moisture. I know one or two people who keep tropical fish; they never seem to have a problem – at least no more of a problem than the one or two very posh places that I know that have a lovely, water feature as part of the house decoration.

It is the area of water or moisture that is needed, which is why I have said that you will need several of the gadgets that hang on radiators.

It is a funny old world. I have been preaching this humidity thing for donkeys years, and it has been highly successful on many occasions. Yet today have you noticed the constant advertisements for de-humidifiers? Makes you think.

Time and time again, I am asked if there is a finish to a piece of furniture that will stop continuously marking, does not need constant attention, in fact, one that is easily and simply looked after. The questioners are usually delighted when I say yes, but are usually not at all pleased when I tell them to try Formica!

In many ways, we have a lot to blame the 18th and 19th centuries for. In the world of furniture, the one that really comes to mind is French polish. As our subject is old furniture, the most common finish on this is going to be just that.

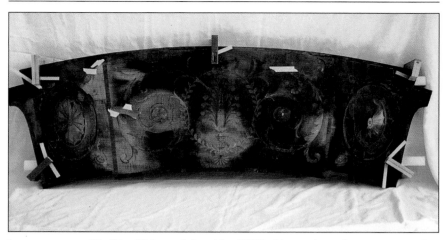

ILLUSTRATION 91: *Top Chippendale table. 1772. I have cleaned areas to see what we had. See page 119, illustration 62, for finished conservation.*

I have been called controversial on one or two occasions! One was when I said that French polish, or shellac varnish, was the worst thing that ever happened to furniture. Having said that, it has over the years earned me a lot of money. Just the vulnerability of it has made sure of that.

I shall have to go into what it is for you to understand my reason for such a statement.

Varnish, in the world of art, is usually based on oils and turpentine. It is roughly that, but can have many other things added, things to help it dry since it can often take quite a long time just to do that. All sorts of things that do not really concern us here.

French polish, is – surprise, surprise – French. I have always said that it came from the brothers Martin, or Vernis Martin, which is a spirit varnish. This is a mixture of alcohol or spirits of wine and shellac. Shellac is an excretion from the lac insect or beetle, the basis of lacquer from the Far East. The difference between this and the conventional sort of varnish was the speed at which the shellac varnish dried and its clarity when new.

A varnish such as this would have been vital to the highly decorated surfaces of high style French furniture. It is quick drying, easily replaced if it was damaged and almost transparent. After all, the one purpose of a finish on furniture is to pick up and reflect the different colours and shapes that that surface has. It is no surprise to me that the first appearance of it in this country seems to coincide nicely with the high style marquetry furniture of the 1770's. The Chippendale table that I was involved with, although the top was in an awful mess from a repair point of view, was untouched and amazingly still carried traces of the original spirit varnish that is today French polish. ILL 91

It is a marvellous finish, except for one thing. It is quite useless for a finish on furniture if you want to use that furniture in a domestic manner. The habit of the 19th century (and when I was a boy) of keeping the front room closed and the table covered does spell out just how delicate the polish on furniture was. A grand piano looks fantastic with its mirror-like finish. You would not dream of dining on it, though, would you?

I can remember asking why the amazing furniture of the continent during the 18th century – the pieces that make so much money today, the commodes, side tables and night tables – always seemed to have marble tops. This furniture, with its marquetry and parquetry surfaces carrying its gilt or lacquer mounts, must have cost a fortune. Yet they usually carried these marble tops. On occasion, when I did see a piece with a decorated and polished top, they were spectacular and could make the marble-topped piece look almost downmarket. The answer I got to my question was that this was the fashion and all part of the design of the time. Me, being of a practical turn of mind, asked if it was possible that a marble would be far more practical than a surface finished with a vulnerable spirit varnish. A marble top would not need the care lavished on it that a varnished one would. After all, these tops were used. A marble could almost be likened to a Formica of the 18th century. The silence was very deafening, and I must confess that the remark did cause me a few problems and one or two closed doors. No matter. All I know is that a French polished surface today is just as vulnerable to water, alcohol, heat and scratching as it would have been then. What our modern ball point pen can do to it is nobody's business.

This was the method of finishing furniture, varnishing if you like. Brushing it on, letting it dry, cutting or flattening it down with an abrasive, then another coat until the surface could be finally buffed and polished. This continued until around 1830. It was long-winded and expensive. It was about this time that the modern method of hand French polishing began. The reason for that happening was the usual one in commerce, speed. I can remember seeing a workshop price book from about 1827. I am afraid that I cannot remember the name. But in there was the price of a dining table at two pounds-ten shillings, to polish it seventeen shillings-six pence – not very good for trade at all.

So the thing that has stopped more trades than you can think about is here again: time. And as we know, time is money.

French polishing is a highly skilled thing to successfully do and quite pointless for me to even go into it. Let us suffice to say that, from the number of complaints that I get today and the near disastrous results that I have seen, I would be doing you one huge disservice if I did try to explain how it is done. Far better for me to tell you the way that you can produce a satisfactory result.

I suppose that I must let you into a small trade secret of my own. I never fully French pol-

ished anything. My success was WAX. Also, it was quite rare for an article from my workshop to mark. However, most any finish put on furniture will be vulnerable in one way or the other. This vulnerability has to be shown. Just by the rarity of seeing a piece of old furniture that still has it's original finish that is in good condition. Remember my forty-eight pieces?

When these study days began, the format of them was quite wrong. I had not seriously thought about it and had tried to put far too much in. I very quickly learned that my workshop vocabulary, the polite one, was of no use here. I had to use the names of things that everyone would understand. Also, when it all began, my audiences were predominately people who had never tackled anything like this before.

It took me the best part of a year to get it all together. It had to be a format that would cover most all eventualities! It did not take very long for me to realise that the problems people had revolved around no more than about four everyday things. Also, I had to be able to explain, and on occasion, show them what to do. You can imagine how very iffy that could be!

One of the perks for the people who attended was to bring in small pieces of furniture that needed attention and I would, apart from giving them advice about what to do, perform on one or two things. Mainly, I showed them what to do but more importantly what not to do. I must confess that it was great fun when a white mark on a table that had been there for years would vanish as they watched. I must also confess that the magician did choose the things he performed on with great care!

During these days, I only used materials that they could buy. There is nothing more irritating for people who attend these sorts of things and then cannot get the materials they want in small quantities. So all the things they need are easily available. I made up a case of these materials and carted them around with me. It really was the sort of polishing and renovating kit that I took with me when I had to work in-house as it were!

I just bought the contents from the do-it-yourself shop instead of filling up my own bottles.

Those four problems that seemed to turn up time and again were:

1. Splitting, warping, shrinkage, fading,

2. Marks on furniture. This was and will always be a problem.

3. Simple ways to refinish a piece of furniture. "How do I finish something?"

4. Explaining to someone that I want my piece of furniture to look as it did before he or she had it in their workshop

Number one. We have gone into this and my views about humidity. Those views have successfully got over the problem on many occasions. Let us put it this way, the continuous visits to tighten things up and put back bits of veneer all seemed to stop after we had got over the dryness problem. Fading is something else and is just caused by direct sunlight. The answer is very simple. Stop the direct sunlight. At least, I thought it was simple. You would be surprised that on many occasions I have been asked how! Without being unkind, it does just amaze me that I have had that response. It is like expecting a doctor to cure everything. I usually ask, "What do you do if the sun is too strong?" They look surprised and say, "Move out of it, or find some shade". Rudely, I suppose, I just shrug my shoulders.

Look at prints of interiors from the early 18th century. You will see that the furniture that could be in direct sunlight is covered or shaded in some way. Direct sun, over a period of time, can cause a surface to appear almost white. This can often be the heavy French polish or varnish that is on that surface, and it could well be that which has faded and the wood underneath will be much darker. Be very careful before any work is carried out, especially the removal of the polish. I learned this in the best possible way by being caught. People like me are supposed to know everything; we do not.

When I first became seriously involved many years ago, a good sofa table from the 1810's came to me, the top appearing to be deeply faded Rosewood. Then I did not know an early 19th century varnish when I saw it. The customer wanted to be able to see more of the top. It was decided that I would strip and repolish it. I learned the biggest lesson of my life. We finished up with a top that was almost brand new. The timber was the rich, purple-black colour of almost new Rosewood. All the fade of the top was in the varnish that I now know was original. It was faked back as best I could, which was not very good. I never got paid. I never had the courage to ask and needless to say I lost a customer.

It taught me a lesson that I shall never forget and without any doubt at all put me on the path of finding out all that I could about how and why these things happen. It was the last serious mistake like that I made. Also, I started to seriously look into the world of REVIVERS.

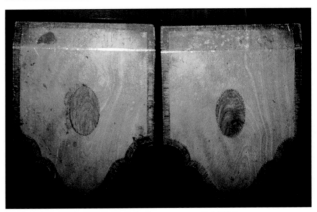

ILLUSTRATION 92: *Knife box tops. C1780.*

Luckily, I can show you exactly what I mean. ILL 92 shows the tops of a pair of knife boxes. They are untouched. Can you see in the top, left-hand corner a darker patch? That is the wood where the varnish is missing. The pale colour elsewhere is the sun fading of the varnish. ILL 93 shows the boxes with the colour West Indian Satinwood should be if left alone. You can see that they are the same colour as the small missing patch. ILL 94 shows the interiors. The

ILLUSTRATION 93: *Knife boxes. Faded varnish on tops.*

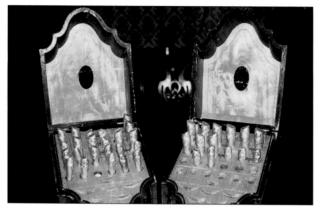

ILLUSTRATION 94: *Knife box insides. 1780's. Untouched.*

colour is as the day they were made. The cutlery is all there. Marvelous things. A classic example of old colour-new colour for you. More amazing, though, is that there are three of them! Could you believe that I ran out of film before I found out – absolutely true. It was such a rare thing, I should have gone back. But this was nearly twenty years ago. Nobody could have envisaged the escalation in things old.

I refused to do anything to them. They are history. They are a lesson to anybody who has an interest in antique furniture. However, they would be perfect candidates for the gentle art of reviving!

So the answer to fading is obvious. I am sure you know, and if you did not, you do now. Shade your furniture.

Number two. Right. Marks on furniture. If I had a hundred dollar bill for every recipe, magic cure, method and old wives tale that I have been given and heard over the years, Sheila and I could go on a long luxury cruise. The problem with all of them is that they could all have worked, just that once.

At a dinner in America, the lady sitting beside me told me that one infallible way was to use Hellman's mayonnaise and Havana cigar ash. I do not doubt for one moment that it worked, just as a lady from our north country assured us all that good, old-fashioned, metal polish would take marks out of anything. It could well work just as long as she did not go through the polish.

Our good, old-fashioned, metal polish has a fair dollop of ammonia in it and what that can do to a wooden surface is sometimes awesome. I am sure that we have all seen what can happen when brass handles are cleaned without taking them off the piece of furniture. While we are here, I cannot recall the number of times I have been asked, "How can I clean them without taking them off?" Well, if you want shiny brass handles, you must pay for it. Take them off. There is no other satisfactory way, just as I have no satisfactory way of correcting the results of cleaning them in situ.

I was going around a collection, and we looked at a nice little side table in Rosewood. It had good colour and so on. But it had a white mark about an inch across on it. The person I was with said, "Shame about the mark". I was innocent in those days, took out my handerchief, damped it with some spittle, rubbed the mark and naturally it vanished. The problem was that I had an audience. "Amazing! How on earth did you do that? What do you have on your spit?" I did not like to say that it could well be a little alcohol. I had been lunched rather well. I just told them, "Have you never heard of spit and polish?" That satisfied them. I never told them that the mark would almost certainly come back when it dried out.

One time, a lady phoned into a radio programme. It was one of those where they had an expert who gave instant advice. I never know whether to admire their courage or feel sorry for

150

their innocence! Anyway, the lady had spilt some water on a card table and had not been able to wipe it up straight away. The inevitable white mark had developed. What could or should she do? The advice was that the mark had been caused by dampness. Amazing. The top had to be dried out. "So take a clean white linen cloth and a warm iron, and simply iron your top to dry it out. All will be well". Easy.

I had heard none of this until a lady called at my workshop with a Georgian card table veneered with the typical butt Mahogany of the time. The whole back of the veneer was badly discoloured and seriously lifted. She was the victim of that sort of advice quite simply because she tried to take a white mark out when it was dry. You only do that to dry a mark quickly before the cause, condensation, can happen.

Anecdotes like this can go on and on.

The first and obvious thing here is like the advice about sunlight. Try and protect your furniture in the first place. Easily said; but did you know this?

Dining tables, when they first began, were dined on, then washed down and probably scrubbed as kitchen tables were scrubbed. It was not really until the advent of Mahogany that the dining table did really become a piece of furniture for furnishing and dining became more of a social event. In those days you would order your table, the top would have been oiled and waxed, delivered and set up. You would also have been supplied with a set of leather covers to put on it before your linen and the table laid for dining. Oiled means that linseed oil was used to seal the surface before it was wax polished. (I have said that you must not put oil near a stripped surface; here I am contradicting myself. Remember that the 18th Century table will be brand new and not carry an old colour.)

The problem is that many people think that oil will be the answer to it all. Few people will know what an oil polish is! I have tried on many occasions to explain that it is probably the only surface polish that will not mark at the slightest

provocation. I have found the best way to do this is to tell people to look at the stock of a top sporting gun. That can stand anything that you will ever do to it and it will always come up smiling. Many people have asked if I could polish their dining table that way. I have to say, "Yes, but you will never accept the cost of doing it". I did one small table once. The time it took was ludicrous. Oil polishing is just too expensive if you want to produce the deep, deep shine of the gunstock.

Why we expect, as a lot of people do, to dine off a table of polished wood without leaving a mark, I will never understand.

So rule one: protect your surface from the possibility of:

1. Heat. This will go through any conventional furniture finish almost as you look at it.

2. Moisture. Water will straight away come to mind. That can have fruit juice in it. We keep flowers in it. The palms of our hands sweat! The ways and means that moisture can get onto a polished surface have never ceased to amaze me. I have to say here that an awful lot are caused quite unintentionally. One of the worst is when a surface is accidently exposed to rain. You will really see what is meant by acid rain if that happens.

3. Alcohol, wine spirits, beer. The normal finish on a piece of furniture from the days we are talking about will, ninety-nine times out of a hundred, have an alcohol-based finish or French Polish. We strip a finish with alcohol. You do not have much of a chance, do you.

A heat mark on a piece will more often than not need a skilled person to rectify. A serious heat mark almost certainly means a repolish. It is well worth the time and trouble to get the best heat resistant table mats or protection that is available.

It is not generally believed that something over-warm to your hand will mark a surface, a waxed one seriously so. Something that is hot to your hand will damage almost any surface, often seriously. The number of times that I have had to deal with the results of just a faintly warm, flat iron you would not believe. I have on three occasions had to try, and I say try, to rectify the results of a hot one.

As an ex-smoker, future generations of my trade will hopefully not have to cope with the results of cigarette and cigar burns. (My way of becoming an ex-smoker was simple. I slipped a disc, and it was just too painful to cough.)

Moisture marks! They will be a part of your life.

Many years ago, I was lucky enough to meet a customer who liked the way that I made things, and how I repaired them. I worked for them during the majority of my time on the bench. They were, when in business, in the world of interior decoration and became world renowned for their products. In fact, I would go as far as to say that they revolutionized the ability of most men and women to do it themselves.

We became more than client and customer, or as close as that can safely be for any client – customer relationship. That is something that is, in my opinion, not thought about today. Anyway, it was many years ago when they suggested that I make up a solution that can be put into a container for marketing. The purpose of the solution? It was to be able to take marks out of the polished surfaces of furniture, no matter what caused them. A magic water in fact. I told them then that it was impossible. Now, all these years later, I will still say that it is impossible, more's the pity. I hate to think of the fortune that I could have made had it been possible, and I very much doubt if workshops like mine would have thrived the way they did!

The mark that must come to mind is the white one, usually caused by condensation. A damp cloth or a carelessly placed tea or coffee cup are favourite causes. The mark from a flower vase stood on something porous. They are painful, ugly and aggravating

ILLUSTRATION 95: *Pembroke and oil stain.*

One of the written-down remedies for the problem is alcohol and linseed or olive oil. This has been around for years and is good when in the hands of a person like me. For you, do not even think about it. ILL 95 is the result of this on a Mahogany Pembroke table. The lady who did it used olive oil. What happened was that the alcohol broke through the polish, and the oil just soaked into the grain. I can remember asking her what sort of mixture she had. It was apparently half and half and was obviously sloshed on. Enough to say that this resulted in a complete repolish.

When this is done and you want to try, the cotton pad has just enough alcohol to feel cold to the lips. The oil is just a very light dab on the pad and is raw linseed. The pressure used over the white mark is considerable. If you do try this one practise on a few before you dive in. If you do dive straight in, I shall not want to know; so do not bother to call!

The cure for white ring marks is to not get them in the first place! However, that is like trying to stop the sun rising. The answer is in a mixture that we used to make up in the workshop, but there is no way in this world that I will give you a recipe. I am not being awkward in my old

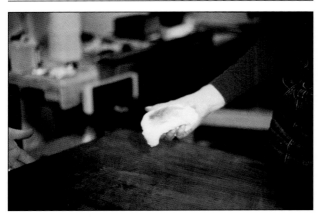

ILLUSTRATION 96: *Nicotine staining.*

age. A recipe for a batch of cookies is one thing; this is something that I just do not agree with. Let me tell you why.

Once on television, an idiot stood up and told us to put 1/4 pint of pure turpentine in a saucepan, add one pound of grated beeswax and heat it up on your gas or electric stove. This was to make wax polish. It would more than likely have burned your house down as well. Another genius told us to visit our friendly chemist and get a 20% solution of nitric acid and use that to clean your ormoulu mounts. And it would work well on your brass handles as well. My God, I bet it would! Another, if you do not like the look of your new piece of pine furniture, just wipe it over with spirits of salts! These were the spoken words of wisdom. I put one in at the end of Chapter 10 that was published!

The answer is so much easier. These days all these things that we used to make up can now be bought. I will recommend a white mark remover which is to all intent and purpose the one that I have used for years. I used it to perform my miracles on my study days. It will be a lifesaver in the kitchen cupboard. There will be an index at the end of all this. We also used a burnishing cream in the workshop that would take the dowdiness off a surface. I do not doubt that you have heard of Tee Cut, a burnishing cream for taking traffic film off your automobile; this is one for furniture and will lead us into the gentle art of reviving.

Number three. I once took on a small bunch of trainees, just five of them. The purpose was to teach wood surface conservation and the refinishing or polishing of furniture. It was a surprise to discover that the first and foremost thought in peoples minds was to strip the finish off and refinish, regardless.

This was in America, and the furniture we are talking about here is just that, American. It does not matter a toot.

The first thing that came our way was a very nice, three-drawer, dressing table from the 1830's. The instructions were – yes, you have guessed it – strip and repolish. Now this piece had the polish or varnish that it started with still on it, or I reckon it had. In my business, it is strange but I have discovered that when you get down to this sort of thing, the customer is rarely right. In this case the surfaces were good, a few marks as you would expect and something called alligatoring. If it was a painting, it would be called a craquelure. This is the surface of the varnish loosing its elasticity and the moving wood causing this cracked appearance. The moment the wood stops moving or breathing it will become, like us when we stop breathing, dead.

When presented with something like this, give it a wash with a mixture of vinegar and water plus a drop or two of liquid detergent. ILL 96 Make sure it is not wet, just over damp. Enough to see what may come off. Do this all over to get the surface dirt and dust off. Sometimes this is sufficient and a good wax polish will produce miracles. By the way, the orange colour on the pad is nicotine, which does surprise people.

In this case it was decided to use a reviver. ILL 97 shows two of the drawers, one as received and the other after a couple of minutes of work with a reviver. It needs no explanation. It does just that; it revives. The illustration says it all. This works on the majority of wood finishes. What it is does not really matter. Enough to say that they are a mixture of almost everything that is needed to clean and brighten up the surface on

ILLUSTRATION 97: *Two drawers, one revived.*

a piece of furniture. Having said that, the surface must be complete. I have had unhappy people who tell me it has not worked because they were expecting it to replace missing areas of polish. Like all things in life, give it a sensible chance.

ILLUSTRATION 98: *Me and pressure.*

Time and again, I am asked, "What sort of pressure do you use?" The answer: "Quite a lot." ILL 98 "Then I should be able to exert far more pressure than you." Do not worry about it; it will just take you longer.

The pad is just cotton wool, covered with a piece of well washed linen. Do not use synthetic cloth.

ILL 99 is this little table when it had been revived and waxed a couple of times. If my memory serves me well, the whole job took about five or six hours. Also, this table has gilding above the feet. I have had many questions about that. Do not do anything to leaf gilding unless you know exactly what sort of gilding it is, oil or water. Because of that I am not going into how you can clean gilding. I have been in this business far too long to even attempt such a thing.

However, as with all things, there is not a general panacea or answer to everything in a bottle. I would not use a reviver on a well-established, wax-polished surface. Often wax can build up, especially with the over-enthusiastic use of it and taken to an extreme. You can result in a surface that looks like this ILL 100. The answer in this case was to thin the wax polish down with turpentine, make it about half as

ILLUSTRATION 99: *Table finished.*

ILLUSTRATION 100: *Over waxing.*

ILLUSTRATION 101: *Wax cleaned.*

ILLUSTRATION 102: *Table attributed to Duncan Phyfe.*

firm as it was, use this with some fine steel wool (0000's) and clean the old, dirty wax back. ILL 101 is after a couple of hours or so. Surprising but true.

Remember me, the housewive's friend. Only wax your furniture once or twice a year. Allow it to dry before buffing it up. The moisture content of the polish is only to enable you to spread it about easily. I hope that I did say to never use those polishes that come out of an aerosol. They are wonderful for lots of things but not antique furniture.

How would I advise you to refinish a piece of furniture? The best way is how I showed my bunch of students. One in particular took to it immediately. ILL 102 is a nice little piece of late, 18th-century furniture that was heavily French polished about sixty or seventy years ago. The polish was poor and had completely discoloured. Revivers did not work. It was decided to strip back and start again.

I have just said the word strip. The image is to get a pot of paint stripper and a brush, cover everything with it and scrape the paint or varnish off. Fine; that is the purpose. It will sound silly, but you will just take too much polish off. This should only be done when you are presented with this ILL 103 – a badly water damaged top. ILL 104 is the top with stripper on. The fan was laid in exactly the same way as the Golle piquet table. You can see the stripper bubbling. Do not scrape it off; wipe it off with a piece of coarse cloth. Wash it with alcohol and then polish. ILL 105

This little piece came from a lady who was at a study day. She phoned and asked if I would please help her out. I collected it as I was passing near her home. One of the conditions was that they collected it. The job was done. I called, and they arrived. We were having a cup of tea, and they asked how much. I said, "That's okay. I was doing one or two other things and photographed the job, which was far more useful to me". About a week later they wrote to me and sent me a cheque for fifty pounds.

The whole job only took about an hour. In those days, that was an accountant's money!

ILLUSTRATION 103: *Water damage*.

ILLUSTRATION 104: *Stripping*.

ILLUSTRATION 105: *Polished*.

Back to polishing. A wooden surface will only polish when you have a surface that is as smooth as a piece of dull glass. In other words, the grain of the wood must be completely filled. I do not doubt you have seen pieces polished that have the problem. The grain is open; we call

it looking wiry. You will also have seen old surfaces that have the grain filled with a completely different colour, usually dull white. These are grain fillers. They are caused by coloured plaster of Paris used to fill the grain. It was coloured in the beginning. This fades and we are left with this ugly problem. Also there is not a lot that can successfully be done about it.

In the shops that sell the revivers, mark removers and polishes, you will see grain fillers. Do not be tempted. The way to fill the grain so that you can produce a polish is to simply fill it with the polish. The problem is that you are not a polisher. It will mean a lot of tedious work of a coat or two of polish, waiting for it to dry, cutting it down as I call it or rubbing it down as you probably will, until the surface is fully choked up and the shine can be put on.

The same problem would have faced Alison, the young lady who took this job on. The answer is the usual one. Do not strip it back in the first place, or find a way of stripping that will leave the grain filled. The answer is as usual simple. French polish is alcohol-based, so use alcohol to gently dissolve the polish off. ILL 106 is after her first fifteen minutes. She was as surprised as I at what was under that dirty shellac. The trick here is to take the shellac off gently so that you leave the grain filled with the old shellac. The top was a mess, a lot of marks and a veneer tear. ILL 107 The tear was treated as the Golle table. It will nearly always work.

The end result of taking the shellac off gently and leaving the grain filled is this ILL 108. Alison put two coats of a transparent shellac polish on and rubbed each coat down with 0000 steel wool. Twenty-four hours was left between each coat, and the piece was wax polished twice with a dark-coloured variety. Three days was left between each waxing. The end result surprised me. It was excellent. The colour still had its integrity. So how would I refinish a piece of furniture? Well, just like that.

ILL 109 shows the top after this young lady had finished it. She is entitled to smile. Notice

ILLUSTRATION 106: *15 minutes of stripping.*

ILLUSTRATION 108: *Polished.*

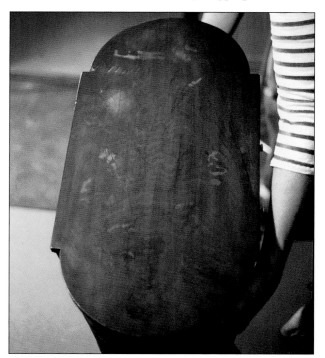

ILLUSTRATION 107: *Tear in the veneer.*

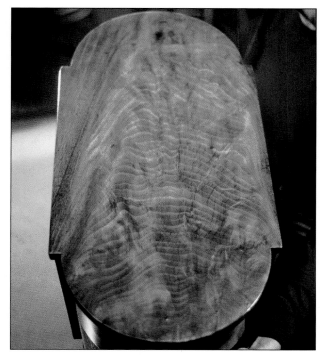

ILLUSTRATION 109: *Top finished.*

how all the marks have gone? They were treated with an age-old workshop solution, oxalic acid.

I do not like acids or even talking about them, but here I must as this one is important. Oxalic is a vegetable acid. You buy it in a powder form and mix an ounce in half a pint of warm water. Now it is an irritant, so have plenty of ventilation and use it, if possible, outdoors. Use gloves (the vinyl ones you can buy in a box of a hundred are ideal). Wear an apron and finally a dust mask or similar. What

am I doing telling you this? I do not really know, because you can buy wood lighteners and bleaches these days with all the other things that you will need. The reason is really that this is the one I have used ever since I began to polish. Another reason has got to be that it works. So do exactly what I say, if you do give it a try.

Treat the marks with a cotton wool bud (Q-tip), and allow it to dry. If it does not go first time around, try it again. You will have times when the marks will not go completely. But at least they will look a whole lot better. Nothing is ever perfect if it is old; do not expect it to be. A near dry wipe with alcohol will neutralise it enough to polish. In this table top, the marks were treated before the shellac was gently stripped back. People ask, "How can that work?" The answer again is simple: the marks were not there when they polished it, were they? Another thing is that oxalic is probably one of the best cleaners of brass that you will find. Look at the handles of the dressing table. Just remember that I said BRASS – brass handles, not gilded mounts or anything else like that.

That does seem to be it. The trick with all of it is to not go mad. Be patient and with everything, no matter what it is, persevere. You will be amazed at what can be achieved. I have.

Number four. How can I explain to someone that I do not want my piece of furniture to look brand new, over-cleaned or harsh? This is one of the complaints that I constantly get. I have seen far more pieces that look like that than I should have.

The first thing, I suppose, has got to be recommendation. I will probably blot my copy book when I say that a certificate or diploma will not impress me very much; experience will. More than anything, it will be how he or she talks about the piece of furniture. Do they talk about it as I hope I have talked about it in all these words that have gone before? Strange as it may seem, it was just this problem that prompted me

to try again; for years people like me went about our jobs, earning a living and raising a family. After all, that is really what it was all about.

We were, I suppose, very much from the era of "my little man around the corner". None of us were large concerns. I can remember what a huge shock it was to me when I discovered that people who I thought should know all the things that I took for granted – just the basic rules of age, how things were and had been for generations – did not seem to know what I was talking about. For me, even worse, they did not seem to think it mattered.

Well, as far as I am concerned, it does matter. That, more than anything, is why I have tried to put this together as I have seen it. That could well be the best answer to number four. If you understand all this, you will know the questions to ask. Hopefully also you will be able to tell people what you want and not what they think you should have.

Finally, this book has proved far more difficult than I could have imagined – and has had its moments of "to hell with it". However, without the backing and encouragement of John and Becky Booth, my Sheila and one or two people who have known me for years, a story such as this would never have been.

One thing I am sure of is that this young couple, within a couple of hours of meeting me, realised that I might – just might – know something that could be a little different about the furniture game!

SUMMARY

To SUDDENLY BECOME SERIOUSLY ILL does sharpen your mind! It happened to me at the beginning of 1998 and for a while I did not imagine that I would be capable of all that is necessary to finally put something like this together. I have learned more about Fax machines, fast air-mail deliveries, long distance phone calls, computers, photo-copiers and the publishing business than should be expected from someone of my age! However, it was more than gratifying to discover that I could cope with it and now have the end result in front of me. For that I have to thank Sheila, John Booth, my publishers, Doctors and modern medicine. Now that it is all together, for better or worse, I realise that I have just scratched the surface of a subject that has in so many places and areas become shrouded in almost a mystique.

My beginnings were humble, to say the least, and how I began would be impossible today. To explain, I had been working in the trade for 30 years when I was offered the job of running the Conservation department in a museum. It came to nothing because I did not have a degree in whatever you should have a degree in. However, that does not matter because my success, and I must be arrogant enough to say that I was successful because I understood my trade and it needed a discipline. In my case that discipline came mainly from my years of World War II. It played a huge part in my survival of those years.

I have been a fortunate man. I had the opportunity, coupled with my curiosity and the need to find out how it was done all those years ago, nothing, or very little has been left to us about those years, most of it was, as with me, in the memories of those who did it. The little that has been written down is often shrouded in mystery, folklore and often vagueness. We had little we could refer to, so, it was down to us to find out, we knew people like me who we could talk it over with. We had our own "old boy" network.

A complicated repair job was simple by comparison to a book like this which could be ten times the size and there would still be room for more. My intention, and I hope that it has worked, has been to try and show how we who made it and repaired it understand it, to de-mystify it if you like. After all, the trade used to be called the mystery.

EPILOGUE

Two or three days ago Sheila and I ticked the last page of our reading of this book before returning it to the publishers. For me it was amazing that it was finished! It was the 100 odd illustrations in it that really made me think. In the main they are unique to me, my mugshots as I call them. I have hundreds upon hundreds of them and it did then dawn on me that I have seen and recorded things that no furniture buff, collector, museum curator, historian, dealer or expert from the salerooms has ever, and in some cases are ever likely to see.

How many of these people would have seen a French ebenistes stamp exactly as it looked when he struck it in 1793?

On the 10th of June 1993 a majestic piece of French furniture was sold at Christies, London. It was Lot 59 at that sale. ILL 110 is my photograph of it. The catalogue tells us in great detail the history of the piece and that it is stamped three times J. PAFRAT. So indeed it was, but, it stays firm in my mind because it was stamped eleven times and I had to replace one of the rather complicated clover leaf locks that was missing. Unless you were told I doubt if you would discover that!

When it first came to me it had not been touched since it had been finished in 1790-94. The marble top was very thin and had to be removed, this marble was supported on the top of the piece by a thin pine board frame which also had to be removed. I then came face to face with the ILL'S 111 & 112. Each corner of the piece had been struck twice by Mr. Pafrat, or one of his minions. What you are looking at here is a stamp exactly as it would have looked when it was struck, in say 1792. Anyway, it is something very rare to see. I come from a workshop, and I have only seen this once before, and never anything like this! It also, I hope, supports my remark in this book that a stamp put on later does not stand a chance.

Mr. Pafrat died in 1794 so it is fair to say that he was the end of an era. Jimmy Little's really good years were those up until the first World War; he was the end of an era. It is one hell of a shock to suddenly realise that the same could well be said about me!

ILLUSTRATION 110: *Commode by Pafrat. Paris C1792-94.*

ILLUSTRATION 111: *Signatures as struck in C1792.*

ILLUSTRATION 112: *Signatures as struck in C1792.*

A FEW WORDS,
SOME COMMON,
SOME NOT

ANTIQUE
Usually applied to something 100 or more years old. Today you will hear it applied to things 25 years old! It does not seem to be significant anymore.

BREAKER
Name from the workshop for a piece of furniture bought to be broken up and used for repairs.

CHASER
Name for the highly skilled person whose art is to finish a casting (usually bronze) when it comes from the mould. Ciseleur in France.

CUT AND SHUT
Name given to the reducing in size of a piece of furniture to make it more saleable, often done to try and deceive, small furniture always deserves a closer inspection than large!

DOVETAILS
The strongest pulling and hanging joint in wood, also the oldest.

EBONY
The origin of ébéniste and more than likely Cabinetmaking. The first true veneer. Possibly the most important wood in the history of the Trade.

FADING
Action of sun and daylight on a surface, it cannot be produced by artificial means.

FACEMARK
Marks in chalk, charcoal, graphite, etc that are found inside furniture, bottom boards drawers, etc., they indicate where everything is marked and measured from.

GLUE
We all know what glue is, but in restoration the glue must be and I repeat must be easily reversible. This means the old fashioned animal glue. Modern glues have no place what so ever in antique furniture.

GRIBBLED
When old wood is used to make up a piece of furniture, often to try and deceive the wood could be wormy. If a surface with wormholes is opened up, the galleries of the worms activities will be exposed, we called this gribbling. If I see this in a piece of furniture I would not touch it with a bargepole.

KNIFE CUT
Knife cut is the name for a veneer cut with a knife, it can be sliced or peeled. Has been in use for the past 140 years and is the method commonly in use today.

LOPER
The name given to the piece of wood that pulls out to support a bureau fall. I have always called it a locum, probably because I got it wrong when I was a boy!

MORTICE

Slot made to receive a tenon, common joint for framework, panels, etc. Most common and the essential joint for chairs.

OLD COLOUR

The colour a piece of furniture takes up if it has been left alone. It will be very rare to see because the thickness of it is minimal. Ignorance, some modern varnish strippers, stripping tanks, etc. will often destroy it. For me an old colour is the authenticity of age. Old colour applies as much to the inside of a piece of furniture as it does to the outside!

PEGGED

Name given to the pegs of wood used to draw up a mortice and tenon joint, these are often called dowells, they are not, dowells are the round pieces of wood used to make a cheaper version of the mortice and tenon.

PIERCING

Name given to the sawing of an intricate pattern in metal. In brass inlay and Boullework you do not saw out the shape, you pierce it.

REVIVERS

Mixtures made up to revive a polished surface that has been, let us say, over used! They are always worth a try before the usual thing that happens, refinishing.

SAW CUT

Simply the name for sawn veneer.

TENON

Tongue cut to fit the mortice.

VENEER

Often regarded as somehow inferior, this is not the case and you will find that almost every piece of high style furniture will have veneer incorporated somewhere. The most important thing that ever happened in the world of furniture.

WOODWORM

At the first sign of an exit hole from this pest have the piece of furniture looked at. The best treatment is fumigation. Remember, THERE IS NO SUCH THING AS A TOUCH OF WOODWORM! If ignored the results can often be tragic.

APPENDIX 1

*T*HEY SAY THAT A BAD WORKMAN BLAMES HIS TOOLS. Fair enough, he has to blame something. I have always found that the skilled man can produce a more than passable job with anyone's tools that came to hand!

It is the same with the materials for finishing, I had my favourite brands, but, it did not matter, as long as I had the correct materials for the job in hand a good result would happen. You cannot be taught experience in a short paragraph printed on the back of a bottle!

To make it easier for those of you who want to try their hand I am going to give just two or three names that will supply all your needs.

W.S. JENKINS & Co. Ltd.
Jeco Works.
Tariff Road.
Tottenham.
LONDON N17 OEN

Write for their catalogue, they supply Harrell's wax polish. I have used that all my working life, also they can supply anything that has to do with the finishing of furniture.

In my opinion the best option of all for the uninitiated has got to be the products of this company.

Liberon Waxes, Ltd.
Mountfield Industrial Estate
Learoyd Road
New Romsey
Kent TN28 8XU   UK

In America.
SEPP LEAF Products, Inc.
381 Park Avenue South.
New York, NY 10016

A final one that I have used as long as Harrell's is Antiquax.
Partridge Fine Arts Ltd.
PO Box 144
OLDHAM
OLD 6WW

APPENDIX II

*H*AVING NOW SEEN THE APPENDIX in print I was rather ashamed at the starkness of it. For those of you, and I hope some of you do chance your arm and try some of the simple things that have been described, remember that we have scratched the surface, just a little, but it will be enough for you to start and see how things happen, and, more importantly to feel confident with these simple things. It is like a seed when it is planted and nurtured, what that can grow into is often surprising.

Do not expect everything to perform miracles, if there were magic potions no one would have ever needed my services.

These days we have a bewildering range of things for this and things for that, however, in the world of old furniture keep it as simple as you can. You know my philosophy: If it is not simple it very often cannot be successfully done.

When Liberon 0000 steel wool came on the market I could not believe that a wool could be so soft. Since then I have used nothing else. I have always used Harrells wax polish, antique and khaki, (Jenkins). My shellac polish, (French polish) has always been Jenkins transparent or the Liberon makes. Revivers, Harrells reviver (Jenkins) or again Liberon versions.

The white mark remover is from Liberon, it is excellent as are their various cleaners.

Alcohol is methylated spirits in the UK. Denatured alcohol in the USA. Raw linseed oil is raw linseed oil, you will need very little of this, in fact some of the oils about the house are fine, ground nut oil is a good example.

There are many other products that have not been mentioned and the catalogues from these companies are well described. Try them and see what happens, but please, I beg of you, if you do this, find an inconspicuous place to try them on, or practice on something else, just do not do what I once saw a guy do with a painting, he cleaned an area about two inches in diameter right in the middle of the canvas, absolutely true, and can you believe that the idiot did it on television.

Finally, when all else fails read the instructions. Please!

BIBLIOGRAPHY

Gilbert, Christopher, *The Life and Work of Thomas Chippendale*, Studio Vista, Christies, London. 1972.

Cescinsky, Herbert, *The Gentle Art of Faking Furniture*, Dover Publications, Inc., 180 Varick Street, New York, NY 10014. First published Chapman & Nell Ltd. 1931.

Wilson, Gillian, *Selections from the Decorative Arts in the J. Paul Getty Museum*, The J. Paul Getty Museum, Malibu, CA. 1983

Furniture History Society Volume XVIII. *The Cabinet Makers London Book of Prices 1793*. Furniture History Society, c/o Department of Furniture & Woodwork, Victoria and Albert Museum, London, UK. 1982.

Bradley, Ian, *History of Machine Tools*, M.A.P. Publications, 13/35 Bridge Street, Hemel Hempstead Hertfordshire, UK. 1972.

Griffiths, Denis, *Brunels Great Western*, Patrick Stephens, Wellingborough, UK. 1985.

Hawkins, David, *The Techniques of Wood Surface Decoration*, B.T. Batsford Ltd. 4. Fitzhardinge Street, London, W1HOAH. 1986.

In America, Sterling Publishing Co. Inc., New York. 1987.

Wiegandt, Claude, *Comment Reconnaitre Les styles du mobilier*, Charles Massin. Paris, 2. Rue De L'Echelle. Written in French, but is one of the best pictorial examples of the development of furniture that I think I have seen. Furniture is very much an International thing.

INDEX

A

Acers, 13, 19
Amalgam, 122
Amaranth, 13, 21

B

Bandsaws, 41, 43, 47, 50.
Beech, 13, 19
Bell metal, 120
Birch, 13, 20
Brass, 99, 103, 104, 117
Breaker, 9
Bumper, 43

C

Chasing, 120
Ciseleur, 121
C. Coronet, 124
Cross banding, 31, 93
Cut and shut, 142

D

Dovetails, 60, 61, 65
Drix, 20

E

East Indian Rosewood, 12, 13, 17
East Indian Satinwood, 13, 18, 137
Ebony, 22, 79, 80
Elm, 22

F

Facemark, 42
Fading, 149
Fire Gilding, 122
Fixings, 108
Flat front, 142
French polish, 147, 148

G

Glue, 74, 80, 81, 82, 108
Gilt bronze, 120
Guinea, 134, 135

H

Harlequin, 134, 135
Horn, 99, 102

I

Inlay, 92, 93, 96
Ivory, 102

Keys, 28, 126

Kingwood, 11, 13, 20, 137

Knife cut veneer, 137

Lost wax, 121

Mahogany, 13, 16, 31, 33, 35

Mercury, 122

Mortice, 45, 60

Mulberry, 69, 22

New colour, 9

Nitric acid, 128

Oak, 13, 14

Old colour, 7, 9, 127, 128

Ormoulu, 123

Partridge wood, 67

Pine, 13, 14

Planer, 45

Purpleheart, 11, 13, 21

Revivers, 149, 153, 154

Sand burning, 93

Satinee, 13, 21, 22

Satinwood, 13, 18

Sawmills, 49, 78

Sawn veneer, 11

Serpentine, 142

Shellac, 7, 147

Tenon, 60

Tortoiseshell, 99, 101

Tulipwood, 11, 13, 21, 31

Veneers after 1850, 79

Veneers before 1850, 76, 77, 79

Walnut, 13, 15, 16

Wax polish, 146, 155

West Indian Rosewood, 12, 17

West Indian Satinwood, 13, 18, 27, 32

White marks, 150, 151, 152

Yew trees, 13, 20

ORDER INFORMATION

Order *Close Encouters with Antique Furniture* from your bookstore.

If unavailable at your bookstore, please send $12.95 plus $2.50 for shipping and handling for each book. Quantity discounts are available. Please contact the publisher.

Michigan residents please add 6% sales tax.

Send _____ book(s).

PLEASE PRINT

Name: _____

Address: _____

_____

City: _____

State: _____   Zip: _____

Send check or money order (payable to Sage Creek Press) plus above information to:

Sage Creek Press
121 E. Front Street, 4th Floor
Traverse City, MI 49684
(616) 933-0445